Food to Grow

Food to Grow

A simple, no-fail guide to growing
your own fruits, vegetables and herbs

Frankie Flowers

photography by

Shannon J. Ross

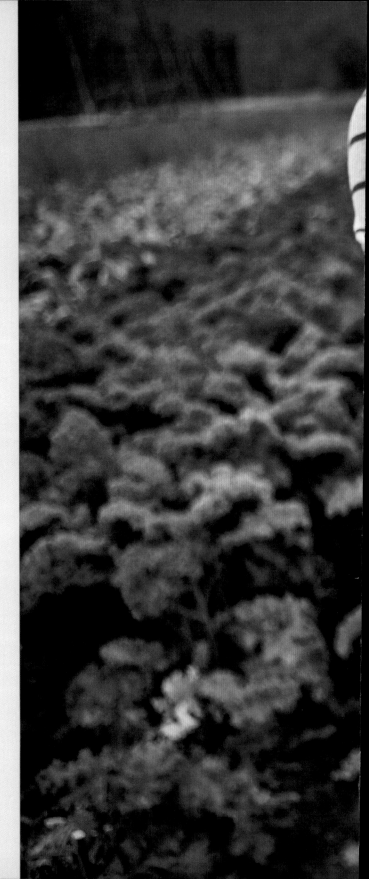

Published by Collins, an imprint of HarperCollins Publishers Ltd.

First edition

HarperCollins books may be purchased for educational, business,
or sales promotional use through our Special Markets Department.

HarperCollins Publishers Ltd
2 Bloor Street East, 20th Floor
Toronto, Ontario, Canada
M4W 1A8

www.harpercollins.ca

Library and Archives Canada Cataloguing in Publication
data is available upon request.

ISBN 978-1-44343-399-0

Printed and bound in the United States
QUAD 9 8 7 6 5 4 3 2 1

For you, my fellow humble gardener

Every seed is just a plant waiting to show itself to the world.
From backyards to school yards, fields to gardens to rooftops,
keep growing and stay dirty forever.

Contents

Introduction

My name may be Frankie Flowers, but I'm about more than just growing pretty blooms. In fact, I grew up a marsh mucker. What's a marsh mucker? The Holland Marsh, which is just north of Toronto, is known for its black soil—marsh muck—which is perfect for growing vegetables. My family emigrated from England in 1956 to be marsh muckers, and they got their boots and hands dirty in the rich earth of the marsh. My grandfather was a marsh mucker, my father was a marsh mucker, and growing up, I was a marsh mucker too. We raised everything from romaine to Boston lettuce, carrots to parsnips, cabbage to cauliflower, onions to leeks, and pretty much anything in between. A passion for growing food has deep roots in my family.

My dad, Tony (left), and my Great Uncle Len (right) in Bradford's Holland Marsh in 1956. They both grew up growing food—and they taught me all about farming.

I wanted to write a book about growing food because I've been doing it my whole life. I've grown food on a large, commercial scale, and in backyards or pots on a patio. Although I've been doing it for years, I know that many people are new to the fun of growing their own and literally eating the fruits of their labour. The local-food and organic-food movements have encouraged us to think about where our food comes from and how it's produced. But if you're not from a food-producing family, or it's been years since you've nurtured a tomato plant, you might need some practical information to get you into—or back into—tending vegetables, herbs, and fruits.

Growing your own isn't all that hard, and most people, even brand-new gardeners, end up with great results. Still, things can go wrong. My goal with this book is to help you, no matter what you know about soil and sun, take those first steps to becoming a backyard farmer—and hopefully get a healthy, bountiful crop even the first year. I will guide you through figuring out why to grow, when to grow, what to grow, and when to harvest. I have suggestions to help you run an environmentally friendly garden that will even look pretty.

Why Grow Your Own

Why not? Food gardening gives you control over what you eat. When you garden, you can count the steps—not the miles—your food took to get to your plate. You will truly know what fertilizer, if any, came in contact with your food, and when or if your lettuce had bugs. You can be sure that those tomatoes were actually vine ripened, because you harvested them right off the vine.

And you get to choose what you eat—you're not limited to the selection at your local grocery store or farmers' market. If you adore a certain variety of tomato or want to eat more greens, you have a big range of choices when you buy seeds or seedlings (small plants ready to grow in your garden). If you are interested in heirloom seeds for their historical value, you can give them a try. If you wish to be an organic gardener, you can purchase organic seeds or seedlings and follow organic practices right to harvest. If you want to make jams or pickles, you can grow the ingredients for your canning projects.

Ecologically, growing at home makes sense. Your food will not log hours of travel time that deplete fuel resources. Having a lush garden or growing food on your patio or deck takes carbon dioxide from the air and converts it to oxygen, reducing your home's carbon footprint.

Over time, food gardening can save you money. There are some up-front investments in equipment, such as tools and buying or building beds or containers, and you may spend more on things like soil in the early years. Like any undertaking, gardening comes with costs. Eventually, though, if you become a skilled grower, you can save by growing just what you want to eat and how much of it you'll want to eat.

But really, food gardening is about more than these practical concerns. I believe growing your own is an important process that engages the body, the mind, and the heart. Seeing food start from a seed or seedling and grow into a plant is a journey that gives you a strong sense of ownership and pride.

Family time in the garden. Gavin, my older son, loves tasting raspberries.

Matheson, my youngest, and Red the chicken. What a gal! She gives us eggs and keeps the garden fertilized.

Gardening gets your body moving and your brain stimulated. It's a healthy hobby that gives back. It's great for stress release or just for passing the time. Like other pastimes, it can trigger that fun competitive spirit: Some people, for example, grow to see who can produce the biggest pumpkin at harvest time or whose homemade tomato sauce tastes the best.

You can share all these benefits with your family. Children in particular thrive getting dirty outdoors. So many kids have no idea where food comes from and how it makes it onto our tables. My two sons help out in the garden, and growing fruits and vegetables gets them excited about eating them. Have a problem with your kids eating their greens? I say grow some together.

Getting out there in a vegetable garden can also involve older generations, and neighbours. Communities used to swap seeds, share tips, borrow tools, and harvest and preserve together—why can't

they again? If you don't have land of your own, join a community garden. You can meet new people, share ideas, and support others in their growing efforts. You can feed yourself and even grow enough to donate to a local food bank.

When growing your own food, the positives outweigh the negatives. The downsides are you might lose some plants to aggressive bunnies and bugs, or you could get a sunburn or pull a muscle in your back from the few hours you will most definitely spend weeding in the hot sun. Not bad trade-offs for the huge benefits of tending and eating your own crops.

What You Need

Space: To grow crops you will need a place to plant things. The space can be as small as a 40 cm (16 inch) container or as large as a half acre. The more space you have, the more you can grow. But the more you grow, the more work required. A small balcony, backyard, or city lot can produce enough food to supplement a grocery bill and create the bulk of many meals. If you live in a basement, though, or in a high rise with no patio, you will struggle to grow things at home without equipment. In these cases, try to acquire a community plot or take over a friend's yard for your growing projects.

Sun: Food-bearing plants love light. Sun equals success! The more sun the better. Some plants such as leafy greens will grow in the quick rays of the morning sun or in dappled light. But the majority of food plants require at least six hours of direct afternoon sun. You can buy grow lights and get a harvest just about anywhere. But this book is about simple, straightforward gardening that's affordable for everyone. Follow the sun when you plant; if your space has zero sunlight, you will labour in vain to grow food successfully.

Soil: You can grow plants in water and other mediums, but I'm just going to talk about growing plants in regular old soil. Some soil types—clay, for example—are challenging to work with. Luckily, you can do things to fix—amend—your soil to make it more food-growing friendly. You can also grow a lot of delicious crops in containers of various types and sizes with soil purchased at a garden centre.

Water: You need it to live and so do your plants. You will want outdoor access to water to care for your crops. If you have that—or don't mind lugging a big watering can from the kitchen sink—I can help you create plots that respect the importance of water and never waste it.

Experience: Gardening isn't rocket science, but it does require some basic knowledge. I will share what I know with you. Be warned—you may have to adapt my advice to work around the challenges of your space. It takes about three seasons to really learn your own garden and figure out which tips lead to a bountiful harvest and which ones don't apply to your garden and your needs.

Let's Do This

My goal with this book is to offer a guide to the most effective and efficient way to grow food in the space you have—big or small. I'll answer all your questions (no question is too basic for me!): When should you plant? What should you grow by seeds versus seedlings? Which vegetables are better to grow rather than purchase at the grocery store or farmers' market? How can you bunny-proof your vegetable garden and squirrel-proof your containers?

You can grow fruits, vegetables, and grains almost anywhere at any time of the year. Did you know NASA has raised radishes, peas, and lettuce in zero gravity on the International Space Station? But let's get real. This book isn't about growing all year long, or growing with a lot of fancy equipment and special technical skills. Or growing foods no one in your household will ever eat. This book is about growing in a way that's straightforward, accessible to almost everyone, and fun (almost) every step of the way.

With sun, soil, water, seeds, plants, and a little time to develop some confidence, you will be amazed at what you can grow, how much you can grow, and how great it tastes. You're going to sweat. You're going to get dirty. But you're going to have fun and eat some pretty tasty things come harvest time.

So—let's get food growing together!

Part one lays the groundwork. It leads you through where, when, how much, and just plain old how to grow. Want to understand your soil and how to get the most out of your garden? Start here. Part two is an A to Z listing that details each of my favourite foods to grow. It gives you all I know (and then some) about your chosen backyard crops. Each entry leads you through the specific requirements for a tasty harvest, including space, light, and the plant's favourite neighbours. I've also organized all of the foods into three different levels for the grower. Easy foods are perfect for the beginning grower and should not give you much in the way of problems. Moderate plants are for those who've been at this gardening thing for two seasons or more and don't mind a few extra steps to be successful. Difficult crops are targeted at the advanced grower who's been gardening a long time and does things like collect seeds. Don't forget to refer back to part one when you get to planting, though. Chapter 2 tells you all about improving and amending your soil to make it perfect for crops, and chapter 7 covers basic prevention and treatment of critters that might attack your plants.

PART ONE

Food to Grow Groundwork

Chapter 1

Food Basics: Where to Grow

Are you so ready for your new food garden that you can taste it? Whoa there. Before you create food-growing magic, you need to figure out just what kind of garden will work for you. Let's face it, everyone would probably like to harvest from one of those sprawling plots you see out in the country, complete with a towering row of corn and vast pumpkin plants that will produce a perfect pumpkin in time to carve that jack-o'-lantern at Halloween. But do you really want to weed that big plot? Water it on sizzling summer days? Even if you do, maybe it doesn't get enough sun or it's a long walk from the water tap. The truth is, most of us don't even have that kind of space.

Time to get real about how much sweat equity you want to put into gardening and what kind of approach suits your space. Maybe you can find a sunny corner in your yard, and it's got the perfect soil and drainage for your crops. But maybe your soil is terrible or your sun only hits your patio. If so, you're best off planting in containers.

I want you to get the most fruits and vegetables from the space you have with the least amount of work. Give me just a seed of passion, a scope of time, and a bucket of effort, and I'll help you figure out what kind of garden suits you.

Types of Food Gardens

Raised beds look great in just about any yard—and plants thrive in them too.

Did you know there are two ways to garden? You can plant your food right in the soil for an in-ground bed. Or you can grow food—not just pretty flowers— in containers. And not just those round planters you can buy at garden centres and hardware stores. Troughs also make amazing food gardens. What is a trough? It's a farm-issue steel or plastic container used to feed or water animals, and it can be repurposed. Troughs range in size from 15 to 250 gallons, and you can find them in garden centres or farm supply stores. (Used ones go for really cheap.) The steel ones look great in a modern-style yard.

As well, you can grow food in a raised bed. This is just a garden set on top of your soil, lawn, or patio. You build a wooden box, anchor it in the earth or place it on your patio, fill it with soil and plant in it. You'll be able to tell from reading this book that I love raised beds! They warm up quickly in the spring, are easy to rig up with irrigation and frost protection, and they're gentle on the old back when you weed them. You can hire someone to build you a raised bed, but they're actually quite easy to put together on your own with basic materials from a home improvement store or a lumberyard.

While planning your food crops, you should decide if you're an in-ground gardener or your plants would be better off in a container. If you don't have a lot of land and are working with a porch or patio only, clearly you already know the answer! But sometimes the answer isn't always so clear. Some of the factors I'll cover next—things like sun exposure, soil type, and convenience—may influence your choice too. The following table shows the pros and cons of each type of garden:

Garden Type	Strengths	Downfalls	Frankie's Tips
Container	Perfect for small spaces Easy to weed Portable—move your garden to catch more sun, or take inside if there's frost Converts any space into a garden—from a deck to a high-rise terrace	Limited in the types of food you can grow—some plants just need more space for their roots Limited yields Dries out quickly	For first-time food gardeners, best to start out with one season of containers, then expand to larger spaces
Trough	Ideal for small lots or large terraces Accessible height—easy to weed and harvest So durable one can last a lifetime Most come with a drainage plug Stainless troughs can look fashionable in a modern garden	Somewhat limited in the types of food you can grow Heavy to move Comes in a limited size selection Large troughs need a lot of soil at set-up	An excellent in-between choice: grows more than a container and is less work to set up than a raised bed
Raised bed	Warms up fast in spring, leading to faster harvest times Looks great and can be integrated into your wooden deck Easier on your back to weed, and develops fewer weeds Good if you have problem soil Easy to cover over for frost protection	You need to be handy to build the bed or you have to pay someone to do it Building the bed comes with materials costs	Particularly when you have clay soil below, be sure your raised bed drains well—line the bottom of the bed with stones or another hard material, or drill holes at the base
In-ground garden	Economical—you can use existing soil With minimal prep you are ready to go Can water less as in-ground beds don't dry out as fast as containers Can plant a large garden if you like	Soil takes longer to warm up in spring Hard to protect against frost Weeding is rough on your back You can struggle to grow food if you have problem soil If you get a serious plant disease, you may not be able to grow in that plot again for a few years	Locate in a convenient place for easy maintenance—you don't want to have to carry the hose 100 feet every time the garden needs water Even if you have ample space, start small

Time and Commitment

Should you go for the big in-ground bed or just try a few containers this year? Your schedule and how much time you have to get down and dirty in the dirt will make the decision for you. Gardening is work! It's fun work, but it does need time over several months.

If you've got a busy season ahead of you and a lot going on in your life—a big work project, a new baby, a major household renovation—take that into account when organizing your garden. Whatever you do, don't forget your travel plans. If you have a cottage, are going on a long road trip, or know you'll be away during the harvest, be sure you can get help from a neighbour or a local teen you can pay to water, weed, and pick ripe produce while you are gone.

How much time do you need? According to a 2009 study by the National Gardening Association, U.S. households who grew food spent an average of five hours per week gardening. And 5 per cent spent over 20 hours every week. I say people with very small container gardens can get away with just an hour a week of gardening. But if you have more, such as a 1 by 2.5 m (4 by 8 foot) garden or a trough or two, you should devote half an hour to gardening every day. If you can't garden daily, you can make up time on the weekend.

And it's not just about time. You can *make* time for something you love. How you feel about gardening is going to affect how often you'll get outside and tend your plants.

Growing in Window Boxes

Rectangular window boxes—the ones that hang off windows or the ones you place on your patio railings—are lovely for annual plants. But they're not my favourite for food gardening. Small, narrow window boxes dry out quickly and don't hold enough soil for many plants. Exceptions: Smaller leaf lettuces such as mesclun mix or arugula will thrive with regular watering. If window boxes are your only option, look for containers that are at least 20 to 30 cm (8 to 12 inches) deep. And please, water them like crazy.

What Kind of Gardener Are You?

Everybody's different, but there are four general types of gardeners. See where you fit, to help you make decisions:

Passive gardener: Loves the idea of gardening but isn't the hugest fan of pulling out the hose or those pesky weeds. Will put in less than an hour per week.

Garden snacker: Adores a nibble of gardening. Usually, snackers love gardening early in the season, but then life gets in the way. Will devote up to

Place food-growing pots along a walkway so they're right at hand for weeding, watering, and harvesting.

three hours a week on the garden in the spring, but up to three hours every other week in summer.

Garden enthusiast: Would garden more if not for the rest of the things on that to-do list. Will devote two to five hours weekly to the garden.

Avid gardener: Lives, breathes, eats, and sleeps plants. Gardening is not a pastime but a way of life. Knows the name of every plant—even some in Latin! Devotes over four hours per week and is always up for more.

How Much to Grow

Bigger gardens take more work, period. If you like gardening but don't love it, and you're super-busy, don't plant too much. The best approach, in my experience, is to start small and expand every season. A handful of containers this year could lead to a larger, in-ground plot next. And while there are no hard and fast rules about how big you should go based on your available time, I can give you a good idea of where to start:

- Passive gardener: No more than two 40 cm (16 inch) containers.
- Garden snacker: Two to four containers; or one garden trough; or one garden bed 1 by 2.5 m (4 by 8 feet).
- Garden enthusiast: Four to six containers; or two to three garden troughs; or two garden beds.
- Avid gardener: As many plants as your space and budget will allow!

Your Time Pledge

Take an honest look at your weekly schedule and decide how much time you can carve out for gardening. Then make a pledge. For example, "I, Frankie Flowers, pledge to spend a half hour each day working in my food-growing garden." (Maybe add a footnote that you may not garden *every* day but will make up time on the weekends.) Write down your promise and post it for the world—or at least the family—to see. Maybe everyone in the family could be in on the promise and share not just the fun jobs of planting and eating but the weeding and watering too. Such pledges can help motivate you on those hot summer days when you'd rather kick back than take care of your plants.

Location

Gardening is like real estate—it's all about location, location, location. You're not going to move just so you can plant a food garden this year. So you have to work with what you've got.

Space

In this book, I talk about a 1 by 2.5 m (4 by 8 foot) in-ground garden. This is a great size that lets you grow a decent crop. (Any bigger, and you will have trouble reaching over to weed your plants!) If you want more growing space than that, plant multiple plots with walkway space in between them, rather than one big plot. If you don't have this much space, you can go smaller, or you can even tuck your food-growing plants among other garden plants.

Ideally, raised beds should be 1 by 2.5 m (4 by 8 feet), but you can make a smaller bed that's 1 by 1 m (4 by 4 feet). Raised beds can go in your garden, on your lawn, or on your deck or patio (you build a wood bottom for those sitting on non-porous surfaces).

If you don't have room for any of these gardens, have a look at a small trough or use pots. Don't go smaller than a 40 cm (16 inch) round container—the minimum size for holding enough soil to support the roots of food-growing plants. You could be successful with 25 cm (10 inch) pots for some herbs. Tiny pots might look cute in an arrangement, but they can stunt plant growth and dry out very quickly.

Sun

Sun equals life in the garden. About 95 per cent of fruits, vegetables, and herbs need huge amounts of sun to grow properly. To know the sun needs of your

Left: A big bounty doesn't need to take up a big space. A 1 by 2.5 m (4 by 8 feet) plot is an ideal size.
Above: Plant tags are every gardener's best friend. They give you important information about each plant's light and water needs, and how long you'll have to wait to harvest.

food plants, read the seed pack or plant tag and look for these terms:

Full sun: This means the plant needs six or more hours of direct afternoon sun daily. If your garden location receives its most intense sunlight between the hours of 11 a.m. and 3 p.m. while facing south or west, you're gold.

Partial sun or partial shade: These plants like three to six hours of filtered or dappled light. They thrive in sunlight, but a long stretch of hot afternoon sun is too much for them. The shorter, gentler rays of the morning or late-afternoon sun of plots that face north or east tend to suit them best.

Shade: This means three hours or fewer of sun on a daily basis. While many beautiful plants will thrive in low light, the only food plant that likes darkness is mushrooms. If the only time you see the sun is at sunrise for an hour, or if your available outdoor space is deeply shaded by buildings or a tree, plant shade-loving perennials for their beauty and seek out a farmers' market or a community plot for your food.

Sun-loving plants placed in the shade will struggle and could become more susceptible to disease. The opposite is also true: Shade plants placed in a too-sunny location will burn up and die.

Don't fool yourself into thinking you have enough light when you don't. And remember, a sunny location that looks just right for sun-adoring seedlings in the spring may transform into a part-sun location once nearby trees and shrubs go into full bloom. If trees are shading your potential food garden, trim them back to let in some light. Do not do this yourself! Hire a professional arborist, who will ensure your trees remain healthy after a

pruning and who can use proper safety gear when working on tall trees. Gardening is very difficult with broken bones.

Soil and Drainage

If you're planning an in-ground bed, you need good, fertile soil that drains well after a rain and when the snow melts in the spring. Having poor soil and drainage might lead you to giving up on an in-ground garden at all and using containers or raised beds instead. Or you can fix your soil (amend it) to make it more food-plant friendly. (I cover soil and drainage and making soil better—amending it—in-depth in chapter 2.)

Convenience

The best-kept gardens are those closest to the door and the water tap! Gardens located in the "back 40" are often neglected—out of sight, out of mind. Farmers know this, and while they may grow cash crops out in their large fields, the family vegetable garden is always right beside the house. Set things up near the water tap and the kitchen door so you can grab some herbs or greens when you're cooking. If you walk through your garden every day because it's by your door, you're more likely to see if your plants are wilting or your tomatoes are ripe and ready to pick.

Wind

Wind can be wicked. Windy locations can dry out because wind increases transpiration—the process by which plants take moisture from the ground and let it evaporate into the air. People who live in windy cities such as Calgary or near the coast must plant in protected areas or create a wind barrier. (For information on how to protect your plot from wind, see page 155 in chapter 7.)

Critters

Whether you have a remote, rural garden or a plot in the city, you probably have furry friends that stop by to check out your garden. Some may even seem cute. But when they are munching on your lettuce or trampling your tomato plants, they become much less adorable. Squirrels, rabbits, deer, birds, raccoons, mice, moles, and groundhogs are all as eager to eat your harvest as you are. In the case of deer, they can—and will—destroy your garden in a matter of minutes!

Speak to your neighbours who garden so that you know what you're up against, then plan how to repel critters. (See chapter 7 starting on page 151 for information on repelling pests using fences and other deterrents.)

Budget

Over time, growing your own food can save you money. But don't do it for that reason. Starting up a food garden, as I've said, comes with costs—containers, soil, tools, and more—and it may take a few years to see the payoff. It's pretty hard to figure out how much a food garden can reap in produce. One estimate: The National Gardening Association says a $70 investment in a garden will yield about $600 in food.

I think you can control how much growing food will cost. If you plan wisely and buy only what you need from a good garden centre, you can keep the tally down. I've been gardening a long time and this chart (below) gives you my best guesses on how much you should be spending.

Type	Size	Soil	Plants	Final Cost
Container	40 cm (16 inch) pot, $10–$100	Two 30 L bags of potting soil, $8–$24	4 seedlings, $6–$15	$25–$140
Trough	.5 by .5 by 1 m (2 by 2 by 4 foot) trough (567 L/150 gallons), $75 used, $250 new	Eight 80 L bags of potting soil (or twenty-one 30 L bags), $80–$120	7–9 seedlings, $20–$45	$175–$415
Raised bed	1 by 2.5 m (4 by 8 foot) cedar planks and posts, $150–$300, misc. materials, screws, filter cloth, $20–$50	Twenty-four 30 L bags of compost or triple mix, or 2 cubic yards if you buy in bulk, $150–$300	10–15 seedlings, $20–$75	$340–$725
In-ground	1 by 2.5 m (4 by 8 feet), no construction costs	Ten 30 L bags of compost, triple mix, or manure, $30–$40	10–15 seedlings, $20–$75	$50–$115

Wait, that's not the end of your shopping list. You'll need a few more tools to help get your delicious harvest. Of course you don't have to buy all these things—you can beg or borrow them from neighbours and family members at the start:

Seedlings vs. Transplants

When you visit the garden centre in the spring and you see shelves full of small tomato, pepper, and lettuce plants, know these are called both "seedlings" and "transplants." The two words mean the same thing. For newer gardeners, growing from seedlings or transplants is often the better choice than starting your food garden from seeds, as they're less work and you'll have a shorter time to harvest.

Essential

- Gardening gloves
- Knife or scissors (for a whole bunch of uses, including cutting seedlings from their pots, cutting string to tie vines, opening bags of soil and more)
- Trowel (a spoon from the kitchen will do in a pinch)
- Plant tags
- Watering can or hose
- Pitchfork or tiller
- Garden fork/weeder

Optional

- Spade
- Pruners
- Rake
- Hoe
- Wheelbarrow

Yield

How hungry are you? If you have a large family who love fruits and vegetables, or you're bent on making tomato sauce from your own 'Roma' tomatoes, then you might want to go big. If you're feeding just yourself, skip the big plot and try a few containers of your favourite salad greens and maybe a pepper plant.

The National Gardening Association estimates that a well-maintained garden can yield 225 g (half a pound) of food for every 900 square cm (1 square foot) of garden area. So, if you plant a 1 by 2.5 m (4 by 8 foot) plot in the garden or in a raised bed, you'd end up with 7 kg (16 pounds) of produce at harvest. Not a lot, but enough to supplement several meals.

But hey, those are basic yields. I have a few tricks when it comes to maximizing the output of your growing space. In chapter 4, I cover some pretty clever ways to increase yields so even the smallest of containers can produce more than one harvest.

Select Your Site

Now it's time to get specific about where (and how) you plan to grow. Perhaps the space for your food garden has already been set aside. Maybe the information in this chapter has caused you to change your plans and you're now thinking of pulling up a flower bed for vegetables or buying a trough.

If you're still not sure and you haven't grabbed your shovel yet, no worries. Information in later chapters about your soil and the needs of your favourite food plants might sway your opinion about how to set up your food garden this year and in years to come. The great thing with gardening is that it's just plants and soil, and sometimes a bit of wood and a few pots. You can always switch things up the next year until you eventually hit your garden groove.

Chapter 2

The Dirt: Getting Ready to Plant

Now that you've given your yard the once-over, you're ready to put things in order. Prepping your garden before you plant involves getting up close and personal with your soil to make sure it's really got the right stuff for growing your summer salads and fall gourds. After that, you'll be flexing your muscles as you add things to your soil, dig up weeds, build raised beds, and wash out containers. Got some bleach? Got a hammer? You're good.

A bit of dirty talk, a bit of dirty work. All for a good cause: making sure things are in place for your plants so you'll have one heck of a growing season this year.

Assessing Your Soil

If you're going to be an in-ground gardener, better know the facts about your soil. Soil is the basic building block for any good food-growing bed. Soil is not the same as dirt. Soil is made up of 50 per cent water and air and 50 per cent minerals and microorganisms. My son Gavin is in Grade 3, and he's learning about soil and its crucial role in supporting plants. A review: From the soil, roots get oxygen, water, and nutrients—the key ingredients for photosynthesis, the process by which a plant keeps itself alive. Poor soil offers a poor flow of these life-giving materials, and if you don't do anything to make it better, you'll have a hard time growing.

Soil Types

Most native soils in Canada are a mixture of three major mineral particles: sand, clay, and silt. These types differ in the size and number of pore spaces, which is the space between the soil particles that gets filled by air or water. Pore space impacts the amount of air and oxygen in the soil, how water drains from it, and how well it can hold moisture and nutrients.

Soil Type	Drainage	Water Retention
Sand	high	low
Silt	low	high
Clay	low	high
Loam	medium	medium

Sand: This soil type has the largest particles. It's very coarse and gritty to the touch and has very large pore spaces, so it is often unable to hold moisture or nutrients—in other words, it drains too well. Sand is often added to clay soils to improve drainage. Benefits: It's easy to work with and warms up quickly in the spring.

Silt: Silt has smaller particles than sand does. Silty soil feels smooth to the touch and has smaller pore spaces, so it retains moisture and often won't drain well after a rain. Since silty soil has small particles, it can compact easily under pressure, so it's recommended you don't walk on a garden with heavy silt content. Benefits: Silt is nutrient-rich.

Clay: Clay has the smallest particles of the three soil types, making it good for retaining moisture—in fact, too good. Clay's tiny particle size limits the passage of air, restricts drainage, and often suffocates plant growth. Clay-based soils are highly acidic (see Soil pH on page 28). Clay soils are challenging to work with, as the soil is so heavy, and the earth takes a long time to warm up in the spring. Benefits: Sorry, not a lot to say here. Clay soils are really hard to work with.

Loam: So what is the perfect soil? We call it "loam." This is soil that's almost an equal combination of sand, silt, and clay. (Sometimes you'll see the terms "sandy loam" or "silty loam"; they mean the soil is still a balanced combination but there's either a bit more sand or a bit more silt in the loam.) Loamy soils have it all in terms of benefits: They retain moisture but also drain well.

Sandy soil drains quickly, drying out your food plants.

Nutrient-rich silty soil can get compacted down.

Few plants like clay (above). Loam (below) is ideal.

What's Your Soil Type?

Feel free to go down to the garden centre and buy yourself a soil test. It'll run you $10 to $100 (the pricier ones tell you a lot more than your soil composition). Or you can try these two homemade tests that are free, relatively quick, and fun to do:

Frankie's clumping test: Go to the centre of your garden bed. Using a trowel or spoon, dig down 5 to 10 cm (2 to 4 inches) and remove one big handful of soil. Make a fist around it and look at how the soil holds together:

- If the soil clumps so tightly that you can shape it like it's packing snow, your garden soil is primarily clay.
- If the soil won't clump, almost slides through your fingers, and feels coarse, you have sandy soil.
- If your handful of soil binds, appears almost slippery or slick, and leaves a residue on your fingers, you have silty soil.
- If your soil clumps easily but also breaks apart easily, you have soil with a balanced percentage of clay, sand, and silt—loam—and you've won the soil lottery because this is the best soil of all!

Mason jar test: This easy home test tells you the percentage mix of your soil by type. Almost no soil is 100 per cent clay or sand or silt. Knowing the balance of the three can help you amend your soil.

- Start by getting a 1 L (about 35 ounces) Mason jar with lid; a spoon or trowel; 5 mL (1 teaspoon) of liquid dish soap; and water.
- Go to the centre of your garden and dig down 15 cm (6 inches). Add a spoonful of this soil to your jar. Fill the remainder of the jar with water. Add the soap, secure the lid, and shake. Then place the jar in a location where it will not be disturbed and leave it for 12 hours.
- The soil will separate. The sand will sink to the bottom, the silt will take up the middle, and the clay will rise to the top. You can see by the thickness of each of these layers the percentage of each element in your soil.

The Thing about Peat

I live in Bradford, Ontario, near the Holland Marsh, which is known for the fertile soil that supplies much of the province with fresh produce, thanks to its richness. The marsh contains a perfect example of peaty soil. This soil type is dark brown or black, soft, absorbent, and easily compressed. Plants love peat, so it's often used to amend (fix) nutrient-poor soils. And since it's very acidic, it's often used to amend soils where the gardener wants to grow acid-loving plants. Peat sounds perfect, but it's not! Only a limited number of plants thrive in peaty soils. Often, gardeners need to amend peaty soil with organic matter and sand to make it better balanced and grow a wider range of plants.

The Importance of Colour

The colour of your soil contains important clues about its nutrient level and ability to drain.

Black soil: The darker the soil, the more organic matter it contains. Black soils are generally nutrient-rich, but they may even be too rich, thus running the risk of "burning" plants because of the soil's high acidity. Black soils are often found in bogs and sometimes lack adequate drainage.

Brown-red soil: Think PEI and its iconic, potato-growing earth. Brown-red soils are often composed of sandy loam, which has good drainage and great growing conditions.

Blue-green-grey soil: Be afraid! This colouration is often a sign of poor drainage, as soil turns this colour when it is continuously wet. You'll struggle to grow without adding amendments.

Yellow soil: Similar to blue-green-grey soil, yellow soil indicates a problem with drainage.

Soil Drainage

Have you ever sat in a tub for 24 hours? Probably not! After even half an hour, your skin starts to wrinkle and your feet begin to feel spongy. Plants also prefer brief dips in water. They enjoy getting their feet—roots—wet, but not for too long. Soil that drains well is a must for any healthy garden.

Your soil type will generally determine your drainage. However, things like wind, sun exposure, air circulation, and slope will change how long it takes for certain parts of your garden to dry out after a rainfall.

Does Your Soil Drain?

To figure out if you have a problem with drainage, try this easy test—it's from the Cornell University website:

Go to the centre of your future garden plot. Dig a hole about 30 cm (1 foot) deep. Fill the hole with water and allow it to drain completely. Refill the hole immediately and measure the depth of the water with a ruler. Fifteen minutes later, measure the drop in water in inches, then multiply by four to calculate how much water drains in an hour.

Less than 2.5 cm (1 inch) per hour is poor drainage, so that part of your garden will retain water after a rain or when the snow melts. No good for your food plants! If you have drainage of more than 15 cm (6 inches) per hour, you have a problem with excessive drainage and will struggle to keep your plants moist.

It's a (soggy) snap to assess your garden's drainage with this hole test.

Problem soils—soils with either slow or rapid drainage—can be fixed, or amended. (See Making Your Soil Better, opposite.) You may also want to adjust your garden plan and put in plants that like extra wet or dry conditions. For instance, leafy greens don't mind their feet wet, whereas herbs such as rosemary thrive in dry soil. Or you may need to adjust how you water your garden (for more on watering and maintenance, see page 111 in chapter 6.) Have a look too at the Food to Grow Plant Guide starting on page 188 for more information about the moisture needs of individual plants.

Soil pH

There's just one more thing you need to know about your soil: its chemical composition. This is measured in pH, which tells you how acidic your soil is. PH matters because some plants love acidic soil and some bask in alkaline. If your soil is too far in either direction, you might want to add some amendments to bring it back into balance before you get growing. Acidity is measured on a scale of 0 to 14. Everything below 7 is considered acidic, or what we call "sour." Above 7 is alkaline, or "sweet."

Most plants like neutral conditions with a pH of 6.0 to 7.5. Below 6.0, the likes of leafy greens, beets, and onions grow happily. But many plants can struggle to absorb nutrients such as nitrogen, phosphorus, and potassium. Over 7.5, iron, manganese, and again phosphorus are harder for plants to absorb. Food plants such as blueberries and potatoes will thrive in these conditions but not much else—acidic soil is really hard on food plants. FYI, clay and peat soils tend to be acidic.

To find out the pH of your soil, you can take a sample to a lab or you can purchase a soil test kit at a garden centre.

Making Your Soil Better

Just leaving your in-ground soil as is probably won't work out, unless it's a lovely, airy loam. You will need to add one or more ingredients to get a better balance for your soil type, or to adjust your pH. This is called "amending."

It would be great if you could add ingredients to soil just once and fix it forever, but you can't. In fact, it's pretty much an annual affair. Many people like to work on their soil in the spring. There's nothing wrong with this, but with spring being so busy in the garden, I find fall a much better time. In fact, try the late fall. That's when gardens are empty and tidied up after the harvest. The frosts and thaws of winter can help the materials you add to your soil naturally mix in over the next few months and the soil will be ready for planting in the spring.

The goal when amending soil is to have a depth of 20 to 25 cm (8 to 10 inches) of good soil to grow in.

Many soil amendments I'll suggest come in bags from the garden centre. You'll notice I don't offer you precise recipes for applying things such as lime and sulphur. That's because every product is different, depending on the formulation. Just follow the directions on the side of the bag, which will tell you precisely how much to use, how to prepare it, and how frequently you need to reapply it. Read the label before you buy and always choose the product that addresses your particular need, offers the right amount for your garden size, and goes on with a minimum of preparation and tools. Never buy based on price. Instead, look on the label for the amount of filler in the product and choose a high-quality product with little filler.

Amending Sandy Soil

Sandy soils just can't hold on to moisture and nutrients. Your poor plants will dry out. To fix this, add in a mixture of humus, peat moss, and compost, which garden centres sell under the name triple mix. Since sand is so light, it will always rise to the top. So you need to amend year after year by adding triple mix to the soil and mixing it in. If your soil is highly sandy and amendments aren't working or staying mixed, you may want to consider a raised bed for food gardening.

Amending Clay Soil

Clay soils are tough—they really are. Many people claim they've successfully amended these heavy soils with gypsum. This is simply calcium sulphate and is sold in bags at garden centres. It can increase the particle size of your soil and improve drainage. You're welcome to give it a try. But in my experience, if you have true clay soil, you're best to dig out the clay to a depth of 30 to 38 cm (12 to 15 inches) and line the bottom of this hole with coarse materials such as stone or broken brick to create a reservoir, and then fill in the entire hole with triple mix or compost. Truck away the soil you removed. This is a lot of work! But either do it or build a raised bed. Even if you opt for a raised bed, you'll need to set up good drainage in it too.

Amending Silt Soil

To make silt perfect for food growing, all you need to do is lighten things up. Just rake in a little triple mix or some organic matter (such as leaves or vegetable clippings; see more on organic matter on page 31) and you should be ready to grow.

Amending Acidic Soil

To fix acidic soil, the traditional solution is to add horticultural lime. In fact, this is so standard that fixing acidity with any ingredient is called "liming." You can also lime with wood ashes—yes, from your fireplace—as they contain calcium carbonate, which is very alkaline, as well as potassium,

Triple mix is the fix for sandy soil.

Acidic soil gets balanced by lime.

Many garden centre products help alkaline soils.

phosphorus, and trace minerals. However, you should use wood ashes with caution; overdoing the amount you add to your soil can actually make it unhealthy for plants and slow their growth. For most liming amendments, use 10 kg (22 pounds) per 100 square m (1,000 square feet) and only apply once every three years.

Amending Alkaline Soil

Many materials can be added to alkaline soil to balance it out. Pine needles and peat moss are popular. However, studies have shown pine needles do not acidify soil. The most commonly used ingredient—and the one I recommend—is garden sulphur. You can easily buy it at your local garden centre. Follow the instructions on the package.

Making All Soil Healthier

I've covered "amending soil"—making problem soil more balanced. But just about all soil can use a boost so it's ready and willing to grow a healthy food garden. This is called "improving soil." You improve soil by adding materials that increase the activity of microorganisms and attract good-for-soil creatures such as worms.

What you want is about 5 cm (2 inches) of material that's all about nutrients for the top layer of your soil. Any more than that or more than 5 to 6 per cent of your growing soil, and you can get soil that's too active—soil that uses up too much nitrogen and takes that precious mineral away from your plants. We need to find balance!

Make your own compost with a barrel or tumble composter. The tumbling action stirs the compost for you, taking kitchen scraps to garden glory in no time.

For your in-ground garden, no matter how great things are going, improve once a year. You can do it in the spring before you plant, but as I said, I'm a big fan of pumping up soil in the fall. Try the following options for improving soil—use just one, or a combination of them, to give soil a nutrient boost:

Organic matter: The term "organic matter" covers a wide variety of living, dead, or decaying plant materials and animal waste: things like shredded leaves, kitchen waste, compost, and manures that are in the process of breaking down and turning to humus, the dirt-like material you get when living things have decayed completely (and not to be confused with hummus, the stuff you eat). Organic gardeners love this improvement. It's all about using what you have lying around anyway, especially in the fall after cleanup. In fact, organic matter does its best work when used in the fall so it has lots of time to break down. Ideally, in the spring you till it into your plot (see more on tilling on page 35).

Compost: Compost is basically organic matter that's already been broken down. It's great for gardeners who like to buy their improvement medium in bags, or who have a backyard composter. Many municipalities compost and they'll often give it away free. Improving with compost is very easy—you just rake it in.

Manure: Manure is garden gold. While it may seem that growing your food in an animal's poo makes no sense at all, trust me, manure is good stuff. The key is to use waste that's been properly composted. Decomposition ensures that pathogens such as E. coli have been killed off. It also makes manure a better fertilizer—raw manure will actually

burn most plants. Most, if not all, bagged manures have been fully composted and some have even been sterilized to guarantee they're extra-safe from pathogens. And bagged manures don't smell. Never use manure from meat-eating animals such as cats and dogs, as there's a risk of transferring parasites or disease organisms. Manure from livestock that graze on vegetables is ideal. In fact, these animals excrete between 75 and 90 per cent of the nutrients of the food they ate. Poultry manure has the highest nutrient content, followed by that of hogs, steers, sheep, dairy animals, and horses. I like to work with sheep and hen manure. Sheep can digest weeds very effectively, so you get little in the way of weed seeds in their waste. Hen manure also contains calcium, which I have found bolsters the overall health of plants and really helps tomato plants with a problem called "blossom-end rot." As a bonus, pelleted hen manures help repel many furry friends such as squirrels, chipmunks, and rabbits.

Triple mix: Everything has been done for you in this blend of humus, peat moss, and compost. It's like combining all the above improvement mediums into one handy mix that's light and full of nutrients. You can't go wrong.

Composted manure—this one is from hens—is a great natural fertilizer for the food garden.

Preparing Your In-Ground Garden

Now that you know everything (well, almost everything) there is to know about soil, you're ready to select the spot for your in-ground garden and get down in the soil and make it happen.

Plotting Your Space

Grab a yardstick, twine, and four (or more) wooden stakes. Use the yardstick to measure out one or several 1 by 2.5 m (4 by 8 foot) plots—or a smaller plot, if that's all you have—leaving at least 60 cm (2 feet) between each bed so you can easily walk between them. Place a wooden stake in the four corners of each plot and mark the plots by wrapping the twine around the stakes. Call me picky, but I like a garden plot that's nice and square, so take your time to do it right.

Clearing Your Plot

You need to get the old plants, grass, and patio or path materials out of the way so you can plant. The more thorough you are with removing old growth from the area, the more weed-free your food garden will be—not just this season, but for years to come.

If you have sod, use a spade to dig down under the roots and strip it from the ground. Some gardeners will tell you that you can simply flip the sod over—the grass will die and you'll have a nice amount of soil left from the roots. As far as I'm concerned, that's the lazy gardener's route. I don't recommend this approach because the grass will just come back and grass is a pain in the ... back. In other words, endless weeding!

It's worth a bit of time at the beginning to start your garden right. Measure out your space, using a yardstick to keep things straight. Once you've measured, roll back the sod and weeds to make way for your new garden plot.

Clearing by Tilling

Tilling is the process of turning over and breaking up the soil. Traditionally, it's been a key step in changing over the use of a garden bed, as it helps get rid of old plants and weeds. It also reduces soil compaction and injects air into the soil, loosening it so moisture and nutrients can reach the roots of a new crop. Particularly if you're converting a high-traffic area into a food garden, you'll want to churn up the soil so it's ready for your plants.

The best time to till is when soil is moist but not wet. Avoid tilling after a heavy rain, as wet soil clumps when it dries, which will be a problem for your seeds and plants later, and can lead to the soil becoming compacted soon after you're done. Really dry soil is also problematic, because it increases the rate of evaporation. To test the moisture level, dig down 15 cm (6 inches), grab a handful of soil, and squeeze it in your hand. If water quickly rushes out of the soil and a clump forms very easily, it's too wet. If the clump just falls apart and crumbles, it's too dry. If a clump forms easily in your palm but gradually falls apart and minimal water is released from the soil in the process, you're at the perfect moisture level to till. Leave wet soils for three to four days before testing again. For dry soils, water them thoroughly and let them dry out for two days, then test.

Before you start to till, remove all sticks, stones, tree roots, and as much vegetation as possible to make the task go smoothly. Till your garden to a depth of 15 to 25 cm (6 to 10 inches), using one of the two methods that follow:

Manual tilling via double digging: For a small plot that's not overly compacted, you can till by hand with a little sweat equity. This is a neat approach that works very well. Using a spade, dig out a row on the far end of your garden to a depth of 30 cm (12 inches). Take all the soil you've dug out and place it along the edge of the garden at the opposite end from this row. Leave it there for now. Next, dig a second row alongside the first, tossing the soil from this row into the empty trench you dug for the first row. Then dig a third row, putting the soil in the second trench. When you reach the end of the garden, fill your final trench with the row of soil waiting for you at the opposite edge you started from.

With this technique, one pass should do the trick. If your soil is impossible to dig with a spade, consider using a rototiller (see next section) or building a raised bed, as compacted or heavy soil that's hard to dig may not be suitable for a healthy food garden. (If your soil is relatively easy to lift, you've got healthy soil great for growing!)

Zapping Weeds with the Sun

Even with a good till, things you don't want can remain in your plot, such as remnants of weeds that could grow back, and microscopic pests such as insects and disease. Some gardeners are fine with using a non-selective herbicide that will simply kill all plants and weeds, clearing the way for a new crop. If you want a more natural approach, a process called "solarization" is a simple way to create a clean slate.

First, take away as much of the vegetation as you can by hand, then till the soil and water it. Next, lay clear or black plastic over the earth for at least four weeks. The soil temperature will rise, killing pests and any lingering seeds or vegetation naturally, leaving it ready for a new planting.

Automated tilling with a rototiller: A rototiller is basically a spade with a motor. If you have a hard plot with soil that's been compacted by people walking on it, or you've got a big plot, you may need motorized help. A rototiller is expensive to buy, but you can easily rent one. (Split the rental cost and the time with a neighbour. I've found that one morning's rental gives you long enough to till four small yards.)

Start off by setting your rototiller to its shallowest depth. This will scuff up the hard crust of your soil. For the second pass, do the same thing. For the third and fourth passes, start increasing the depth gauge. Keep going until you create a workable depth of 20 to 30 cm (8 to 12 inches). Three to four passes should be sufficient for most gardens.

No-Till Method

Tilling has been around for years and is pretty much the accepted way of clearing land. But new studies now say that tilling can negatively affect soil's natural micro-organisms, disturb creatures such as earthworms, even make the soil more compacted over time. I have to agree that deep tilling is not always ideal, especially in areas that get large amounts of rain, where tilled soil can get really compacted.

The so-called lasagne method is a no-tilling technique that takes a page out of Italian cookbooks. Start by collecting newspapers—nothing glossy, just your usual newsprint, and cardboard too. Remove any tape, adhesives, and staples. Cut or mow your plot and remove any large weeds by hand. No tilling!

Using a wheelbarrow half filled with water, dampen your newspaper and place three to six layers of it (or just one layer of damp cardboard) on your plot, covering the entire surface. Just like building a lasagne, now layer again by placing 20 to 30 cm (8 to 12 inches) of coarse organic matter or mulch such as shredded leaves, straw, or sawdust on top of the newspaper or cardboard. (This is your "brown" layer, just like the one you'd place in a composter.)

Now do your "green" layer, 5 to 10 cm (2 to 4 inches) of grass clippings, kitchen scraps, seaweed, or composted manure. This layer puts nitrogen into the soil. Next, spread blood meal (purchased at a garden centre) over the whole area. Finally, top it all with one layer of 5 to 10 cm (2 to 4 inches) of bark mulch.

Over time, this layered concoction will break down and both kill off the old plant growth and enrich the soil. (If you do this, you don't need to improve the soil that year.) However, it really does take some time. The process is very much for the patient gardener, since no-till tilling needs at least four months to be effective. Ideally, lasagne your garden in late fall and it'll be ready for new plants in the spring. Did I mention this approach is organic? Just a bonus.

Time to Amend and Improve

Once your plot is cleared of debris and old weeds, you can get your soil tip-top for the growing season. First, amend your cleared garden plot to help your soil's composition, drainage, and pH. Then, improve the top layer of your soil with a nutrient-rich medium. (See Making Your Soil Better starting on page 28.)

Need More Soil?

If you need to improve your garden with a few additional layers of soil, go ahead and purchase some bags at your garden centre, or if you need large amounts, maybe even buy some in bulk. Remember that improving your soil can plump up your beds as well—that's usually enough for most food gardens. If you want even more soil, purchase a good-quality product and use one 30 L (cubic foot) bag for every 60 by 60 cm (2 by 2 foot) section of garden.

Building Fences

With your plot ready to roll, consider now if you need a fence. A wooden, plastic, or metal structure can be a useful tool for plants to climb, but it may also protect against wind and, most critically, furry critters that may visit to eat your plants.

Decide whether you will build, then what, precisely, you will build, with those criteria in mind.

Soil: You Get What You Pay For

That $1 bag of soil seems like such a great deal. Resist. Like most things, with soil you get what you pay for, and discount bags often don't lead to good results in the garden. As a general rule: the heavier the bag of soil, the poorer the quality. (Unless it's been raining—then they're all heavy!) Soil weight is harder to gauge with bulk sellers. Ask around and find out who has seen good results in the garden with a bulk seller's product and which bulk sellers offer good service. Also, ensure that the soil has been screened and shredded—otherwise you might end up with sticks and stones in your brand new soil.

Preparing Container Gardens

If your yard lacks sufficient sun or all the news about your soil is bad, perhaps you've decided to make food garden magic happen in containers instead. Good stuff—let's get them ready.

Best Containers

You can grow a lot in containers. But they are not all created equal. On the page opposite is an overview of the types of container materials and which might be best for your prized plants. (Remember, aim for no smaller than 40 cm (16 inches) for a round pot for most plants, or you'll get stunted growth and a plant and soil that dry out too quickly. For herbs you can go as small as 25 cm (10 inches.)

Choose containers suitable for your plants and location. These two are cute, but are too small for great growing—choose function over fashion!

Cleaning Containers

I'm a firm believer that to be a successful container gardener, you need to start off right—which means, start off clean. Old pots can carry diseases from the year before. They can also have a buildup of salt or other materials that are no good for your food crops. Clean the pots outdoors by removing all soil from them using a hose or brush. Next, create a cleaning solution of water and 10 per cent bleach. Submerge pots in this solution for at least 10 minutes, or wash them with the solution by hand—wearing gloves. Rinse off the pots thoroughly. I recommend doing this on the driveway, as bleach can burn lawns. Then, let containers dry for a day before planting in them.

Brand new pots just need a quick wipe. And if you gardened the year before in your containers and everything grew beautifully without a trace of disease, you don't have to wash these. In fact, you don't even have to toss out all the soil. Just dump out the top third, replace, and you're ready.

Soil for Pots

Soils that are ideal for in-ground gardens are too heavy for growing plants in pots. You cannot simply take your existing garden soil, throw it into a container, and expect your tomatoes to thrive. They will drown and die. Instead, you need a medium that can absorb moisture and then quickly dry. You need potting soil. It's often referred to as "soilless mix." It looks like soil and feels like soil, but it is mostly peat moss, bark, vermiculite, and perlite. These, in combination, act like a sponge that absorbs and evaporates water quickly so plants never sit in water—thereby avoiding root rot.

Container Type	Advantages	Disadvantages
Clay or terra cotta	Breathable Rustic-looking Attractive	Break easily Can be damaged by frost and cold so they cannot be left outside in winter
Concrete	Long-lasting Wind-resistant (they won't blow over) Durable	Heavy Can be pricey
Plastic	Inexpensive Come in many colours Lightweight	Become brittle with age and from the cold Wind can blow them over
Foam (polyurethane)	Lightweight Look like concrete Winter-resistant	Chemically produced
Wood	Sturdy Custom shapes (you can even build your own) Natural appearance Insulated containers that can help perennials survive winter	Woods might be treated with creosote, which can be toxic, so you must be careful to choose woods treated with non-toxic waterproofing or use cedar instead
Metal	Sturdy Long-lasting Wind-resistant Winter-proof	Conduct heat Heavy Not recommended for edibles
Stainless steel troughs	Long-lasting Rust-free Safe for foods Large capacity Winter-proof	Not ideal for very small spaces

Potting soil does not contain humus or minerals, which helps with absorption of water but means the soil is poor in nutrients. You need to fertilize often to keep your potted garden healthy. (See more on fertilizing on page 124.)

Soil for Troughs

While troughs are just large containers, they do best with slightly heavier soil, something that will retain some moisture and hold on to nutrients. My favourite way to create the ideal medium is to add one bag of triple mix for every six bags of potting soil. If you scale up or scale down the amount of soil you're using, just keep that six-to-one ratio and you'll have the perfect mix.

Soil for Raised Beds

Since raised beds drain into the ground, you can use nutrient-rich soil in them. If you have your own compost, it's the ideal growing medium because it's a great weight and full of nutrients. If not, just buy triple mix, which is perfectly balanced for raised beds.

Bag It

A bag of potting soil is all you need to get growing. Just take a large bag of potting soil, lay it on its side, and cut out holes for planting in. You can grow everything from tomatoes and peppers to lettuce and kale in a good old bag of soil. Since soil bags come with holes already, you don't even need to worry about drainage. In my opinion, this is a lazy gardener's approach, and these garden bags aren't all that pretty. But you'd be surprised how many people use them!

Drainage for Containers

Most plants do not like to sit in a bath for a long time. You need to make sure your container garden drains or you will end up with unhealthy plants. There are two main ways:

Drainage holes: Most pots and troughs come with a hole or a few holes for drainage. (Troughs come with a plug; just take it out.) The holes are an escape route for water. Some plastic pots don't have any holes, or enough holes to let water drain away. Get out the drill and make some before you plant. Raised beds sitting on a patio will have a solid floor; such beds, as well as those sitting on clay soil, might require some drilled holes to let the water out.

Reservoirs: Another way container plants can stay happy and dry is to have a reservoir to collect water beneath their roots. Look around your garden, house, and garage for coarse materials you can use, such as empty or broken grower pots, bricks, stones, even empty water bottles. Fill the bottom third of your pot, trough, or raised bed with these materials before you add the soil. As a bonus, if you're using plastic pots in a windy location, the coarse materials at the bottom can help weigh the pots down and keep windy blasts from knocking them over.

Depending on the situation, choose one or the other of these options—and both if water ends up lingering in your containers. Getting drainage right takes trial and error, sometimes over a few seasons.

Drain, baby, drain! Rocks create a reservoir.

If you have a drill handy, and you're handy, make some drainage holes.

Preparing New Places to Grow

Building a Raised Bed

I do love a good raised bed. Initially, they take some work to set up, but in the end your efforts pay off in spades. Here's how to create a raised bed garden for your food plants. It's essentially a rectangular box with no bottom or lid. (You will need a wooden bottom if this bed is part of your deck or sitting on your patio, but these instructions are for making a bottomless bed.)

Also, this bed is 1 by 2.5 m (4 by 8 feet) in size and 45 cm (18 inches) high. Plants need just 20 to 30 cm (8 to 12 inches) of soil to thrive, but to be kind to the human back, I like a bed that's 45 to 60 cm (18 to 24 inches) high. Any higher and your wooden structure might require additional support, so don't go there.

1. Choose your site. Sun, sun, sun. Nothing matters more!
2. Purchase your materials. You will need:
   - One 2.5 m (8 foot) long four-by-four white cedar post for corners; nine 2.5 m (8 foot) long white cedar two-by-six planks for sides and ends
   - 1 lb box of 3½ inch galvanized nails or 3½ inch galvanized wood screws
   - Landscape fabric, 1 by 2.5 m (4 by 8 feet)
   - 1.5 cubic yards of compost or triple mix
   - Circular saw
   - Level
   - Carpenter's square
   - Drill and drill bits
   - Eye protection
3. Mark out the beds on the ground using a yardstick, wooden stakes, and string; or by using orange contractor paint (which washes away).
4. Remove vegetation from the area.
5. Rough up the top layer of the existing ground with a spade to a depth of 10 cm (3 inches).
6. Dig a trench around the exterior of the bed to a depth of 10 cm (3 inches). This trench will allow you to bury the lower half of the bottom boards (which will stabilize the bed), so dig it a bit wider than your wood. Rake and level the ground.
7. Build your bed on a flat surface not too far away from the bed's final home, such as your patio or in your garage.
   a. Make corner posts. Cut your 2.5 m (8 foot) four-by-four plank into four 60 cm (24 inches) lengths. These will stand up vertically and sit on the inside of your bed's walls.
   b. Build one of your long bed walls. Using a drill and screws, attach the ends of one 2.5 m (8 foot) two-by-six plank to your posts. The bottom of this plank should be flush with the bottom of the posts. Stack the next two-by-six on top of the first and screw it in, then the third. One wall is done. The post should stick up about 18 cm (7 inches) above the top plank.
8. Build the opposite long wall the same way.
9. Cut the remaining 2.5 m (8 foot) two-by-six planks in half. Use them to build your two short 1 m (4 foot) walls.
10. Carry the raised bed to your garden and put it in place. Using a level to get things flat, tamp corner posts in place with a mallet or small sledgehammer.
11. Line the bottom with landscape fabric. Fill the bed with compost or triple mix, and plant!

A: When you screw your 1 m (4 foot) planks to your corner posts, make sure to keep things straight and flush.

B: Once all of your two-by-six planks are screwed in, the structure of your raised bed is pretty much done.

C: Place your new bed in the garden and get it as level as you can. If you have two or more beds, leave a walkway between them.

D: Landscape fabric lines the bottom of the bed, keeping soil and nutrients in, and weeds out.

E: Fill 'er up! Load your beds with compost or triple mix. Each bed will take about one and a half cubic yards. If you're doing lots of gardening this year, consider ordering in bulk. Save some money and save your back!

Preparing Pots

1. Choose a sunny location.
2. Purchase new containers or clean existing ones.
3. Assess drainage. Drill additional holes, or add coarse materials to improve drainage.
4. Fill containers with potting soil, water it, and you're good to go.

The following season, provided your potted food plants developed no diseases, you can keep much of the soil and use it again. (Now that's a money saver!) Just replace the top third with new potting soil. If there was any disease at all in your plants, discard both the plants and the soil, clean the container thoroughly (see page 38), and put in all-new soil.

Setting Up Troughs

1. Determine the best location in your garden or on your deck or patio. One more time—think sun, sun, sun.
2. Purchase trough(s).
3. Place in selected location, remove drainage plug, and decide if you need to create a reservoir for additional drainage.
4. Fill with a potting soil/compost mix, moisten, and plant.

The following season, just plant your trough again, perhaps topping up the upper part of the container with some new potting soil and compost. You do not have to empty troughs year after year. However, if you had diseased plants, you must empty them out entirely, disinfect, and start with brand new soil. (Pricey and a bit of work, but worth it, or you'll spread that disease.)

How Much Soil Do You Need?

Figuring out how much soil, triple mix, mulch, or other ingredient you need for a container or in-ground bed is not rocket science. But it does require a little math. You need to know the dimensions of the space you want to fill. Use this calculation: length (in feet) times width (in feet) times depth (in inches). Divide by 12, then divide by 27. That will get you the cubic yards of soil you need. (If you really don't like math, take comfort in the fact that if you buy in bulk, most sellers will just ask for your garden or container dimensions and will crunch the numbers for you.)

$$L' \times W' \times D'' \div 12 \div 27 = X \text{ cubic yards}$$

One cubic yard equals about 765 L, or twenty-five 30 L bags

For a 1 m by 2.5 m (4 by 8 foot) raised bed where you want a depth of 40 cm (16 inches) of soil you'll need 1.5 cubic yards of soil.

You can buy bagged soil—or compost or manure—from the garden centre if you can carry the bags. If you need a lot of soil, it may be more convenient and cheaper to order from a bulk seller who will deliver the soil right to your garden. Once you're ordering three cubic yards, you'll definitely save money—and save yourself some back-breaking work.

A soaker hose (far right) makes sure water gets where you want it to go—into the ground, not onto plant leaves or evaporating in the wind.

Irrigating Your Garden

When your in-ground or container garden gets dry—and it will in the summer—you can pull out the hose or the watering can. But if you have a large garden or you know watering will be an issue, consider setting up some kind of irrigation system that stays in place all the time and allows you to water easily and sometimes automatically.

When planning an irrigation system, the goal is to install one that avoids top watering—just getting the plants wet—and instead gets moisture to the roots of your delicious crops.

Irrigation systems can be professionally installed, or you can purchase kits at most home improvement and some garden centres. Prices range widely. Some systems include electronics and software, and some are even Wi-Fi enabled to monitor the weather. You probably don't need to go there for your small food garden and can spend as little as $20.

If you have an in-ground garden, you can set up a soaker hose on a basic timer to water your garden. If you have troughs or containers, consider drip irrigation. It's exactly what it sounds like: a system that waters individual plants slowly by a gradual drip. This approach uses water efficiently, as the water stays in the soil close to plant roots. Such systems are not expensive, and easy to set up. You often just attach the soaker hose to an outdoor tap or garden hose and place it on a timer. Many home improvement stores sell drip systems in a kit, or you can buy the individual components.

Ready to Go

Your beds and containers are now prepped and ready to start growing whatever tasty delights you have in mind this year. You're set to start learning about the many wonders of the food plants that thrive in our Canadian climate.

Get Organized: Your Garden Plan

The most bountiful and delicious food gardens are backed by a secret weapon: a plan. Putting careful thought into what you are planting and knowing in advance where you are going to put it—and why—makes for great growing. An organized foot plot gets lots of sun, has airflow, stays moist, and, most crucially, grows crops that its owners actually want to eat.

Here are my steps to plotting out a really smart food garden this year:

1. Ask your family what they want to grow and eat, and get each family member to come up with their top five. Narrow the list to seven to 15 foods.
2. Edit your final list based on your available light, your space, and what's good to grow. (See what I have to say in chapter 3 about the best foods to grow.) If you have a small space, eliminate any requests for pumpkins and promise a trek to a pumpkin farm in the fall instead. If you plan to grow in containers, whittle down your list to plants that suit pots. If you have a lot of shade, modify your list to add plants that don't mind it. (This means tomatoes are out—sorry!) If you are just growing in a few pots this year, keep your list of 15 as next year's wish list and just grow the top five instead.
3. Based on the size of your family and how often they will enjoy eating the crops on your list, and taking into account any plans to can or freeze your produce, determine just how much to grow. (Look to the Food to Grow Plant Guide starting on page 188 for information on individual plant yields to help figure this out.)

4. Draw up a chart to indicate some key characteristics of your winning plants. Use the seed pack or plant tag to gather information, and put it in the chart: how long the plants take to mature, their height, and how many you'll plant. (See my sample chart on page 49. I don't include the growing height and width of the plant, but you could include that information, as well as watering and fertilizing needs.)
5. Draw a picture of your garden bed or containers, making your rows run north to south. Make your drawing to scale (if you use graph paper, one square could equal 30 cm/1 foot, for example). You can also look to the internet to find an app that helps you do this task. Tall plants should be on the north side of the garden so they don't shade others. (But you might want to put your leafy greens under the shade of pole beans to help them endure the summer heat.) Put slow-growing, large plants close to small, fast growers and the big plants can take over the extra space once the little ones have been harvested. You'll notice that in my garden plan I do this with tomatoes and leaf lettuce, zucchini and spinach. (Refer to chapter 4 for information on planting companions so you are sure to put plants that like each other side by side.)
6. Draw a garden plan for the later stages of your garden if you're practising multi cropping (an important yield-maximizing technique outlined in chapter 4 starting on page 84). Enter your estimated sowing, planting, and harvest dates in your calendar (a paper one or your digital calendar). These dates are goals only. The weather can change the growing season, as can your own busy schedule. You'll see on page 50 that I've included a plan to show what my summer and late summer will look like. Yep, I'll be harvesting all season long with this plan.

Frankie's Family Garden

Here's how I might plan a 1 by 2.5 m (4 by 8 foot) garden for my family based on those steps. I like to grow tomatoes, cayenne peppers, basil, Swiss chard, and kale. My wife, Laurie, requests tomatoes, herbs, kale, leaf lettuce, and cucumbers. Gavin, my oldest son, likes beans, cherry tomatoes, basil, zucchini, and eggplant. And Matheson, my youngest, asks for potatoes (for fries), cherry tomatoes, peas, lettuce, and cucumber.

Based on what we like, the size of the plot, and what's easy and smart to grow, we made our final list. I added spinach for a quick-to-harvest leafy green. I eliminated eggplant and potatoes. We don't eat much eggplant, and potatoes are cheap to purchase and finicky to grow. Here's what we settled on growing:

Food to Grow	Time to Harvest	Height	Number
Tomatoes	slow	tall	2–4
Cherry tomatoes	slow	tall	1–2
Herbs	fast	short	multiple
Kale	fast	short	4–12
Leaf lettuce	fast	short	4–12
Beans	slow	tall	2–4
Peas	slow	tall	2–4
Cayenne peppers	slow	tall	2–4
Cucumbers	slow	short	1–2
Swiss chard	slow	tall	2–4
Zucchini	slow	short	1–2
Spinach	fast	short	1 row

Our Springtime Plot

This is a "sketch" of our 1 by 2.5 m (4 by 8 feet) plot. Each square represents 30 cm (1 square foot) in my garden. My mom, Alyce, created these illustrations where each drawn plant represents one of that plant in the garden. Thanks, Mom!

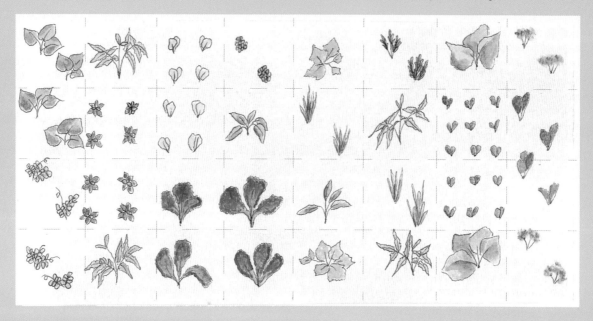

Our Summer Plot

Once my greens—leaf lettuce, kale, and spinach—are done, I'm going to let some of those 30 by 30 cm (1 by 1 foot) areas remain empty, to be taken over by neighbours like now-tall tomato plants. And I'm going to plant a little spinach.

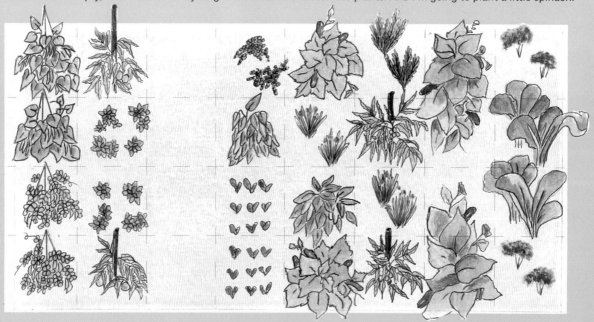

Our Late Summer Plot

The harvest is in full swing in my little plot. My summer spinach grew so quickly that I'm able to put some kale in its place. Also, my zucchini, peas, and beans are done, and I'm now going to grow some leaf lettuce, mesclun mix, and radishes for fall salads.

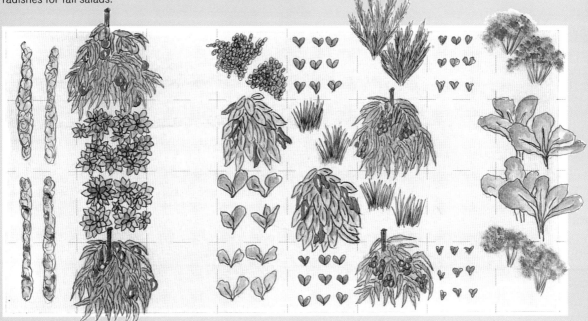

Key to the Plots

Our Springtime Plot
Row 1: Beans, tomatoes, leaf lettuce, oregano, cucumbers, rosemary, zucchini, parsley
Row 2: Beans, basil, leaf lettuce, cayenne peppers, chives, cherry tomatoes, spinach, Swiss chard
Row 3: Peas, basil, kale, kale, cayenne peppers, chives, spinach, Swiss chard
Row 4: Peas, tomatoes, kale, kale, cucumbers, cherry tomatoes, zucchini, parsley

Our Summer Plot
Row 1: Beans, tomatoes, empty, oregano, cucumbers, rosemary, zucchini, parsley
Row 2: Beans, basil, empty, cayenne peppers, chives, cherry tomatoes, empty, Swiss chard
Row 3: Peas, basil, empty, sow spinach, cayenne peppers, chives, empty, Swiss chard
Row 4: Peas, tomatoes, empty, sow spinach, cucumbers, cherry tomatoes, zucchini, parsley

Our Late Summer Plot
Row 1: Sow leaf lettuce, tomatoes, empty, oregano, sow spinach, rosemary, sow radishes, parsley
Row 2: Sow leaf lettuce, basil, empty, cayenne peppers, chives, cherry tomatoes, empty, Swiss chard
Row 3: Sow mesclun mix, basil, empty, sow kale, cayenne peppers, chives, empty, Swiss chard
Row 4: Sow mesclun mix, tomatoes, empty, sow kale, sow spinach, cherry tomatoes, sow radishes, parsley

Chapter 3

Tasty Choices: The Best Food to Grow

You're all ready to plant. The seed racks and seedling trays at your garden centre offer many options. Too many, in fact. Choices are good; choices can be fun. But choices can also be overwhelming. If you're new to food gardening, you don't want to choose wrong. You want your hard work in the garden to be successful so that your time, energy, money, and space result in a bounty at harvest, not a sob story to share around the water cooler.

With this in mind, let me limit your choices. It seems bossy now, but you'll thank me later—really you will. I've handpicked some of the best vegetable and fruit growers going. Foods that grow easily, give you the best bang for your small-garden buck, and have great yields. Delicious choices await.

Choosing Your Crops

Selecting what to grow can be an exciting but intimidating task. Options are endless, from different coloured carrots to different sizes and shapes of eggplant. Even something as simple as mint comes in different shapes and flavours. In order to grow successfully, you need to be selective in what you grow. Due to space, climate, and soil type, some plants will not be suitable for your garden. I've developed my own criteria to determine if a plant will make its way into my garden and onto my table:

- Will my family eat it?
- Does it fit my space and soil type?
- Is it easy to grow?
- Does the plant produce good yields or allow for multiple crops?

If you've answered yes to many or all of these questions, you've probably got a winner. Here's how I know what to avoid:

- Is it hard to grow?
- Is it a space hog?
- Can I buy it inexpensively at the grocery store instead?
- Will it attract critters such as bugs, slugs, and bunnies?
- Is its maturity date (the number of days until harvest listed on the seed package or tag) longer than my growing season?

If the answer to one or more of these is yes, I'd say walk away—unless we're talking about a sentimental favourite, like the potatoes your aunt Marjorie used to grow. This food plant is probably just not worth your energy.

Time Enough to Grow

It takes time for a tomato to go from seed to tasty burger topping. In Canada, that can be a problem, as many parts of this country have somewhat short growing seasons. How long is the growing season in your area? You can easily find first and last frost dates for your region on the internet, or check the Food to Grow Plant Guide on page 188. Choose your food plants accordingly. Many varieties of peppers, for instance, take too long to mature for Canadian growers, as do foods such as peanuts and artichokes.

Green beans rule: delicious and easy to grow.

Frankie's High-Yield Favourites

Particularly when you're growing in a small space, you have to be selective. These are my favourite high-yield, money-saving, minimal-fuss vegetables that, as a bonus, grow in many parts of Canada. They're pretty tasty too.

Green beans and peas: The more you harvest, the more these plants will produce. Go for the bush style of these green vegetables. Pole beans, which grow on a vine, might be tempting, as they have a small footprint. But since they grow up and need a structure to climb on, they can end up shading the rest of your garden. (See more on vertical gardening on page 70.)

Salad greens: Greens like leaf lettuce, arugula, and mesclun mix keep on giving. If you harvest the young side leaves when you want to make a salad, avoid removing the entire plant and more will grow back. These useful plants mature so quickly they're often ready to pluck before anything else in the garden. Be sure to stagger when you plant (see more on this in chapter 4 on page 80) so you'll have greens all summer long.

Kale: This super-food is a super-producer. Just like salad greens, if you only remove the young side shoots, kale will keep growing. Kale can also grow in cool weather and will withstand a light frost, so you can get a jump-start on the growing season with a spring planting.

Small garden? Grow salad greens like leaf lettuce.

More on What to Grow
This chapter lists my favourite food crops. For detailed information on all these foods, and on dozens more that may catch your eye, see the Food to Grow Plant Guide starting on page 188.

Kale looks as good as it tastes.

Swiss chard.　　　Yum ... cherry tomatoes.　　　Go on—grow garlic!

Swiss chard: A leafy green that just keeps giving and giving; the more you cut the more it grows! (Notice a trend: Leafy vegetables are just plain smart to grow. Plus, they're really good for you.)

Spinach: This green is quick to harvest and it grows well from seed. Spinach will start growing quite early in the season, as it likes the cool nights and warm days of early spring.

Herbs: Parsley, basil, sage, and oregano, among others, grow well in most parts of Canada. You can snip off what you need for dinner, and as a bonus, the more you harvest herbs, the better they grow. Since herbs can cost a few dollars each at the grocery store and you rarely use a whole bunch, I consider them a financially smart crop.

Cherry tomatoes: Both the vine and bush varieties yield lots and lots of sweet, small tomatoes with a minimal amount of care. If you have kids, you can't go wrong: I call cherry tomatoes "garden candy," as kids will scarf them back like sweets. Grocery stores charge a premium for these, so they're a frugal choice too.

Cayenne peppers: One plant goes a long way. Although cayenne peppers take some time to mature, once they produce, the yields are great. As well, the peppers dry nicely and can spice up your cooking all winter long.

Garlic: This cooking essential has good yields in small spaces. The garlic scapes—the chive-like growth from the top of the bulb—come up in summer and are great in cooking. Garlic actually repels insects, so it acts like a protector for the rest of your garden. Garlic from the grocery store is often imported and has travelled ever so long to get to you. Nothing tastes like fresh out of your own garden!

Frankie's B-List Vegetables

These veggies take a bit more work, maybe aren't quite as space efficient, or come with a few more quirks. They also take more soil amendments or fertilizer to grow, or they may be just fussy enough that you need a few seasons to get things just right. In other words, I *like* these vegetables in the garden, but I don't *love* them. Still, no harm in giving them a try.

Slicing tomatoes: These are by far the most popular food crop in Canada and in the world. They are incredibly versatile and folks from salad fans to those who love to make big batches of salsa and spaghetti sauce want one or more varieties in their garden. Full-size tomatoes can take up a fair bit of space and require feeding with fertilizer to do their best.

Beets: Because beets need space, they're not for a very small garden. They also get mixed reviews at the dinner table: Some people just don't like them! Many varieties have a long date to maturity, so choose early varieties for a slightly quicker harvest.

Growing Heirlooms

It's become increasingly popular to seek out traditional foods that have not been tampered with by humans. Heirloom seeds are just that: old varieties of food plants that have not been hybridized or cross-pollinated. But be warned: The reason gardeners started changing plants was that some old varieties have flaws. Heirloom plants may be at risk for common disease, take too long to harvest, or taste bitter. So by all means seek out heirloom seeds and give them a try, but know you may find growing heirlooms a little more challenging.

With nutritious roots and greens, beets are a healthy double-whammy—but not everyone agrees they are a tasty one!

Zucchini: This vegetable is quick to germinate from seed and one zucchini plant is enough for a family. But zucchini are prone to mildew. They also sprawl. Many new gardeners make the mistake of growing several plants and then give away half the harvest or scramble to find decent zucchini bread and relish recipes.

Cucumbers: Like zucchini, they grow easily right from seed and are so quick to harvest you can pick them in midsummer. And they're prone to mildew too. Grow them vertically to save space, as these can be space hogs.

Carrots: Since carrots are so cheap to buy, they're not the most cost-efficient growers. But they are easy to rear and they occupy little space—you can get up to 16 carrots in a square foot. You can harvest your crop early and have small, sweet baby carrots. But carrots don't grow well in containers. And rabbits—as you know—adore carrots, so don't grow them if those critters lurk in your garden.

Zucchini grow like mad—plant them somewhere that gives them lots of room to stretch out.

Now that's a great-looking carrot!

Raising Chickens

I love the Netherlands. It's not just the flower bulb hub of the entire world, but everyone there seems to have a chicken coop. It's a smart and resourceful thing to do if you want to be a true backyard farmer. Chickens not only produce a regular harvest of eggs, they also eat almost everything you don't want in the garden: leaves, weeds, and even bugs, as well as kitchen scraps. Place your edibles in the coop and the chickens just peck away at them. Chicken poop can be composted into a wonderful, rich amendment to feed plants, and if you let chickens loose around your yard, their pecking aerates the soil.

But before you buy some birds and build a coop, do your research. Many municipalities have bylaws restricting these birds. Plus, chickens only lay eggs for five to seven years. This is a picture of my friends' the Mackies chicken. Her name is Red and she's a Silkie, a breed known for their friendliness but not their ability to produce eggs—they only lay about three a week. Pick a breed that works for your needs and don't adopt a rooster, as most bylaws ban them because they are really, really loud. You may need to protect your birds from local dogs, and coyotes and wolves if you live in a rural area.

Frankie's Fave Fruits

Strawberries: This tasty perennial is easy to grow in the ground but also thrives in hanging baskets, bags, and other containers. Select everbearing varieties that will offer fruit from spring into summer.

Blueberries: Jam-packed (get it?) with antioxidants, blueberries can be a little picky about soil type (they like it acidic). If you can give them the right soil, these tasty, purplish-blue treats grow easily and thrive in small spaces. Some will even overwinter in a pot.

Apples: This go-to fruit tree is a challenge to grow organically but is one of the hardiest of all the fruit trees. If you are already thinking of planting a tree in your yard, why not an apple tree for fruit as well as shade? Most require a friend (another apple tree/pollinator) to maximize yields.

Haskap berries: Something old is new again! Also known as blue honeysuckles, haskap berries are exceptionally hardy. They're one of the first shrubs to flower in early spring and one of the first to bear fruit. Haskap require pollination (so you need two plants) and are honestly not all that pretty to look at. Who said this was a fashion show—it's a food garden!

Rhubarb: This perennial, once established after a few seasons, will keep on giving. But the plant takes up a fair bit of space and does not like containers; plus, it's not that expensive to buy. Some gardeners find they don't use much, so only grow it if you're actually going to eat or preserve it, and will be doing so year after year.

Rhubarb starts small but gives you years and years of harvests.

Frankie's First-to-Harvest Picks

If you live north and have a short growing season, you have to select your food plants very carefully. Unless you can rig up frost protection or start growing in a greenhouse, you run the risk of getting your prized foods ruined by an early frost. Here are some foods that don't take long to grow:

- Watercress—24 to 48 hours when using sprouts
- Radishes—25 to 30 days from seed
- Spinach—30 to 40 days from seed
- Lettuce—45 to 55 days from seed
- Kale—55 to 75 days from seed

Above: Who doesn't love the idea of picking an apple from their own tree? Top right: Plant radish seeds and they'll be ready for salads in a month. Bottom right: Strawberry shortcake, strawberry jam. Take your pick with this versatile fruit. The chicken wire here helps to ensure that you—and not furry or feathered garden visitors!—get to enjoy your harvest.

Shade Crops

I know I said you need six hours of afternoon sun for a happy food garden, but there are plants that thrive without quite that much sun. Know this about shade: Not all shade is equal. Only mushrooms will grow in total darkness. Most partial sun or partial shade food plants need one to two hours of direct sun a day followed by indirect light or sunlight filtered through the canopy of a tree or shrub. Wherever moss grows, that's a sign there's not enough light for a food plant—put in a hosta instead. If you're going to push it and plant some food in an area where you have some sun but not much, make certain everything else is in order. Be sure the soil is healthy by adding some compost, manure, or triple mix before you plant. Once your food shade garden is up and running, water in the morning only. Slugs adore shady areas and soggy nighttime meals, and will munch up your garden if you keep it wet in the evenings.

Frankie's Top Shade Plants

- Salad greens: leaf lettuce, mesclun mix, arugula, and watercress
- Cooking greens: Chinese cabbage, spinach, Swiss chard, kale
- Root vegetables: radishes, beets, and leeks
- Legumes: peas, beans
- Herbs: lemon balm, chives, mint, parsley, oregano, and golden marjoram

Shade-loving mint will thrive even in less than six hours of sun a day. Leeks (opposite) are also a great shadier option.

What to Grow in Containers

Containers offer a great way to grow a wide variety of fruits, vegetables, and herbs, and often you can locate your crop right near your kitchen so you'll be sure to eat your garden plants as soon as they ripen.

As with a larger garden, you want to pick the most suitable plants. Select a variety that can thrive in the space you have available. Look for types that say bush, dwarf, or compact, and avoid those that say vigorous, heavy feeder, and invasive.

Frankie's Container Picks

Beans: Dwarf varieties of bush beans will actually grow in very small containers 25 cm (10 inches) in diameter with little fuss. Try 'Contender' (green bean), 'Tendergreen Improved' (green), 'String-less Green Pod' (green), 'Golden Wax Improved' (yellow), 'Pencil Pod Black Wax' (yellow). Want to have a go at pole beans instead? You need to support these vertical growers (see page 70 for more on growing up), but you can get lots of beans in a small space. One of my favourite varieties is 'Scarlet Runner'—a delicious pole bean that also produces beautiful red flowers.

Beets: This colourful vegetable will grow right from seeds and can adapt to containers of all shapes and sizes. Try a window box (a deep one) or even old recycling bins. Select 'Early Wonder' or 'Detroit Red', both of which are ready to eat in just under 60 days from sowing.

You might never eat strawberries and eggplants together, but they grow beautifully in a shared container.

Swiss chard: Swiss chard is a healthy green that also looks sharp in a container, so I'll often mix it with ornamentals for a pretty but practical container alongside a front walk. 'Bright Lights' (which has multicoloured stems) and 'Rhubarb Chard' (with red stems) are attractive versions that keep on growing if you pick the outer leaves.

Salad greens and lettuces: Mesclun mix, arugula, and mustards like 'Red Giant' are probably the easiest and fastest to grow of all edibles. Lettuces like Boston, endive, and escarole too. Start early spring, skip the deep heat of summer, and sow a final crop in late summer for fall.

Eggplant: Eggplant is one of the most underrated plants of the food garden. With its felt-like foliage and fabulous purple flowers, it looks great. It grows well in containers with a little staking. 'Little Fingers' and 'Hansel' are my favourite varieties, as their size is perfect for slicing and grilling.

Kale: This leafy green thrives in containers and dazzles during the process. Even those fall plantings of flowering kale you get for decorative containers are edible. Just one warning: In late fall, remove and discard all the foliage from your containers, particularly those right at your front door. The smell of rotting kale will drive away your whole family during the holidays—unless you're okay with that.

Peppers: Bell, sweets, hot, even very hot peppers, thrive in pots and planters. For northern gardens, look for peppers with fewer days to maturity, including 'Northern Bell' and 'California Wonder' (a bell variety). For hots, try 'Yellow Wax Hot' and 'Long Red Cayenne'.

Radishes: These crunchy treats are ready to harvest before just about any other crop and do well in containers. Plant them straight from seeds in early spring and late summer. I like 'Cherry Belle', 'Sparkler White Tip', and 'French Breakfast'.

Spinach: In spring and fall, spinach grows well from seeds in containers. But during the summer heat, I would avoid the frustration of growing spinach; it tends to bolt (shoot up and flower, turning the leaves bitter). Try 'Bloomsdale' and 'Matador'.

Tomatoes: The first food I ever grew in a pot was a tomato plant: a popular cherry tomato variety known as 'Tiny Tim'. Tomatoes come in two main varieties: indeterminate (vine style) and determinate (dwarf/bush). To make growing container tomatoes easy on yourself, choose determinate varieties such as 'Early Girl Bush', 'Celebrity', or 'Patio'.

Cucumbers: Just one variety, 'Spacemaster', takes well to containers—but it performs very well in just about any pot, even hanging baskets. It produces a slightly smaller fruit and is resistant to common diseases such as cucumber mosaic virus and scab.

Herbs: Herbs are a natural fit for containers: You can move them around to follow the sun, and place them right next to where you're cooking and eating. On my deck, I keep 25 cm (10 inch) and 30 cm (12 inch) pots of basil, parsley, mint, rosemary, chives, and oregano right beside the barbecue. Instead of mixing all the herbs in one big container, where they can crowd one another or steal nutrients (think of an aggressive herb like mint trying to interfere with basil, which needs lots of moisture and care), separate them into their own pots.

Frankie's Best Fruits for Containers

Strawberries: This perennial fruit shrub does very well in containers and will even survive the winter in a pot. Some people actually put the pot into the ground to overwinter it. For fruit all season long and pretty flowers, choose 'Tristan' or 'Loran' varieties.

Blueberries: This acidic-soil-loving plant will require some TLC, and you need to be careful in choosing the right variety. Pay attention to hardiness and look for plants that are both dwarf and self-pollinating. 'Jelly Bean' and 'Sweetheart' will grow well in containers.

Tropical fruits: Warmth-loving fruits such as oranges, tangerines, lemons, limes, even pineapples, will grow in large pots if you bring them inside over the winter. You won't get a lot of fruit and the fruit will be small, but growing tropical fruits in containers is a fun way to experiment with food gardening.

Figs: My family has been growing figs in containers (below) ever since I can remember. Most varieties can handle a light frost, and easily overwinter in an insulated cold cellar or garage. Recommended varieties include 'Brown Turkey' and 'Chicago Hardy'.

What's *Improved*?

If you see the word *improved* on a seed package or plant tag, it means the plant has been hybridized to make it better. Perhaps this plant variety had a flaw—it was susceptible to a common disease or it needed too much fertilizer—so someone used traditional practices such as cross-pollination (letting the seeds of two varieties mix to make new plants) to include more attractive properties from another variety. This does not mean genetically modified food! The only genetically modified crops available in Canada are some varieties of corn, canola, zucchini, and soya.

What to Grow
If You Want a Challenge

I want you succeed as a food farmer. So while you can try anything you like in your garden, some plants are more likely to fail. They occupy too much space, they're invasive (will spread everywhere and are hard to get rid of), and may take several years to harvest. Plant the following if you really must. But if things don't go well, remember: I told you so.

Asparagus: This perennial takes several years before it's ready to harvest. If you're willing to wait, asparagus does have good yields in due course. But the amount of space this vegetable needs (one stalk equals one spear), and the amount of time, makes growing it not worth the effort in a small-size plot. While the seed heads are attractive, these plants really do best in a large garden.

Brussels sprouts: If you've never seen Brussels sprouts as a plant (below), you have no idea how funky-looking and large one is. A single plant takes up a lot of space—the stems themselves can grow up to a metre (3 feet) high—and needs 100 days to mature. Buy Brussels sprouts at the farmers' market.

Cauliflower: The plants start out small but get big quickly. One mature plant can measure up to 60 cm (24 inches). They're also fussy to grow: Cauliflower can be sensitive to temperature, requiring you to tie back the leaves to protect the florets (the part you eat) from the sun. Cauliflowers taste great, but these space hogs are too much work.

Celery: Celery needs a lot of fertilizer and loads of water. This space hog takes 100 to 120 days to mature—meaning you can't even grow it in cooler regions of Canada. It's a no.

Coriander: Cooks who love Indian and Mexican cuisine always want to plant this fragrant herb. Yet it's one of the most frustrating herbs to grow. It does fine in cool, spring weather, but as soon as it gets a blast of heat, it starts to bolt, lose its flavour, and go to seed.

Corn: This big plant shades small gardens and attracts rodents like raccoons. Corn is also a heavy feeder and will steal nutrients from the soil and deprive other plants.

Mint: This perennial herb is easy to grow. Too easy. If planted in a garden, it is hard to control. It soon becomes invasive and a nuisance. Plant in containers only or you'll be surrounded by mint forever.

Potatoes: Based on space and economics, it's cheaper to buy potatoes than grow them. They require acidic soil, and planting and caring for them are somewhat involved. The best way to grow potatoes is to opt for a mini variety and use very deep containers.

Raspberries: Small-space gardeners beware: Raspberries grow rapidly, and their canes (stalks) can easily overtake a garden and a yard if not maintained. For the lazy gardener who has a small space, visit a pick-your-own raspberry farm instead.

Squash: Left to their own devices and not tied or staked, most varieties of squash will overtake a small garden in a matter of weeks. Squash and many other vine-type plants are not suitable for small spaces. The only way to grow squash is to grow it vertically (see Going Up: Gardening Vertically on page 70).

Raspberry picking in your own backyard sounds dreamy until the brambles take over! Plant and prune with care.

How Much to Grow?

You've likely worked up a plant list by now and have a sense of what you're going to grow this year. So, how many seeds or seedlings should you put into the soil? This is one area where new gardeners can really go astray. You don't want to get overwhelmed with cherry tomatoes, zucchini, and hot peppers at harvest, while coveting the very few garlic bulbs and beets you were able to harvest. There are two key factors to take into account when planning how much to grow:

What you eat: Track your family's produce-eating habits over a few weeks. Do you go through heaps of salad greens? Do apples go rotten? Your written notes on what you actually eat will give you a sense of both what to grow and which foods will get eaten in volume at harvest. If you plan to make up some pesto or can tomato sauce, know you can plant more basil and tomato and come out fine.

Plant yields: While one pepper plant and one zucchini plant can produce a lot, one carrot seed just makes one carrot. See the Food to Grow Plant Guide starting on page 188 for the yields of your chosen crops.

Planting a lot of one crop may seem easier, particularly if you're planting from seed, but resist the impulse. Overplanting can lead to waste later on, and you will end up giving away half your harvest when you just can't get through all that rhubarb. On this count, less is definitely more.

Green beans are easy to grow from seed, but make sure you sow just enough seeds for the number of plants you want, and not the whole package!

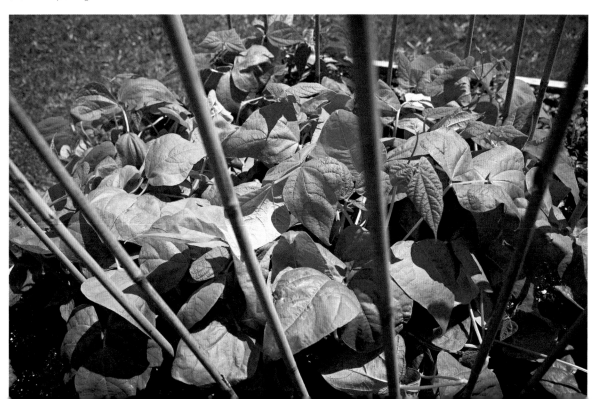

Going Up: Gardening Vertically

Small space? No room to grow out? Then grow up! Vertically, I mean. Vertical gardening maximizes square footage by staking the stems and leaves of plants, enabling them to grow high into the air. This approach frees up ground space, but it also allows for lots of air circulation in and around plants, so as a bonus, vertical gardens attract fewer bugs and diseases. Often, foods grown in the air develop fewer blemishes and grow bigger. I think vertical gardens are ideal when you are growing on a very small yard or patio, as the added height frequently adds privacy—and these gardens are pretty. The one downside: Vertical plantings cast shade, so always remember to locate your tall plants carefully; that way the rest of your food garden gets to bask in the sun too.

Best Foods to Grow Up

Beans: Pole beans are wonderfully easy to grow, and you can choose green or yellow varieties. They have a very tiny footprint, but they really do grow tall, so be ready to support this vegetable. People with small patios they want to look nice will love 'Scarlet Runner', which has a delicious bean and a pretty red flower as well. Also try 'Kentucky Wonder Pole', 'Lazy Housewife' (seriously!), and 'Romano Pod'.

Cucumbers: This vegetable is such a space hog when grown horizontally. Seedless varieties such as 'English' or 'Asian' are much more efficiently grown on a trellis. While cukes get fewer soil-borne diseases when grown vertically, no matter what you do they're at high risk for powdered mildew late in the season. If they get it, harvest what cucumbers you have and move on. It happens to everyone.

Grapes: This perennial vine is somewhat aggressive and must be supported on a strong pergola or arbour. Only plant grapes if you want that particular variety year after year and you're sure you'll use your bountiful harvest for eating or winemaking. Another warning: Grapevines attract raccoons. Try 'Reliance', 'Cayuga', and 'New York Muscat'.

Kiwi: Sound too exotic to grow in Canada? You might be right. The hardy variety should do fine growing upward, but I personally was not impressed with the very low yield of this plant. Another kicker: You need both a male and female plant to produce. Try if you like, but I'm buying my kiwis from the grocery store.

Peas: These are incredibly easy to grow and kids love to eat them right off the vine. So many varieties grow well: 'Lincoln', 'Green Arrow', 'Sugar Snap', and 'Tall Telephone' (also called 'Alderman').

Squash: This space hog has no place in small gardens, but acorn, delicata, buttercup, and yellow summer squash all grow beautifully as vertical vines. Be careful with heavier squash varieties, as the fruit itself may need support or it could pull the entire vine down as it reaches maturity.

Tomatoes: Indeterminate, or vine, tomatoes thrive on trellises or stakes, or you can even string them up on a wire. I like 'Brandywine', 'Big Beef', or 'Better Boy'. Cherry tomato varieties you might want to try include 'Juliet', 'Sun Sugar', or 'Sweet 100'.

Supporting Plants

Just about anything solid, strong, and well put together will support a vertical food plant. You can buy pretty arbours, trellises, obelisks, spirals, and tomato cages. You can simply use wooden stakes. Handy people can nail together beautiful pergolas to drape long vines over, or rig up structures using found items such as rebar, old pipes, and hockey sticks. You know you're in a Canadian garden when you see hockey sticks holding up plants!

Choose your support based on your garden space, but make sure the support will work when the plant is fully grown—read the seed pack or plant tag, as some of these vines get very tall. Your support should be able to bear the weight of the fruit too.

You also need to find a material for tying that won't cut into the stems of your plants. Avoid wire, especially if it doesn't have a protective coating, as it will harm plants, as will kitchen twine. Try old nylon stockings, cut into strips. Or just purchase green staking tape from the garden centre. You can reuse it year after year if you collect the strips at the end of the season and store them.

Vertical Leafy Greens

Okay, I know leafy greens will not climb up a trellis or over a pergola. But they do have shallow roots, so they're perfect for growing in small, stackable spaces. Leaf lettuce, mesclun mix, and arugula can be grown high above the soil in reclaimed eavestroughs. Paint up the troughs, fill them with potting soil, and you have long, attractive planters that you can mount on a fence. Or try them in garden pockets, which are just sacks made from fabric, filled with soil, and hung on a wall or fence. Kale and spinach will grow in small, high-up containers too.

When to Support

I recommend putting trellises, bamboo poles, arbours, cages, and spirals into the soil before planting or immediately after. This way plants can grow into the supports and you won't disturb the soil by installing cages or poles while your plants are growing.

Once you've got your supports in place, the work is not done. Growing a vertical plant is an ongoing process of training and tying. Check on your vertical plants weekly to be sure they're attaching properly to their structures. Keep your eye on heavy fruits; you may have to get creative about holding them up by the time the harvest nears. You might even wire a squash to the support structure till the squash is fully ripe.

Growing in Containers

Just about any plant you can grow up you can anchor in a container. The only exception is grapes, which grow on a thick, perennial vine that should go into the ground. Use a large pot or trough for your vertical plantings—the bigger the better, as the roots must dig deep to support a tall plant. Be sure your container is heavy, or weigh it down—you don't want it getting knocked over by wind or the sheer weight of the vine.

Decide whether you'll put your supports right into the soil of the container, which you might do for a cherry tomato plant. But beans could grow up a fence with their roots in containers. Just be sure your container is firmly anchored on the ground (a few stones in the bottom, or a heavier container, works well here) and won't be knocked over or moved by accident, tearing down your vines and support structures in the process.

A Homemade Trellis

This inexpensive trellis looks great and goes up easily if you're at all handy. Just purchase five 2 to 2.5 m (6 to 8 foot) bamboo poles. Place the poles in a circle on the ground, creating a starburst shape, and tie the tops together with garden twine. Use your trellis for tomatoes, beans, or peas.

Chapter 4

Maximizing: Getting the Most from Your Garden

My family grew vegetables in the Holland Marsh in Ontario for over 40 years, and I learned that to get awesome yields you must plan smart, plant right, and keep things growing as long as you can. It's also about how many times you can turn over the land, or get multiple harvests off one field in one growing season. I promised you that this book would help you get the most vegetables, fruits, and herbs from the smallest space possible. I promised, and I will deliver!

Even if you're new to food growing, there are tricks the seasoned pros use that you can use too, to help you increase yields and ensure you have produce almost all growing season long. The bonus of this approach goes beyond filling your plate. Most of these yield-upping ideas have environmental benefits—they reduce waste, help the soil, even conserve water. In my book, when it comes to yields, more is more.

Grouping Your Plants

The simplest way to get plants producing a whole lot of food for your kitchen is to give them good pals. Plants love being part of a healthy community where there's lots of give and take. Sharing space with helpful friends means swapping nutrients, helping each other conserve water, and repelling pests both big and microscopic. There are three key ways to grow plants together to increase yields:

Companion Planting

Some food plants like existing side by side—they play together nicely like two happy kids in a sandbox. Other pairings spell disaster—by attracting similar diseases or insects or stealing essential elements from the soil that the other needs. What you choose to plant and where you decide to put it should be influenced by who gets along and who fights. For instance, peppers thrive next to basil, which repels some garden beetles, aphids, and spider mites. Onions and carrots help peppers taste better. Two of the worst fighters in the garden are tomatoes and potatoes. They are actually from the same family and attract the same insects and diseases, and each is a heavy feeder that steals nutrients from the other.

Here are some food plants and their best and worst neighbours (see a comprehensive listing of companion plants for each fruit and vegetable in the Food to Grow Plant Guide on page 188):

Food	Friends	Enemies	Helpers
Beans	beets, cabbage, carrots, cucumbers, potatoes, radishes	garlic, leeks, onions, shallots	Marigolds repel bean beetles Catnip repels flea beetles
Beets	broccoli, beans, cabbage, chard, kohlrabi, onions	pole beans	
Broccoli	beets, carrots, onions	strawberries	Marigolds repel cabbage moths Nasturtiums repel aphids
Cabbage	broccoli, sprouts, chard, spinach, tomatoes	strawberries	Tomatoes and celery repel cabbage worms
Carrots	cabbage, chives, leeks, lettuce, onions, peas, radishes, rosemary, sage	dill, parsley	Onions and leeks help repel carrot flies
Cucumbers	beans, cabbage, radishes	potatoes	Radishes repel cucumber beetles
Eggplant	green beans, peppers, tomatoes		Green beans help deter Colorado potato beetles
Garlic	cabbage, tomatoes	peas and beans	Garlic helps others, as it repels aphids and some beetles
Kale	cabbage family (collards, Brussels sprouts, kale)	pole beans, strawberries	Nasturtiums keep insects busy
Lettuce	beets, carrots, radishes, strawberries	cabbage family	
Peppers	basil, chives, coriander, garlic, tomatoes, spinach	beans, fennel, cabbage, kale, kohlrabi	Nasturtiums attract aphids, keeping them away from other plants
Tomatoes	basil, beans, borage, chives, dill, onions, parsley, peppers, spinach, thyme	broccoli, Brussels sprouts, cabbage, cauliflower, corn, kale, potatoes	Planting basil close by might improve flavour (not proven, but I say give it a shot)

Intercropping

Think of this as companion planting, but where the plant buddies are really, really close together. Inter-cropping—also called "interplanting" and "partner planting"—puts crops so close together they're almost touching and often intertwining.

The most popular North American example is the Native American tradition known as "the three sisters." Corn is the centrepiece, providing support to pole beans that grow up the tall stalks. The beans help the corn stalks stay strong and put nitrogen back into the soil. Squash goes at the base of the corn and the beans, and its vines cover the soil just like mulch, keeping it moist. You'll remember from chapter 3 that I don't recommend corn or squash; they make a good intercropping, but they are still best for people with larger, in-ground gardens. Plus, if raccoons frequent your neighbourhood, corn isn't the best plant to grow!

But you might try these two together: radishes and carrots. You grow both right from seed and plant both at the same time in the spring. The faster-growing radishes will be harvested before the slower-growing carrots mature, so you get two crops in one small space.

The key to successful intercropping is to ensure that the requirements of plants (sun, soil type, nutrients) match one another and that harvest times complement too. Pair fast-growing crops with ones that are slower to fill out.

Fast-growing: Arugula, bush beans, green onions, lettuce, radishes, and spinach.

Slow-growing: Broccoli, Brussels sprouts, cabbage, cauliflower, corn, eggplant, kale, and tomatoes.

By the time these tomato plants (in cages, top left and right) grow big enough to shade their neighbours, we'll have already harvested the kale (top centre) and radishes (bottom rows).

Flower Companions

Lastly, you can arrange food growers with flowers. And not just for looks. Some pretty flowers are also hard-working, and serve as protectors for food plants.

This is why I love nasturtiums (bottom left). They are my absolute favourite flower to grow. They look great, they're edible, and they help with plant health and yields by acting as a so-called trap crop—that is, they draw in most garden insects and can protect most food crops. In midsummer you can almost hear aphids eating your nasturtiums. And these tough flowers don't mind at all—they keep thriving even after such a feast.

I recommend planting a few pots close enough to your food garden to lure insects away but far enough away that bugs, when they're done snacking on the flowers, won't go on back to your vegetables.

Marigolds (bottom right) also get hyped for their helping properties. But in my view, they're over-hyped. A common practice among food growers is to plant a border of marigolds around the garden so the flowers will distract insects—marigolds seldom get bothered by insects—and repel animals such as deer and rabbits. The reality is there's no good science showing marigolds distract insects. In fact, they might attract spider mites to a garden. And these pretty annuals are often devoured by rabbits and rarely repel deer. I once saw a deer walk right over a border of marigolds to eat a head of romaine. For my money, a fence is a whole lot more effective than this flower.

Science vs. Experience

Gardening theories about how to improve the flavour of plants and reduce insect damage or disease are often based not on true science but on practical experience. And some ideas about growing plants come more from folklore than anything else. For instance, old-school gardeners say never plant food crops that sound alike close together. That works for tomatoes and potatoes, but not much else. If you hear something works and it seems to make sense, I say no harm in giving it a try.

Timing Your Crops

To be really smart about handling limited soil space, a calendar is your best friend. Using information such as the likely last frost date in your region in the spring and the likely first frost in the fall (see page 396 in the Food to Grow Plant Guide for more on frost dates), plus the time-to-maturity information noted on seed packets and tags, you can map out a plan so your garden works hard every growing season.

Staggering

This is the simplest approach to timing your crops right. It's not so much about yields, but about making sure you have a longer harvest. Nothing worse than having all your salad greens ready for the plucking concurrently. For a few weeks you've got arugula and endive everywhere, your family starts getting tired of all the salads, and some of your plants have started to bolt. A few weeks later, it's all over and you're off to the grocery store to buy

lettuce! Staggering your plantings gives you a steady diet of the foods you love and reduces food waste.

Simply put seeds or seedlings of your favourite food in the ground at different times. If you're sowing seeds into a garden, plant a round early in the spring, and another round seven to 14 days later—and do this three times if you have the space. When the first round is done harvesting, the next will be ready for your plate. Staggering works with salad greens, cooking greens, radishes, carrots, beets, and cabbage.

Mixing Varieties

This approach works similarly to staggering. Say you love tomatoes. Find two varieties with different maturity dates. Plant both varieties at the same time and treat yourself to a longer harvest. Instead of tomato overload for a short time—and maybe even wasting a few—you get a slow, steady supply. As a bonus, this approach has you trying new varieties with different tastes and growing needs—this is how you can land upon the perfect type for your garden and your family. With so many varieties out there, it's great to test a few and find a good fit. You can do this with just about any plant, particularly those that offer early varieties, or larger types that take longer to mature.

Note: If you love to preserve your fruits and vegetables, don't stagger your crops or mix your varieties! Get all your tomatoes, zucchini, and basil going at the same time so you have a bumper crop in your kitchen. Then sanitize those jars and get to work. But still keep in mind the maturity date on your canning crops and make certain they're ripe and ready for your jams, chutneys, and sauces when *you* are—not while you're on vacation or at the same time in August your sister is getting married.

Multi Cropping

Multi cropping, also called "succession planting," is a surefire way to turn your teeny plots into models of efficiency. You see, some plants have a short time to maturity, shorter than your growing season—sometimes much shorter. So you can sometimes plant a new food crop after the first one is done. Using this technique, you can get two or maybe even three rounds out of the same small space.

Multi cropping also caters to plants that like certain conditions. Some adore the cool soil and nights of spring but wither in summer. Others thrive in heat. Still others want what fall has to offer and even tolerate early frosts. When you time out your crops and mix them up, you can make everyone happy.

You need to know a few things to pull this off: the date to maturity of the crop (look on the seed packet or tag and see below), the season the crop likes (see below), and which crops the one you want to plant doesn't mind preceding or following in the garden (see Crop Types opposite).

Short-to-maturity crops: These guys grow quickly and are key crops for a multi-cropping plan. Baby carrots, kale, radishes, all lettuces, spinach.

Cool-loving crops: Carrots, kale, radishes, spinach, lettuces, parsley, cabbage-family foods such as cabbage, cauliflower, broccoli, and Brussels sprouts.

Warm-loving crops: Summer squash, zucchini, peppers, tomatoes, most herbs.

Crop Types

If you are going to multi crop, you need to understand what can follow what. Some plants work well together and some don't—except this isn't about neighbours sitting beside each other; it's about a rotating lineup. Basically, you don't want to plant the same crop twice in the same spot in the same season (or the next season, as part of crop rotation, see page 84). That includes crops from the same family that need the same soil nutrients. Take cabbage, collards, and kale. They're all from the brassica family and affect the soil in the same way.

Most plants fall into four easy-to-remember groups according to how they succeed each other in soil:

Group 1: **Plants grown for flowers or leaves.**
Flowers: cauliflower and broccoli. Leaves: lettuce (head, romaine, Boston, leaf, mesclun mix), cabbage, kale, kohlrabi, Brussels sprouts, and spinach.

Group 2: **Plants grown for fruit.** Tomatoes, peppers, eggplant, squash, cucumbers, corn, and potatoes (this may not make sense, but potatoes are related to tomatoes, which is why they made this list).

Group 3: **Plants grown for their roots.** Carrots, beets, parsnips, radishes, onions, garlic, and leeks.

Group 4: **Plants that feed the soil.** Beans, peas, cover crops (which are sown in late fall, see 86), and peanuts. These plants come last because they feed the soil. Most of the plants in this group are legumes, with nodules along their roots that contain bacteria called "rhizobia," which help the soil absorb nitrogen from the air.

Group 1: Plants grown for flowers or leaves.

Group 2: Plants grown for fruit.

Group 3: Plants grown for their roots.

Facing page: A slow-growing tomato peeks out between two fast-growing lettuce plants. By the time the tomato shades the lettuce, it will have been harvested and enjoyed. Perfect inter cropping.

Group 4: Plants that feed the soil.

How to Multi Crop

Using all you know about your food plants—how long they take to mature, what season they like, and what group they belong to—you can now plan out your growing season of successful multi cropping.

You do this by dividing your plot into four sections (or four containers) and slotting in your food plants. See, in the chart below, how you can start radishes early in the spring in the first part of your garden and, when they're done, put in tomato seedlings to harvest in the fall.

The goal is to avoid planting foods from the same group in the same section of your garden right after each other. This seems limiting, but it's got great benefits. Check out what happens when you plant group 1 after group 4. Once those legumes in group 4 have put all that nitrogen back into the soil, greens such as lettuces, spinach, and Swiss chard will flourish. That's why, in section 2 of the chart, you're okay to plant spinach again after those soil-enriching bush beans grew all summer long. That will be some fine spinach.

I know, plotting out crops is a bit of work. But you'll be amazed at what your garden can produce when you try this idea.

	Early Spring	Spring	Summer	Late Summer/Fall
Section 1	radishes	tomatoes	tomatoes	tomatoes
Section 2	spinach	bush beans	bush beans	spinach
Section 3	carrots	carrots	carrots	leaf lettuce
Section 4	kale	kale	zucchini	arugula

Crop Rotation

While multi cropping happens in one growing season, crop rotation is about what happens the *next* season. Multi cropping and crop rotation work together like the ultimate plant-yield tag team.

Growing the same crop time and time again in the same plot will deplete the soil of the nutrients used by that particular plant, and it can enable the spread of disease. If you grow tomatoes in the same corner of your garden every year, you'll soon find your plants stop doing well. If your plants developed a disease one year and you planted that same crop again—or a plant at risk of getting that disease too—you're pretty much doomed to seeing that disease rise again, unless you move things around.

Farmers change crops every growing season and sometimes even let fields go fallow (without a crop) for a year to allow the soil to regenerate. It's a key technique for smart farmers, and smart gardeners should use it too.

Crop rotation becomes essential if a disease affects your plants. When that happens, you want to carefully clear the land of all debris after the harvest. Then, avoid planting that food there for one or even two years. And do some research to be sure the blight that infected your food plant won't be spread by your new crop. (If the disease is really serious, you may need to leave that plot fallow for a year or two.)

Rotating with Containers

The rules of rotation shift a little with containers. With smaller pots, you don't need to bother. That's because you are using a soilless mix already that has almost no nutrients (you add fertilizer to feed your plants instead); plus, you are either tossing all the soil every year or replacing the top third. So plant those same cherry tomatoes in your favourite clay pot every year—no problem. If you get a disease, throw out all the soil, disinfect the container, and grow what you like the next year.

With a trough, it's up to you. Since you're using a lot of potting soil and feeding, you can probably get away with putting your pepper plants in the same spot at least two years in a row. If you find your yields are starting to diminish, you may want to start doing some rotation, or tossing out the top third of soil mix and putting in new.

Raised beds can act like garden beds. If you're leaving the soil as is, you should rotate your plants.

With these two larger containers, always discard any diseased plants and avoid growing that same crop there the following year. If you have a serious disease in a container, you may need to get rid of all the soil and start again.

Blending Multi Cropping and Rotation

For the very best yields of all, you combine these two smart gardening techniques. That means holding on to your multi-cropping chart from one year and building the following year's chart with it in hand. Again, don't repeat crops from the same group. If you look back at the multi-cropping chart on the opposite page, you'll see that during the next growing season you can move your section 4 plan (kale followed by zucchini and arugula) to section 1, and then bump the other multi-crop rotations down to the next section, so section 1 moves to section 2, and so on.

Cover Crops

Happy soil leads to happy crops that will give you generous yields. Cover crops—plants that you put in the ground after the growing season is over, which are really winter crops—can help. Farmer and gardeners with large plots, particularly windy ones that lack nutrients, will do this. Cover crops reduce soil erosion, reduce weed growth, increase organic matter, reduce soil compaction, attract beneficial insects, and, above all, feed the soil by capturing nitrogen. They also act as a kind of crop rotation and allow you to plant the same crops again in the same space next growing season, as this interim crop has replenished the soil.

This is a lot of effort! It's not for everyone and certainly not for city gardeners with small, protected plots.

Here is how it works. You plant—only using particular crops such as winter wheat or rye—after the fall harvest. The seeds will often germinate and give you tiny sprouts before the frost and snow. In the very early spring, they'll grow a little more. Then you till the ground (see page 35 in chapter 2 for more on tilling) and let the crop become a kind of natural compost in your soil before you plant your spring crops. Some call cover crops "green manure."

My favourite cover crop is winter wheat. It's an annual that puts a lot of nitrogen into the soil when it sprouts in the very early spring. However, it does have a strong root system, so it requires a rototiller in the spring to pull it up. Soybeans, clover, and other members of the legume family work well too because they put nitrogen back into the soil.

For newbie gardeners, I wouldn't recommend cover cropping. While the benefits are huge, it demands a lot of labour and might not be necessary if you are taking good care of your soil in your small plot. It may be something you try in the future, particularly if your soil needs the nutrients and you're getting erosion on your good-size, in-ground garden.

Warming the Soil

When it's cold in the morning, I don't want to get out of bed, and when it's cold in the spring, seeds and seedlings don't want to get going either. If your plants have a slow start, they won't have great yields or reach harvest fast enough for multi cropping. Using a few tricks to warm up the soil in spring helps increase yields by getting in-ground crops producing food as early as possible.

Ideal Soil Temperatures

For seeds placed right in the ground in spring to properly germinate, you need toasty temperatures. Any colder than those I've listed—find out with a soil thermometer or by touch if you're good with temperatures—and germination could be delayed, or worse, it might not happen at all and you may not get a crop.

Covering Soil

I have a few techniques to help you warm up the soil in your in-ground garden. One of the simplest is to just cover up the ground in the early spring—before you've planted—with a black tarp or black plastic. Hold the plastic down with whatever you have lying around—bags of soil or bricks usually work well. Leave the plastic down for six to eight weeks in the early spring. The longer the better! Even if it's not terribly sunny during that time, the soil will warm up, and as a bonus, the barrier will kill off any lingering weeds.

Type	Approximate Minimum Temp	Approximate Optimal Temp
Beans	15°C / 60°F	15–29°C / 60–85°F
Beets	5°C / 40°F	10–29°C / 50–85°F
Carrots	5°C / 40°F	7–29°C / 45–85°F
Corn	10°C / 50°F	15–35°C / 60–95°F
Cucumbers	15°C / 60°F	15–35°C / 60–95°F
Lettuces	2°C / 35°F	4–26°C / 40–80°F
Onions	2°C / 35°F	10–35°C / 50–95°F
Peas	4°C / 40°F	4–24°C / 40–75°F
Peppers	15°C / 60°F	18–35°C / 65–95°F
Radishes	5°C / 40°F	7–32°C / 45–90°F
Spinach	2°C / 35°F	7–24°C / 45–75°F
Squash	15°C / 60°F	21–32°C / 70–90°F
Swiss chard	5°C / 40°F	10–29°C / 50–85°F
Watermelons	10°C / 60°F	21–35°C / 70–95°F

Black Pail Technique

This traditional trick is an easy way to heat up a small garden. All you do is fill black pails with water and place the full buckets around your garden. They work like mini heaters. The pails attract spring sunlight, which warms up the water. At night the water releases heat, warming the garden.

Black Tire Growing

Think back. Do you ever remember seeing a food plant growing from inside a tire sitting in the garden? This is really old school. You just place a tire on its side and fill the hole in the middle with organic matter and composted manure and then plant a heat-loving crop such as tomato, watermelon, or squash in the centre. The raised soil warms quickly and the black tire attracts sunlight and traps heat. This practice fell out of favour due to concerns over hazardous materials leaching from the tire into the soil (and into the food). While it's been proven that tire rubber is inert when just sitting in the garden, so there are no health concerns gardening with it, tires have just never come back into fashion. I'm not against the method. I just think gardens full of tires are ugly and there are other ways to warm the soil.

Cold Frames

Cold frames are any rig-up that you use to cover over your soil—and often your plants—in the early spring and late fall. They are designed to both warm up the soil and protect small plants against frost.

A cold frame can be many things: a small greenhouse structure placed over the garden, or a makeshift A-frame made from an old window. This second approach works very well with raised beds. You just attach the window, via a hinge, to the wooden side of the bed and lower the window over your crops like a lid—don't grow anything tall—and you have an instant greenhouse. Using a cold frame, you can grow some crops almost to maturity while the weather outside is inclement: beets, radishes, lettuce, kale, spinach, chard, wheatgrass, and broccoli sprouts. Erecting your cold frame in a sunny location so the sun can heat things up inside is key.

More Is More

Because I grew up on a farm, a lot of these maximizing techniques are everyday stuff for me. Perhaps as a new gardener you're not quite as keen. Maybe you're worried your plants won't yield at all, and something like multi cropping just seems like too much to take on. Fair enough. I urge you to try maybe one of these ideas this year, and once you get more comfortable as a food grower, test out a few more ideas the following growing season.

Chapter 5

Dirty Work:
Sowing and Planting

Enough assessing, planning, and testing already—it's time to get this garden thing growing and put some plants into the soil. Trowels at the ready! The goal of this chapter is to give your plants the best start possible. To get maximum yields in a small space and to avoid frustration, I'm going to take you through the early stages of the growing process. I have to warn you: there are some decisions to make. Do you want to grow right from seeds? Are you fine with buying seedlings (also called "transplants") from the garden centre and growing them? Either way, you can be successful, especially if you know how to start your plants right.

Seeds vs. Seedlings

Decision time: How do you want to grow? Your choice should be based on your level of experience and how much time you have, but also what crops you are growing. Some foods have a long time to maturity and simply take too many days to grow from seed outdoors in most parts of Canada—you need to buy seedlings or start them indoors from seed. Other foods grow beautifully from seeds in the ground. Here are your choices for how to get growing with your food:

Seed starting: This is the process of sowing (planting) your seeds indoors while it's still cold outside. In this undertaking for experienced gardeners, you start seeds for things like tomatoes and peppers, which need a long time to mature. While starting with seeds indoors is not overly expensive to set up—and seeds are really cheap—it comes with a high failure rate and can be very frustrating for newbies. As a result, I don't recommend this type of growing until you've been a food gardener for a few years. (For everything you need to know on seed starting, see page 100 later in this chapter.)

Direct sowing: This just means planting seeds in the ground after the risk of frost has passed. It's done with seeds that like to germinate (start growing) in a cool place and will go from seed to a mature, harvesting plant rather quickly. Anyone can direct-sow! But you need to do it with the right crops. (See page 96 for more.)

Planting from seedlings: Anyone who wants to grow food can, regardless of experience, grow from seedlings purchased at the garden centre. (If you seed-start indoors, you will eventually plant those crops when they reach the seedling stage, so it's the same process from that point on.) You can grow from seedlings for just about any food plant, even those I recommend for direct sowing. (For more on how to plant seedlings and ensure they get a good start, see page 104.)

Seed Basics

Before I explain how to get seeds (and seedlings) into the ground, let's talk seeds. If you understand seeds, you'll be able to decide if you want to seed-start, direct-sow, or just go the seedling route this year.

First, you should know seeds are great. The choices are (almost) endless. There are dozens of varieties available. You can find heirlooms, organic seeds, quick growers, and fun-coloured carrots and beets. If you love choice, seeds are for you.

Buying Seeds

As early as January, seed companies start advertising their wares. Find a reliable retailer (ask your friends!) and start browsing seed catalogues. While seeds are inexpensive, costs can add up. Since you don't need 10 varieties of tomatoes or seven types of peppers—and you will be tempted—I suggest making a list before you even look at a seed catalogue. You do not want to overbuy.

Assessing Seed Viability

Brand new seeds should germinate easily. Avoid buying any seed package that looks like it's been damaged by water or sun.

If you've gardened in the past and have old seeds lying around, or you got a pack as a wedding favour years ago, you'll want to know if you should plant them or toss them. Here are two tests to see if they are viable:

Glass of water test: Fill a glass with water, place all the seeds you're assessing in the glass, and let them sit for 10 to 15 minutes. Any seed that sinks is viable and should grow into a plant. Any seed that floats is no good and should be thrown away. Since you soak most seeds anyway before planting, take the wet ones that sank and sow them inside or outside.

Paper towel test: Remove 10 seeds from a pack, place in two rows of five on a damp paper towel, and fold the towel over on the seeds. Put this in a sealed

Seeds are inexpensive, but avoid the temptation to overbuy (left). The glass of water test (right) will let you know if old seeds are still good. These floaters should be discarded.

plastic bag and place in a warm, dark location. Check daily to see if the seeds have germinated; you'll see them start to crack and show some greenery. If the towel dries up, spritz it with water. Read the seed package to see how long germination should take. Once that date has passed, make an assessment. If more than five of the seeds have germinated, you have a viable package. If fewer than five have done anything, just throw the whole pack out.

Read the Label

If you're not sure whether you should seed-start or direct-sow, how far apart to plant your seeds, how long to germination, preferred soil type, and more, just read the seed packet. Every variety of food is slightly different, but the label will tell you most things you need to know about how to grow the food plant at hand.

Storing Seeds

If you overbuy this year, hold on to the extra seeds. They'll last for about two to three years. But a warning: The fresher the seed, the better your chances the seeds will turn into healthy plants. Leftover seeds should be stored in an airtight container in a cool, dark, dry location. To reduce humidity in the container, add some paper towel and a packet of silica gel (the packets come in vitamin bottles and other purchases, or you can buy them at craft or floral supply stores).

Seed Preparation

Some seeds need a little boost before they go into soil and start germinating. These are known as "the three S's" of seed preparation. I'll tell you all three, but be careful: not all of them apply to annual food plants. But best to know them anyway! Some of them take time. If you are keeping track of your planned sowing dates on a calendar, add extra time to prep your seeds.

Soaking: Many food seeds, such as beans, peas, and corn (and nasturtiums, a beloved plant of food gardeners), benefit from soaking in lukewarm water for 12 to 24 hours before sowing. Soaking softens a seed's outer shell and improves germination. This works best with large seeds with hard shells. You can soak small seeds too; it won't harm them, but once wet, very tiny seeds are really annoying to work with!

Scarification: Some seeds have a tough outer shell and need some encouragement to germinate. Scarification involves scoring, scraping, or nicking the outer shell of a seed. This is often done by using sandpaper or another rough surface and rubbing it over the seed (below). Scrape until you see a minor colour change on the surface of the seed—don't go too deep—and that's it. Scarification is not a common step for food gardeners when planting annuals but is a seed-starting trick for many perennial plants.

Stratification: Many seeds for perennials require a period where they are cool and dormant before they germinate. Direct sowing outdoors offers this naturally. If you are seed starting, you need to follow a few steps to get the same effect. Stratification involves taking a sealable plastic bag and filling it with a moist handful of sand. Put the seeds in the sand, seal up the bag, and place it in a refrigerator for two to four weeks, then remove the seeds and plant them. Check to see that the sand does not dry out—moisten it if it does.

Direct Sowing

Planting seeds directly into outdoor soil is easier than you think. Many crops like to get into the ground when the earth is still cool and will germinate quickly under this condition. Even if you're not an experienced gardener, you can find success if you choose the right crops. You can direct-sow into the garden or containers. If you don't want to deal with seeds at all, and prefer just buying seedlings and placing them in the ground, go for it. Many crops that grow well from seeds are available in seedling form at your garden centre and will grow beautifully in your garden.

Best Seeds to Direct-Sow

Cool, early-season crops: Sow these in early spring to mid. A good time is when you see the forsythia bloom (forsythia is a bush with bright yellow blossoms). The early-season crops below—except for carrots, onions, and Swiss chard—can be sown again once the first crop harvests, as part of a multi-cropping plan:

- Spinach
- Radishes
- Carrots
- Beets
- Onions
- Lettuce
- Mesclun mix
- Arugula
- Kale
- Swiss chard

Warm-season crops: Sow these in mid-spring to early summer:

- Beans
- Peas
- Cucumbers
- Squash
- Corn
- Pumpkins
- Zucchini

There are a few plants that grow better with direct sowing: carrots, radishes, beets, spinach.

Preparing Soil for Sowing

You are ready to sow. Is your soil set to go? You will need to get out your trowel or shovel and move things around a little before your soil is ready to receive your seeds.

Hill method: Just as it sounds, the hill method calls for mounding or hilling soil for planting. The raised soil gets warm in the sun, which helps seed germination. Using a trowel or your hands, move the soil to create a hill 45 cm (18 inches) wide and 15 cm (6 inches) high—your hill might be an actual round hill or could be a raised row of soil. Sow the seeds in the hill, being sure to follow the recommended depth and distance listed on the seed pack. Use this approach for large seeds such as beans, corn, sunflowers, and peas. Also sprawling plants such as pumpkins, squash, and melons.

The hill method helps seeds warm up and germinate faster.

Trough method: Instead of raising the soil, you lower it. You plant your seeds in a shallow trench. You create your trench by using a garden hoe or, if the soil allows, simply dragging two fingers along the soil. In soft soils I sometimes use the handle of a shovel or rake to draw out a trough. Read the seed packet label to be sure you have the right depth as you create your trough. Sprinkle seeds evenly along the length of the trench and then cover with a thin layer of soil. Use for mid-size seeds such as those for lettuce, chard, arugula, cabbage, and cauliflower. Potatoes require a trough too, but a really deep one. (See page 68 for more information on how to plant potatoes.)

Rows: Using either the hill or trough method, plant in long, tidy rows if you have a larger garden. Mark out your rows using stakes and a string line. Or use chalk string, which you can snap against the soil to help you get a straight line. Label the end of each row with a plant tag.

I do like my rows straight and tidy.

Ways to Sow

Your soil is ready to receive. Now it's time to decide, based on the size of your seeds, which of the following four methods of sowing is best:

Hand: Large seeds like corn, beans, pumpkins, melons, peas, and cucumbers can easily be seeded by hand, placing each seed, one by one, in the soil at the right depth. I like to plant two seeds in each location—seeds are inexpensive and you can sacrifice a few in order to increase success and guarantee good yields. If both germinate and pop up, pull out the smaller one.

Broadcasting: Also called "agitating," this style reminds me of my dad, who used to sow onions by simply opening the seed pack and shaking them across the soil surface. This process sounds messy, but it works well for tiny seeds where dropping them in one by one just won't fly. All you do is sprinkle seeds where you want them to grow and cover over with a light layer of soil. Later, when seedlings pop up and have three to five leaves, you thin out the least healthy plants and leave the ones you want, thereby guaranteeing them enough space to grow. Onions, carrots, and lettuces do well with this approach.

Seed tape: You can purchase seed tape, which is strips of biodegradable fabric with seeds stuck to them, evenly spaced apart, for tiny seeds such as beets, carrots, and onions. Since these seeds are so small and are hard to handle, seed tape makes your life easier. Seed tape costs more than seed packets, but it saves you the step of thinning out later.

Mechanical: Farmers with large country gardens may use mechanical seeders to get their seeds into the ground quickly and efficiently. It's not an approach many new gardeners with small plots will try—at least not yet.

Sowing Depth

However you decide to sow, make sure you get the seed depth just right. Read the seed package label to find out how deep to plant, and bring a ruler into the garden if you're not good at guessing. Many new gardeners place their seeds too deep in the soil, whereas tiny seeds don't require much coverage at all. The general rule is you sow a seed a minimum of three to four times as deep as the seed's width. So if your seed is just 3 mm (about ⅛ inch) wide, it should go into the soil about 9 mm (⅓ inch) down. Also, follow the directions on the package for how far apart to space from neighbours.

Mark It!

Always remember to label or tag your garden. Sounds basic, but it's easy to forget! When your seedlings first come up and they're the same size as your weeds, you want to know precisely what you've planted so you accidentally don't yank out your crop. If you planted from seeds or lost the tag from the garden centre, you can be wondering how you'll ever remember what's where. So, make your own! If you or someone in the family has some old vertical blinds sitting around, just remove the string from the blinds and cut them with scissors to about 10 cm (4 inches) in length. Use a permanent marker to write on the strips, and plunk them into the ground. You can also rig up your own tags using Popsicle sticks—write on them or add a waterproof label—or even the empty seed packet, mounted on a twig. Anything goes. It doesn't have to be pretty— it just has to identify your plants.

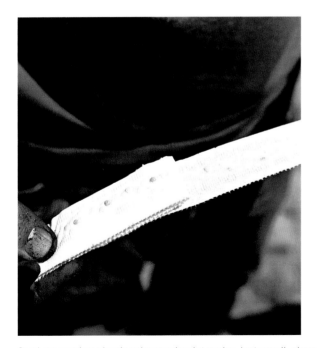

Seed tape makes planting tiny seeds a lot easier. Just unroll, place, and don't bury too deep.

Seed Starting

Sowing your plants indoors and raising them into seedlings while it's still chilly outside is called "seed starting." It's a way to get a jump on the growing season! But it's not for everyone. I don't suggest new gardeners try seed starting for at least two seasons—it takes up a lot of time and can be frustrating. In the meantime, buy seedlings instead.

Benefits: When you start your seeds inside, you are truly the master of your food garden. If you want to grow organic, it's much easier to find organic seeds in a wide array of varieties—as opposed to just what's available at your garden centre when you want to start planting seedlings outdoors. If you are a successful seed starter, it can also be more affordable than buying seedlings.

Drawbacks: This process takes space, time, effort, and experience. Seeds don't always germinate. Seeds come in packets and you may end up with more seedlings than you really need—there's no point in starting a whole packet of tomato seeds if you're a family of two with a container garden on a patio. You must water your germinating seeds often, sometimes daily, or they can die. You also have to watch them for disease.

Best Plants to Seed-Start

You seed-start plants that take a long time to germinate from seed and/or need a long growing season. Also, many seeds will only germinate in warm soil, meaning they won't do well in cool Canadian gardens in spring. Best starters include tomatoes, cabbage, broccoli, kale, leeks, cauliflower, and Brussels sprouts.

Trouble starters: While rosemary, celery, peppers, and eggplant need a long growing season, these plants are really hard to grow from seed unless you're really experienced. Buy them as seedlings.

What You Need

Seed-starting soil: Do not just use garden soil! You need a special seed-starting mix made with vermiculite and perlite, a weed-free medium that absorbs moisture easily so your seeds stay moist but also dries out enough to avoid root rot in your new seedlings.

Containers: You can start in anything that holds soil and has drainage, including recycled toilet paper tubes. Your containers must be at least 8 to 10 cm (3 to 4 inches) deep. I prefer to use grower trays designed for this job. These trays are often reusable and have divided slots (called "cells") for each plant; plus, many come with a clear plastic lid. After you sow your seeds, lower the lid and you'll get a mini greenhouse effect because the lid traps humidity inside, which speeds up the germination process. If you're reusing containers, soak them in a solution of bleach and water overnight, then rinse and dry them before you plant in them.

Timing

You might be excited about your new seeds, but you don't want to start growing too early. First, find out what the last frost date is in your area—the last date, on average, that you'll see a frost in your region. (See page 396 in the Food to Grow Guide for a list of last frost dates in major cities across Canada.) Then, read your seed packet for instructions such as "plant six to eight weeks before last frost date." Get out your calendar—electronic or paper, doesn't matter—and do the math. Write that date down and do the same for all the different seeds you plan to start this year. Follow these dates and you're halfway to success.

Sowing and Early Care

Sow your seeds following the instructions on the seed packet; make sure not to bury them too deep. Put about three seeds to a cell to increase your chances of getting a healthy plant. Keep your seeds and soil moist and warm. Spray your germinating seeds daily or even twice a day with a spray bottle—a watering can isn't gentle enough and can overwater your seeds—depending on the dryness of the air in your home. (Newer thermostats will tell you the humidity level of the indoor air.) Cover your seeds and soil if you have a lid, and keep them in a room with a temperature of 20 to 25°C (68 to 77°F).

Many people think seeds need light for germination, but they don't. A dark, warm room is best. You can buy a heat mat specially designed for seedlings for about $50, which will also keep the soil temperature nice and warm.

Rest Your Water

Some gardeners say you must let tap water rest for 24 hours before using it on seedlings. The logic used to be that this resting time would naturally filter out chlorine from municipal water. Most cities now use a lot less chlorine. Nevertheless, I still prefer to let my water sit overnight before I use it on seedlings.

The Seedling Stage

Once two or three leaves emerge on a tiny seedling, they need light—lots of it. Move your plants to a bright room, or buy a grower light and place your seedlings very close to it, about 10 to 20 cm (4 to 8 inches). Give your wee seedlings 12 to 16 hours of sunlight every day. Like us, they require a rest period, so don't leave the lights on all night. If you have weak seedlings with long, skinny stems, they'll need more light.

As soon as your seedlings develop three to five leaves, you have to be careful not to overwater and rot the roots. If you have a lid over your seedlings, take it off now—earlier if the seedlings have started to touch the lid. Also, this is the time to thin your seedlings. If you have two or more in a cell, pull the smallest ones out. Air flow is important now too; some growers will even use a small fan to keep the air moving.

At this point, you must feed your seedlings. Use a general purpose fish emulsion fertilizer. I recommend feeding them once a week by diluting fertilizer to one-third its normal strength and including it in your normal watering.

Although your seedlings are getting big and it looks like you might be home free, you're not. A condition

called "damping off" appears at this stage. If you wake up one day to seedlings slumped over at the stems, they're not just sleeping—they're suffering from this common condition. It's caused by several soil-borne fungi that set in under circumstances of high humidity, poor air circulation, or crowding. Once your seedlings are affected, it's over for them—you need to throw them out.

Hardening Off

It's now spring! Time to get outside. About 10 to 14 days before your last frost-free day, start introducing your seedlings to the outside world by placing seedling trays outdoors for a few hours every day in indirect light or shade. Choose a spot protected from strong winds and visiting squirrels. Each day, make the visit a little longer. Outdoor daytime temperature should be above 15°C (59°F).

A healthy seedling that's going to survive the transplanting process usually has a well-formed root. If you pull the seedling out of the tray and the base of the plant crumbles, the seedling is not likely to survive (but plant it anyway and see; you can always replace it with a purchased seedling). A viable seedling has a strong root that lifts out of the tray with some soil clinging to it. (For more information on helping your seedlings take root, see Planting Seedlings on page 104.)

Growing from Seedlings

The easiest way, hands down, to grow your crops is from seedlings (also called "transplants"). You buy these small plants ready to go and simply put them in the ground after the risk of frost has passed.

Buying Seedlings

Going to a garden centre on a beautiful spring day is like visiting a grocery store hungry. You run the risk of buying far too many plants. Stick to your plan and only go shopping with a list.

Just like when buying seeds—or buying anything—read the label. Note the days to maturity and make sure the number works with your garden plan and plans for maximizing yields through succession planting (for more on this approach to increasing yields, see page 81 in chapter 4).

Look for healthy seedlings. Unhealthy plants have yellowing foliage, or insect chew marks, black tips, weak stems, or roots growing out the bottom of the container (a sure sign the seedling has been in the pot too long). Healthy plants have lush, vibrant foliage, strong stems, and healthy, white roots.

Imprinting a grid into your soil can help you space plants evenly—much like the seasonal plots we illustrated starting on page 50.

Planting Seedlings

People think it's best to plant in warm, sunny weather. Wrong! Heat and drought are stressful, especially for cool-season crops such as lettuce, broccoli, and cabbage. The best time to plant your seedlings—either the ones you bought at a garden centre or those you seed-started indoors—is during a period of cool, cloudy weather with a risk of rain in the forecast. In a perfect world, you plant one day and a long, gentle, soaking rain falls the next.

If the only time you have to plant is on a hot, dry day, plant very early in the day or very late—ideally, just after sunrise or just before sunset. Experts often recommend using bone meal or transplant fertilizer to ease the transition from small container to garden. This may be true for large shrubs or fruit trees, but if you've prepared the soil properly—with lots of nutrient-rich material such as triple mix or compost—and water sufficiently, your transplants will transition just fine.

When planting seedlings, read the label. Measure out the distance between your plants as suggested on the packet. Take note of which crops will shade over your other plants. A good rule of thumb: Plant tall crops on the northern edge of the bed.

Steps to Planting a Seedling

1. Water your transplants about 10 minutes before planting.
2. Dig a hole with a trowel or a kitchen spoon.
3. Place the transplant in the hole at the same soil depth it was in its pot. (Note that tomatoes like their stems covered. See the Food to Grow Plant Guide on page 188 for more on specific planting needs.) Space apart your seedlings based on what it says on the tag.
4. Pat down the soil around the transplant.
5. Deeply water 10 to 15 minutes after planting.
6. Continue watering regularly to give your seedlings a good start.

A: Give your seedlings a good soak 10 minutes before you plant. **B:** Dig a hole deep enough to let the plant sit at the same depth it was in its pot. **C:** Gently place your seedling in the ground. **D:** Put the tag in the ground as a reminder of what you've planted and how to care for it.

Planting Fruit-Bearing Trees and Shrubs

Fruit trees such as apple, apricot, cherry, peach, pear, and plum go into the ground the same way as small, fruit-bearing shrubs such as currant, blueberry, gooseberry, haskap, and goji. The job isn't a difficult one, but doing it properly can be the difference between getting healthy fruit and raising a struggling plant.

When to Plant

The best time to plant any tree or bush is in spring or fall. At all costs, avoid planting during the hot, dry weather of late June, July, and early August. Summer heat can stress trees and shrubs and you risk losing them. My favourite time to plant trees and shrubs is in early fall, when the soil temperatures are still toasty, the days are warm and the evenings cool, and we tend to get more rain—perfect conditions for establishing roots. The downside is garden centres tend to stock a poor selection of these plants this time of year, and the ones they do have on hand often look dismal. Spring is a better time of year for finding healthy plants and good selection.

Choosing Plants

When purchasing food-bearing trees or shrubs, look for leaves free of marks, spots, or yellowing. Avoid purchasing trees or shrubs that have roots growing out of the pot. I prefer buying container-grown stock (grown in a pot from the start), as these plants are less at risk for transplant shock, versus field-dug (taken from a field), as these plants often struggle after planting. Some field-grown trees have a burlap sack around the root ball, but otherwise you can't tell. If you shop at a good garden centre, the staff should know.

Planting

1. If you are planting in a part of your garden that hasn't been improved recently, add some triple mix or compost to the soil.
2. Dig a hole twice the width of the root ball (that's the root system, and is the same as the size of the container) and one and a half times the depth.
3. Soak the hole.
4. Measure the depth of the root ball and put in enough soil at the base of the hole that the tree or shrub will sit slightly above the soil when you're all done. This is really important—many trees and shrubs die because they've been planted too deep. Be sure those planted in heavily compacted or clay soils sit nice and high.
5. If the tree or shrub is container grown, remove it from its container and score/tease out the root ball by lightly cutting into the exterior fibrous roots using a knife. (I've also used a spade to do

Beware of Frost

Your small, delicate transplants are sensitive to frost. A zap of icy cold could spell the end. So, after planting, be aware of what's going on with the weather. If the temperature is expected to drop below 5°C (41°F) overnight under clear skies and light winds, cover your seedlings with anything you have on hand—a sheet, a blanket, a tarp, even a bucket. Just be sure that if you're using plastic, it does not touch the leaves of the plants. Remove the cover in the morning. For more on frost protection, see chapter 6, page 122.

this.) You want to get the roots ready to expand and grow deep and wide. If you're planting field-dug trees and shrubs with a burlap sack covering the root ball, keep the sack on until after the tree is placed in the hole. Untie it and leave it in the hole—it will biodegrade.

6. Once the tree or shrub is in, fill the planting hole, then tamp around the tree (just use your feet) so there are no air pockets in the soil. In windy locations, stake fruit trees with a wooden stake, wire, and a small section of rubber hose to protect the tree (wire alone will cut into the tree trunk). Shrubs do not need staking.

7. Water deeply. Apply a water-soluble transplant fertilizer to avoid planting shock. If you prefer to garden organically, add bone meal to the soil during step 2. Keep watering deeply and infrequently for up to three months.

The Early Days

In the first few weeks after your seeds or seedlings go into your outdoor in-ground or container garden, they'll still need lots of care. Water often so everything gets a good start. Visit your new plants daily to be sure they're receiving the light and air flow they need. Celebrate every new stalk and leaf. Soon enough, roots will set down, flowers will emerge, and your future feast will be well on its way.

Planting Roots and Canes
Rhubarb, strawberries, and raspberries all require special treatment at planting time. See the Food to Grow Plant Guide on page 188 for more information on how to plant them.

Chapter 6

Keep at It:
Maintaining Your Garden

Seeds and transplants are in the ground; nothing left to do but wait for the harvest. Wrong! During what I like to call "the waiting phase" of food gardening, there's still plenty to do. Your food crops need ongoing care on a weekly or even daily basis: watering your plants, dealing with annoying weeds, fending off frost, and feeding (or fertilizing) those crops that are hungry.

Remember your pledge to devote a certain amount of time each day to gardening? Particularly during the dog days of summer, when your patio lounge chair beckons, gardening can be a bit of a slog. Just envision the bounty of the harvest to motivate yourself to keep your crops moist, weeded, and well fed. A cared-for garden will offer garden gold at harvest time.

Water

Water is awesome. Water does more than just hydrate your crops. A plant draws in water through its roots, and at the same time takes in nutrients from the surrounding soil. Once the plant is full of water, it expels moisture through its foliage—automatic plant air conditioning. Heat from the sun vaporizes this water on the leaves, cooling the plant on hot days. When the plant senses it's dry, this essential process—cooling and feeding—starts all over again.

But with water, more is not always better. Overwatering throws off a plant's evaporation cycle (called "transpiration"). It can lead to disease and root rot, and eventually even kill your plants. The trick is to find a balance of moisture for individual plants, and for your garden overall. The challenge is that every plant is different. And weather, soil type, location, and wind impact how water is absorbed into the soil and the frequency with which it gets used by food plants. You might have to go through a few seasons and a lot of trial and error to really groove into your garden's moisture needs.

A Healthy, Pest-free Garden
Garden maintenance is also about fending off and/or treating diseases and insect and critter infestations. See chapter 7 for more information on keeping your plants safe from invaders.

Soil and Water

Your soil type determines how quickly your plants can absorb water, how long moisture will be available in the soil, and how quickly the soil will dry out. In chapter 2, I covered how to determine your soil type and how to amend it so it will be welcoming for food plants. But even after amending your soil, your soil type will likely influence your drainage. Slope, elevation, air flow, and exposure to sunlight will also influence how quickly your garden dries out.

Clay soils: They don't drain. Or sometimes water runs off clay soil that is impacted. So you either get too much water or not enough. Working with clay soils is a guessing game and you rarely win.

Silt soils: They don't drain particularly well and they turn to muck after rain. While they drain better than clay, avoid overwatering.

Sandy soils: They drain too much. You will need to water a lot. The more sun and rain you get, the more you'll have to water.

How Much to Water

In the world of gardening, you'll often hear the phrase "water deeply." What exactly does that mean? It means to water your garden long enough that water will soak down to the roots of your plants. That's about 15 to 20 cm (6 to 8 inches) down into the soil, which is the depth at which the roots of most food plants reside. When you water deeply, plants send their roots down into the soil, where they stay cool and moist even during dry spells.

When you water shallow, you're casting moisture just on the surface of the soil, which is dangerous, because plants will naturally send their roots in search of moisture and will develop shallow root systems. During hot, dry days, plants with shallow roots are most at risk of dying.

To figure out how long you need to water, take your soaker hose and place it in your garden. Water for a set time, perhaps an hour. Using your hand or a trowel, dig into the ground until you hit dry soil. Measure the moist part using a ruler. If you find 10 cm (4 inches) of moisture, you know you need to water for about two hours to hit root depth.

Best Way to Water

I'm not a fan of overhead watering with a sprinkler. You can increase the risk of disease and unnecessary evaporation. When you water with a handheld hose, aim for the base of the plant. If you shoot a jet of water at the delicate flower of a zucchini plant and you knock it off, no zucchini for you. I prefer drip irrigation, particularly for containers (get more information in chapter 2 on page 47) or a soaker hose. Both approaches get water right to where it can nourish the roots of plants.

When to Water

Simply put, water when your soil is dry. You can purchase fancy moisture meters if you like, but your finger will do the trick. Stick your index finger into the soil below the surface. If the soil there feels dry to the touch, you need to water. If the soil at your fingertip is moist, leave watering for another day.

As for what time of day to water, I say water when you can. If your garden is dry and you have a moment, do it then. In a perfect world, you want to water when plants reach the stage in their transpiration cycle where they can easily accept moisture and the conditions are such that water will evaporate from foliage, minimizing the risk of attracting disease and insects. That means morning, preferably right after sunrise, when your garden is cool and the morning dew has opened your plants and got them ready for even more moisture. Morning watering is not only healthy, but you may need to water less—good news if you're trying to conserve or are under a water ban during a hot, dry summer.

Beware the Droop

During periods of excessive heat, plants will naturally seek to protect themselves by drooping. This helps them minimize the surface area exposed to the sun, slowing evaporation of moisture through their leaves. Your plants aren't about to give up the ghost if they droop—they just need some more water, preferably in the morning, preferably right at the roots. Just check first that the soil isn't already wet— overwatering can cause drooping too.

When to Water Often

- When your seeds are germinating in the ground right after planting.
- Immediately after planting. Seedlings have shallow roots, so they need frequent watering.
- When your plants are flowering or forming fruits.
- All season if you have a windy location. (To protect your garden against wind and its dehydrating effects, see chapter 7, page 155.)

When to Water Infrequently

- Once seedlings are rooted and established.
- Close to harvest for crops such as carrots, beets, and onions.
- Later in the season for your cabbage plants. The heads can split into two if the plants are overwatered close to harvest.

(See the Food to Grow Plant Guide on page 188 for the specific watering needs of food plants.)

Watering Containers

Pots: You filled your pots with potting soil, a light, fluffy medium that does not hold water for very long. That means you must water your container plants differently, allowing the soil time to soak up what water it can. Water your containers once, aiming for the soil, not the plants. Wait five minutes, then water them again. They're properly soaked now.

Raised Beds and Troughs: Water them deeply, wait 15 minutes, then put your finger into the soil to see how far down the moisture soaked in. Since you're aiming for 15 to 20 cm (6 to 8 inches), do the math and figure out how much longer you need to water to reach the roots.

Watering Before a Trip

If you're going away for just a long weekend, you can take a few steps to leave your garden in a moist, happy state. Any longer and you'll have to enlist a neighbour to do regular watering, or use an irrigation system on a timer.

- Soak the garden the morning of your departure. If there is no rain in the forecast, consider setting a soaker hose or sprinkler on a timer. (For this one instance only, I will allow overhead water via a sprinkler!) Timers can be attached directly to the end of the hose.

- Move containers to a partially shaded, wind-protected area of the yard or deck. Grouping will minimize moisture loss. Soak the containers, wait five minutes, and soak again so they're truly moist. If rain is in the forecast, you could be okay not watering. But the weather guy isn't always right, so I would water anyway. How do I know about weather guys? I'm the weather guy in Toronto, and the only thing I know with 100 per cent certainty is my forecasts have been wrong!

Weeds

Weeds are amazing little living things that can grow anywhere, anytime, and exactly where you don't want them. Basically, any plant that you do not want is a weed. You get rid of them not just to make your garden pretty. Weeds can choke out other plants, hog water and nutrients, and they can provide a welcome home for insects and disease.

How to Reduce Weeds

- Create a weed-free garden at the start by solarizing (see chapter 2, page 35), or by spraying with a non-selective herbicide, which is a weed killer that will kill any plant it comes in contact with.
- Cover up the soil by mulching (see page 115).
- Weed often. Weeds left today become more weeds tomorrow, and next week even more. The bigger they get, the harder they are to remove. You need to weed a food garden on a weekly basis.
- Get the whole thing. Nipping off the top of a weed won't do much good; the weed will grow back. Use a dandelion fork, trowel, or just a kitchen knife or fork to help you get the whole root.
- Weed after rain or watering. Pulling weeds out by their roots is easier when they're in moist soil.
- Remove weeds before they flower or set seed. Weeds broadcast their seeds via wind and by attaching themselves to furry friends that frequent the yard.
- When removing weeds, place them immediately in a container, bag, or wheelbarrow. If you walk across the yard with a weed that has seeds on it, you will disperse those seeds as you move.
- Use plain old white vinegar, full strength, to zap young, tender broadleaf weeds such as lamb's quarters and stinging nettle. Just spray on during the hottest part of the day and within a few hours the weed with shrivel. Never do this on a windy day, and avoid overspraying, as vinegar can burn the foliage of your wanted plants.
- Grow in raised beds and containers. As discussed in previous chapters, raised gardens develop fewer weeds and are easier to weed because they're at human height.
- Notice what's nearby. If your neighbour's yard is full of weeds, you'll be weedy too. Place edging between your food garden and any poorly cared-for areas. You can't do much about the airborne seeds from nearby lots—sorry.
- Be a smart waterer. Water the plants you want, not the weeds you don't want. This is why sprinklers aren't that great—they nourish weeds too, whereas soakers or drip systems can target your crops.
- Avoid hoeing or tilling perennial weeds like creeping Charlie. Sometimes this approach doesn't get rid of the weed at all and just stimulates growth. Hand-remove all weeds, including the root. Hoeing and tilling will get rid of young annual weeds only.

Mulch

Putting a layer of material on top of your soil cuts weeds in half by providing a barrier that blocks sunlight from getting to weed seeds, hampering their ability to germinate. And then it acts as a physical barrier that weed seedlings must push through in order to grow.

Mulching also reduces a garden's watering needs—studies suggest it does so by about half. It holds moisture in the soil by slowing evaporation, and it keeps plant roots cool by blocking the sun.

My favourite mulch for food growing is wheat straw. I find that other mulches come with flaws. Freshly shredded bark mulches can draw nitrogen away from plants and slow their growth; grass clippings can mat and reduce the flow of moisture; using fallen leaves as mulch is free (most yards have leaves lying around), but sometimes leaves can carry disease.

Wheat straw rarely carries weed seeds (unlike hay, which is full of seeds), and it's cheap and is available at garden centres and farm supply stores. It breaks down over time, adding organic matter back into the garden. It's not all that pretty, but it's still the best in my book.

How to Mulch a Garden

1. Remove all weeds, ensuring desired plants have germinated and seedlings have been planted. (Mulch is difficult for germinating plants to pop through.)
2. Loosen the soil around plants.
3. Water the garden.
4. Put down a weed barrier such as newspaper, cardboard, or landscape fabric. Cut holes out to allow desired plants to grow through.
5. Layer 5 to 10 cm (2 to 4 inches) of mulch on exposed soil. Avoid placing mulch on top of plants; place close to the stem but avoid touching it.

Weed Barriers

Weed barriers are placed underneath mulch to inhibit the growth of weeds while allowing moisture, nutrients, and oxygen to reach the roots of desired plants.

Cardboard: In large, food-growing gardens, cardboard is perfect for keeping walkways between your plants weed-free. But since it blocks moisture from getting to the soil, cardboard is not recommended as a weed barrier close to plants.

Newspaper: Layered newspaper does the trick. It's thick enough to reduce weed growth but also permeable enough to allow moisture to flow through. Do a quick search online to be sure the newspaper you're using has been printed with non-toxic pigments (most in Canada are these days). Put down about five to 10 layers around desired plants and place mulch on top. If you're tilling at the start of next season, you can till the newspaper right into the soil. The only flaw with this barrier is you need to put down a new layer every season.

Landscape fabric: This is readily available in various thicknesses at most garden supply stores. It allows water, nutrients, and oxygen to flow to plants easily and will last several seasons. But you must remove it to amend or till the soil for the next season.

Common Canadian Weeds

The weeds I list show up in many gardens for good reason: They're tough little plants that spread easily and know just how to take over a garden if you don't keep them at bay.

Lamb's quarters: The triangular leaves of this annual, edible plant have a white, mealy coating—they do look a bit like the skin of a cute little lamb. Pull this pretty but pesky weed up before it sets seed. A single plant can produce as many as 100,000 seeds.

Lamb's quarters

Purslane: This annual, fast-growing weed has red stems that often creep along the ground, and oval, shiny leaves. It can really spread—a single plant can produce up to 240,000 seeds. Remove it by hand before it flowers.

Purslane

Fire and Weeds

I love using a weed torch, also known as a flamer—which is basically a propane tank attached to a torch—to blast weeds from a walkway. They work like fiery magic on stone, brick, or concrete walkways, zapping any weeds that pop up through cracks between stones. And the process makes you feel all-powerful. But any soil with a high percentage of peat can be flammable. Keep away from such soil and be extra-safe around your garden, which can catch on fire pretty easily if you're not careful.

Creeping Charlie: This member of the mint family—indeed it looks a little bit like mint and it sure does spread like mint—has round, scalloped leaves on long stalks. In spring, it sprouts small, violet flowers. Be warned—creeping Charlie may be the most aggressive weed you ever encounter. It reproduces via seeds and sets down roots along its stems. Remove by hand or by applying a non-selective herbicide. Be careful when removing, as any fragments of the plant left behind will grow and spread. Never cut this weed with a lawn mower unless you use a bagger, as creeping Charlie will spread all over your lawn and garden.

Pigweed: There are three types of this fast-growing, edible weed: redroot, green, and smooth. And all three are somewhat similar looking. Pigweed can grow up to 2 m (32 feet) high on strong stems that can be slightly reddish near the base, while the upper stem is green with short hair. The leaves set the weed apart. They're oval to diamond shaped, with pointy tips. Pigweed has small, green flowers. Here's an interesting fact: As a young gardener and entrepreneur, I used to harvest this weed and then sell it at the Ontario Food Terminal. A weed in demand! This European delight steams up like rapini.

Crabgrass: This annual, grass-type weed loves gardens and lawns. You can identify it by its reddish to brown grass-like blades. In early spring, it responds well to pre-emergent herbicides; in the growing season, remove it by hand.

Chickweed: This fast-growing annual weed is rather pretty and delicate. Its stems have tiny white hairs, its flowers are small, white, and star shaped, while the leaves are oval with pointed tips. Remove by hand.

Quack grass: This pesky grass gets its Latin name (*Agropyron repens*) from the phrase "sudden field of fire," which speaks to its rapid ability to take over. It spreads quickly via seeds and underground rhizomes (roots). It has thin, flat leaf blades and gets extra aggressive after its seed spikes appear in July.

Plantain: Not to be confused with a type of banana, this is one of the most common perennial weeds in North America, as it will grow in almost any soil and in sun to shade. You know the look of this weed well. It grows low, sending oval leaves out in a wheel, and shoots up small, green spikes. It flowers in late summer to fall and spreads via seeds.

Edible Weeds

If you can't beat them, eat them! Some weeds are a culinary delight. Be cautious, and never eat a weed unless you're sure you know what it is and that it's edible. Eat only a small amount at first to check for allergic reactions. Here's what's edible:

- Burdock—roots
- Chickweed—tender shoots
- Chicory—leaves and roots
- Dandelion—all parts: root, leaves, and flowers
- Lamb's quarters—leaves and stems
- Pigweed—leaves and seeds
- Plantain—leaves only
- Purslane—leaves and stems

Crabgrass

Quack grass

Chickweed

Plantain

Dandelion: I don't have to tell you how invasive this edible plant is. Of course remove it before it flowers and goes to seed and spreads absolutely everywhere. Dandelions have what's called a "tap-root," a big central root with offshoot roots. Getting the entire root out when you weed is really important—dig deep with a fork or a dandelion weeder and ease the root out without yanking.

Stinging nettle: This weed gets its name from the stinging hairs that cover it. The hairs irritate skin—you will know you found a stinging nettle when you touch one! The base of each hair contains formic acid, and burning from this acid can last several minutes to several days. Leaves are somewhat heart shaped and fine toothed. Stinging nettle is edible—it tastes a bit like spinach.

Canada thistle: This delicate-looking but rather mean little weed has hairy, spiked stems and oblong, jagged leaves covered with barbs. Removing the

weed is no fun. Use gloves, of course, and be careful to get the whole root; if you rip the weed out and split the root in half, the weed will just come back.

Burdock: Ever go on a hike and come home with a burr on your clothing or in your dog's fur? Then you've already met burdock. This weed is stout, with wavy, heart-shaped leaves that are green on the top and whitish on the bottom. The flowers form into prickly balls—those are the weed's burrs.

Canada thistle is the worst to weed. Ouch!

Get rid of dandelion by pulling out the long taproot, too.

Above: Beware the burrs of the burdock weed.
Facing page: Weed-free gardens make for happy, healthy plants!

Frost

A nip of frost on seedlings early in the year or on a plant close to harvest can spell the end. Frost damages a plant's cell walls: Water inside the plant expands when it freezes, harming or killing it. Signs of frost damage include white or black markings on the leaves.

If more than 50 per cent of a plant gets damaged by frost, the game's over. Pull out the plant and discard. If only the top third, such as the upper leaves, got zapped, remove those leaves and your plant might rebound.

The riskiest nights are those with clear skies, light winds, and temperatures that hover near the freezing mark. I get nervous with an overnight temperature of 5°C (41°F) or lower. Warmth-loving crops like peppers, tomatoes, squash, cucumbers, basil, and zucchini are at high risk for frost damage. Newly sown seeds, if they haven't germinated yet, will be just fine. Tiny seedlings in the ground can't tolerate any frost at all.

Frost Covers

The best way to keep your crops from getting frozen out is covering them on potentially frosty nights. Any blanket-like item will do. A bedsheet, tarp, newspaper, cardboard, cloth, or a light blanket draped over your plants will protect them from light frosts. Ideally, find something to hold your cover in place and hovering above your plants (not touching them), such as overturned buckets or stakes. You can create a frame around your plot and hold the cover down with bricks or old pots. Or place a very tall stake in the middle of the bed and drape the cover over it like a tent.

For small seedlings, you can use upside-down glass jars, plastic milk jugs, or buckets as covers—anything to keep frost from touching tender leaves.

Remember, don't let anything plastic touch leaves—if you use a tarp, make sure it's high over those plants. And cover up before dusk. By the time it gets dark, much of the stored heat in the garden has already been lost. Remove your frost cover after sunrise, when temperatures are safely above freezing.

More Frost Protection Tips

- Know the average last frost date for your area and only plant after that date. If you're having an unseasonably cold spring, keep your eye on the forecast before planting.
- Watch the weather. Frost can still be a threat past the last frost date in spring. In the late summer and early fall, keep your eye on the forecast again, as a frost this time of year can impact yields by killing some of your plants before you've harvested them.
- On evenings where there is only a slight risk of frost, water the garden thoroughly before nightfall. The soil will release moisture into the air around your plants during the night, keeping the air somewhat warmer so it won't frost in your yard.
- If you don't have time to create a frame, lay a protective cover directly on the plant. But it must not be plastic!
- Container gardens are particularly susceptible to frost because they're higher off the ground—they'll be hit first. Either move your containers indoors or cover them. Since the roots can also be susceptible to frost, wrap the pot with burlap or bubble wrap or bury the pot in your garden.

My friend Daniel and I get our raised beds ready for a frosty night. We're using a plastic sheet to cover our delicate plants—we'll remove it in the morning. Tender tomatoes need protection if they're at risk of being hit by a late frost.

Fertilizing

A healthy food garden is a well-fed one. Plants actually need 16 nutrients to grow properly, and a lack of just one could result in unhealthy plants. Major nutrients include carbon, oxygen, hydrogen, nitrogen, potassium, calcium, magnesium, phosphorus, sulphur, iron, and chlorine. Micronutrients that plants require include manganese, boron, zinc, copper, and molybdenum. Do you need to concern yourself about every one of these? The good news is, no! Most of these nutrients are already plentiful in soil, water, and the air itself. But if your soil lacks nutrients, you've been gardening a small space for a long time, you have high-needs crops, or generally things don't look healthy, you may need to add some fertilizer to get strong crops for the year.

Read the label. The three numbers in a row on a fertilizer package tell you its percentage of nitrogen, phosphorus, and potassium.

Fertilizer Basics

Key nutrients: Out of all 16 essential plant nutrients, you should focus on improving just three: nitrogen (whose chemical symbol is N), phosphorous (P), and potassium (K). I refer these to as the "up," "down," and "all around" of fertilizer. Nitrogen, the up, promotes green foliage or top growth; phosphorous, the down, aids in root establishment and the production of flowers or fruit; and potassium, the all around, encourages the overall health of a plant.

Put together, these key fertilizers are N-P-K. They're often listed on the bag as three numbers, separated by hyphens, in that order. Note that the three numbers seldom add up to 100, even though they are percentages, as the fertilizer usually contains small percentages of a wide range of other nutrients as well.

Lawn food is often 30–0–4, as your grass is all about green! An all-purpose food growing fertilizer will be something like 24–8–16.

Fertilizer types: Most fertilizers either come in granular or water-soluble form. Water-soluble can be purchased in liquid or powder form; the powder form you mix in water before applying to your plants. Granular fertilizers come in pellet form. You shake the pellets onto the soil and they release nutrients every time it rains or you water. You can buy regular or slow-release formulations of granular; the slow-release versions can last a month or even several months. Personally, I prefer water-soluble fertilizer, because I find that granular offers inconsistent fertilizing.

Plant needs: Certain food crops just insist on fertilizer. Heavy feeders need lots of it, and if you don't feed them, they simply won't grow as well. Tomatoes are the most popular heavy feeder out there, demanding lots of nitrogen. Light feeders, meanwhile, need very little to grow well. Greens and foods from the cabbage family fall into this category.

Overfertilizing: It's possible to go too far! If you give your plants too much food, they'll grow big and tall. But their stems can end up thin and weak and the entire plant might topple over. If using water-soluble fertilizer, be sure you mix at the right ratio, and don't apply too often (I think every two weeks is ideal). With granular, be sure to scatter evenly over your soil.

Do You Need to Fertilize?

No—no need to feed: Your food plants are great! You're planting light feeders, you want to grow as naturally as possible, and you've done a good job of amending and improving your soil before the start of the growing season. You've even done some soil testing after amending and everything looks good.

Yes—fertilize: The crops you grew last year just didn't perform all that well. You want maximum yields. You're a competitive gardener who wants to pull off an award-winning pumpkin or tomato yield to enter in the fall fair (this will require a special formulation for the plant at hand; see more on the specific nutrient needs of food plants in the Food to Grow Plant Guide on page 188).

But the main reason to feed is to deal with problems. If you see these signs, consider adding some food to your garden (for a longer list of worrisome plant problems, see SOS: Signs Your Plants Are in Trouble, page 156.)

Yellowing older leaves

Combined with slow growth and stunted leaves, this is a sign of nitrogen deficiency.

Bluish-green leaves

If you see lines on the leaves combined with slow growth and minimal flower production, this could be a sign of a lack of phosphorus.

Yellowing lower leaves and overall poor health

This, along with slow growth, indicates your plant and soil could need more potassium. Yellowing of leaves could also be an indication of an iron deficiency known as iron chlorosis.

Rotten bit on the bottom of tomatoes

This is blossom-end rot and could be a result of a calcium deficiency.

How to Fertilize

Granular: Before your crops go in, you can simply lay down a granular fertilizer on your plots and let it do its work, or till it in. Once your crops are growing away, you follow a method called "side dressing." To do this, you scatter granular fertilizer about 15 to 30 cm (6 to 12 inches) away from the base of plants, using 1 kg (2 pounds) per 3 by 3 m (10 by 10 foot) area, and rake the pellets in.

Water-soluble: Using the ratio suggested on the container, you mix this fertilizer in with water—just like it's a pitcher of Kool-Aid—and water your crops. You can either mix it in a watering can or use something called a "hose-end sprayer," which is what I do. You place the fertilizer in a container that you attach on your hose and you simply water your garden. You want to aim the fertilizer at the roots of plants, not the foliage—always.

Granular fertilizers are really easy. Just shake them onto the soil—rain or watering will release food to your plants.

When to Fertilize

Granular: Anytime. For a regular formulation, you can use it every two weeks. If you have purchased a slow-release granular, follow the instructions on the label (some only require one or two applications during the entire growing season). Rain or watering will make the fertilizer release from the pellets.

Water-soluble: Right after a rain or watering. This is when roots are most accepting of fertilizer. Through osmosis, the nutrients will be absorbed into the plant more efficiently. Avoid fertilizing in the middle of the day, as applying fertilizer under the hot afternoon sun can burn plants. Fertilize every two weeks, or less often if you wish.

Fertilizing Organically

If you're avoiding chemicals in your garden, there are many other options for feeding your food plants:

Fish-based fertilizers: You can purchase fish emulsion and kelp-based fertilizers at garden centres. These natural choices—which come in granular, water-soluble, and powder forms—put a healthy amount of nitrogen back into the soil and stimulate

Now That's Natural!

I once visited a Greek family in Toronto who kept a classic Mediterranean vegetable garden. The family let nothing go to waste. After eating fish, they would bury the bones and fish bits right in the garden. The soil masked the smell, so raccoons (and unpleasant al fresco eating) were never a problem. The family reused and recycled everything, including rainwater, but they credited their bountiful garden to those fish bits.

the development of micro-organisms. The problem with them? They stink.

Natural amendments: Just ensuring your soil is healthy with things like compost, triple mix, or organic matter early in the growing season might be enough to avoid needing fertilizer at all. For centuries, farmers and gardeners have been adding nutrients to the soil with a range of natural ingredients such as leaf mould; green kitchen scraps; and manures from chickens, sheep, cows, and horses. Get creative with what you have around the kitchen and yard.

Teas: You don't drink them! Compost or manure teas offer a really effective way to fertilize food plots. Instead of adding compost or manure directly to the soil, you water it in via a homemade tea that will be absorbed easily by plants. You make a classic manure tea by taking 2 L (about .75 of a cubic foot) of composted manure and placing it in the middle of a 60 by 60 cm (2 by 2 foot) square of burlap. Tie the burlap together with twine, creating a sack with the manure inside. This is your teabag! Put the bag in about 20 L (4 gallons) of water in a large bucket and let it steep for seven to 10 days, stirring occasionally. Remove the burlap bag (discard it or return it to the composter) and pour the tea into a watering can. Water the garden with water first, then water again with the tea. To make a tea with compost, follow the same instructions but use 2 cups of compost. Steep in water for five to seven days and then use.

Fertilizers help maximize yields, but use them wisely. Too much of any new substance can upset the natural balance.

Cleanliness

Growing up, your mom always told you to keep your room clean. Now I'm hoping you will keep your garden clean too. Successful food-growing gardens are tidy. They are free from decaying, dead, or diseased plant material. They are organized so that air will easily circulate between plants and containers, which minimizes the risk of disease. These same gardens are weed-free—or close to weed-free—as weeds harbour insects, compete against existing plants, and in time will take over. To keep a garden clean, follow these steps:

- Weed, and weed often.
- Mulch.
- Always remove any spent flowers, yellowing foliage, or any leaves left behind after harvest.
- Remove damaged or broken stems immediately. Doing so will allow a plant to repair itself faster and focus its energy on the good parts of the existing plant, not the bad ones.
- Get rid of any insect- or disease-ridden plants to limit the exposure of these pathogens to other plants.
- Use clean tools and sharp knives. After use, wipe your shears, knives, or pruning tools and wash them with bleach, and then give them a quick rub with vegetable oil. The bleach sterilizes and the vegetable oil keeps things lubricated. Remove dirt from shovels with a wire brush.
- Wash your hands, or remove your gloves and wash them after dealing with an infected plant.
- Fence your garden to limit furry friends visiting. Many insects will travel on them—and critters big and small will eat your plants. (See chapter 7 starting on page 151 for more on critters and fences.)
- In fall, when tucking your garden in for the winter, clean up and be thorough. Do not give insects or disease homes to harbour in throughout winter.
- Do not crowd plants. You want to fit a lot in the least amount of space, but planting too close together in a garden, raised bed, trough, or container leads to insects, disease, and dead plants.

Out, dead leaves! Diseases and insects love rotting things, so clear them from your garden.

A barrier of chicken wire will keep birds and critters like rabbits away from prized plants.

Chapter 7

On Guard:
Protecting Your Garden

Just when you think it's time to kick back ... The planting is done, your weeds are a bit of work but mostly under control, you're watering and feeding just like Frankie told you. It's mid-season and you feel like a master gardener! But wait. You can't let your guard down, even now when all seems well. There are enemies lurking just beyond your garden, waiting to invade so they can take down, infect, and eat your prized plants.

Pests both large and microscopic adore gardens. Deer, bunnies, bugs, black spot, mildew, and even the dreaded blossom-end rot are but a gardener's error away. (Wind and other natural phenomena will harm your plots too; I'll get to that later.) An infestation, I believe, is not a matter of bad luck—it's a case of not being prepared. In this chapter, we will consider a preventative approach to pests and problems. It means some ongoing work, just when you hoped to let your garden be and start planning your harvest menu. But trust me, fending off the arrival of pests—both furry and bug-like—and diseases is a whole lot better than trying to nix them once they're in your garden and doing major damage.

Preventing Problems

Stuff happens. Pests and diseases show up in yards and on patios. Don't think your plot of yard or containers are immune and nothing will try to chew them up. It will. But you can't corral or harm furry invaders. And many parts of Canada—including where I live—have cosmetic pesticide bans that restrict the chemicals you can use to protect your garden from pests and insects. Even if you do have access to killing chemicals, you may have kids or pets, or may worry about the environment, and may not want to use them.

The solution? Be proactive. Proactive gardeners plan for invaders and make sure their soil, plants, and garden environment are ready for anything. As a bonus, many of these preventative measures also lead to a healthy and delicious food garden.

Insecticidal soap is a safe powerhouse that can tackle many common garden problems.

Prevent—Don't Always React

Things like tidying up, crop rotation, and watering smart all play a role in preventing bad things from happening to a garden. You'll notice that I've already mentioned many of these habits. They're good for plants *and* they fend off problems:

- Keep the garden clean. A clean and tidy garden, with few weeds and no dead plant debris, offers an inhospitable home for bugs and disease.
- Water in the morning, not at night. Watering at night encourages pests like slugs and diseases like black spot.
- Water the right amount. Dryness will kill a garden; overwatered plants can develop root rot and other diseases.
- Water the roots, not the leaves and stems. Wet greenery can lead to disease.
- Rotate your crops. This leads to healthy plants and soil and discourages the spread of diseases.
- Sacrifice unhealthy plants. One diseased plant can infect the whole garden. Pull it out and toss it in the garbage right away—don't put diseased plants in your backyard composter.
- Spray with insecticidal soap. This natural product, which you can buy or make, can get rid of many bugs. (See page 135 for more information.)
- Use yellow sticky strips. These strips, which you can buy at garden centres, attract insects, which will stick to the glue-like paper. They help you catch bugs and monitor which ones are in the garden.
- Repel furry friends—don't react to them. Making your garden an unwelcome place from the start for deer, bunnies, and squirrels reduces the risk that you'll ever have a problem with them.

Monitor

Be there. Look at your garden, touch it, and work on it regularly. Notice even the smallest changes potentially caused by bugs, disease, or larger critters. Do the rounds in the morning, in the heat of the daytime sun, and at night, to know what's going on. Examine the leaves to see if any culprits are hanging out there, and note the size and shape of any chew marks. Check the top, underside, and stems of plants for bugs or disease. In particular, inspect your garden at night, since many insects are nocturnal.

Once you have bugs or ill or chewed-up plants in hand—or photos of garden disruptions large or small—you can set to the task of identifying them. (Place all plant or bug evidence in a sealed bag so you don't spread the problems farther.) Do some online research, or send your pictures to your gardening friends or even me @frankferragine or frankie@frankieflowers.com for identification. (Check out the troubleshooting guide on page 156 for a longer list of food plant problems and their causes.)

Don't ignore early signs of infestation. These holes mean a bug has been making pesto from your basil!

Set a Breaking Point

Create thresholds that trigger you into action for an array of situations. If you have a few aphids, you can simply wash them off. However, if your stems are crawling with aphids, it's time to put in tougher measures such as using an insecticide. A good threshold is about 20 per cent; if that much of your plant is at risk, I say start getting really tough. I think this is a good breaking point, because if 50 per cent of a plant has a disease or bug, you need to throw it out.

The Last Resort—Control

You've done everything right and you notice caterpillars are munching up your plants and they're not going away despite your gentle measures. It's time to act.

But don't just ramp up aggressive tactics from the start. Because here's the big catch with finally pulling out the sprayer (if you can in your region) and hitting an infestation with the big guns. Problem solved? Not quite. If you spray bugs, they'll just move, and may target another part of your garden. Also, many pests adapt to human deterrence methods over time and could return. You must keep up every aspect your preventative routine—following good garden hygiene and monitoring, even at this stage, to prohibit recurrences and keep your garden healthy in the long term.

The kale is so under attack by slugs or possibly cabbage moths that it's almost unrecognizable. Pull and discard the plant before the infestation spreads.

Natural Protectors

The best way to fend off insects and disease, in my opinion, is to try the natural way first. Many of these approaches work for both bugs and diseases and can be used as part of a prevention plan.

Natural Killers

BTK (Bacillus thuringiensis): This bacterium is toxic to the larvae of some leaf-eating insects but harmless to humans, birds, and other animals. It is available in powder or liquid form, and you must apply it on your plants when the bugs are present. It will also harm beneficial bugs such as bees and butterflies, so use it with caution. Reapply every one to two weeks, and after rain. Works for: cutworm, wasps, ants, moths, beetles, flies, and sawflies.

Diatomaceous earth (DE, or silicon dioxide): This powder is made from the fossilized remains of tiny aquatic creatures called "diatoms." It scratches the bodies of insects as they crawl over it, causing them to dehydrate and die. Sprinkle it on plants in the morning when they are wet with dew so it will stick to the leaves. This very safe substance has few downsides. You do need to apply it after rain, however, and in rare instances you could harm a praying mantis, which is a good garden bug. Works for: crawling pests, including beetles, ants, aphids, whiteflies, and slugs.

Insecticidal soap: This is a gentle product that even organic gardeners can use. It damages the cell membranes of insects and actually dries them out and kills them. You spray it on a plant until it appears wet, targeting both the tops and bottoms of leaves. Avoid using this product during the day because direct sunlight may burn the foliage of your plants. You need to reapply regularly, about once a week. You can buy it at garden centres or make your own by dissolving 5 mL (1 teaspoon) of liquid dish soap in 1 L (4 cups) of water. Works for: aphids, spider mites, Japanese beetles, mealy bugs, caterpillars, whiteflies, and chinch bugs.

Dangerous Naturals

Just because a pesticide or herbicide is natural, organic, or homemade doesn't mean it can't harm a plant. Or humans, pets, and other animals. Always test a product on a small part of a plant first and wait three to five days to see if it has harmed your plant. If all seems well, then you can do a wider application across your garden. Know the overall safety profile of the product before using it and letting kids or pets have free roam of the yard.

It just looks like powder to us, but to slugs diatomaceous earth might as well be a barbed-wire fence.

Neem oil: This natural pesticide comes from the neem tree of South Asia. Neem oil stops young insects from maturing. It also makes plants taste bitter, which makes bugs stop eating them. Neem oil needs to be sprayed weekly—and after every rain—for as long as evidence of the infestation exists. It's banned in some jurisdictions simply because it's not been tested enough, although in my view it's very safe—still, you may not be able to buy it in your region. Works for: fungal disease and chewing insects, including aphids, whiteflies, chinch bugs, and mites.

Sulphur: Deadly to many fungi as well as mites, sulphur is also a key ingredient in many disease-controlling products. Spray on foliage at the first sign of disease and reapply if the issue persists or re-appears later in the season. When you apply it, you must wear gloves, as it's not great for your health at high concentrations. Works for: mites and harmful fungal infections, including black spot, powdery mildew, and rust.

Pyrethrin: An organic insecticide extracted from the chrysanthemum plant, it kills a wide spectrum of insects and breaks down after a day, leaving no residue. It's harmful to people, pets, birds, fish, and bees and other beneficial insects, so it needs to be used with caution and as a last resort when no other remedy is working. To protect bees, use in the evening when they're less active (and keep your pets inside). Works for: fleas, mites, aphids, mosquitoes, moths; almost all insects are affected by pyrethrin.

Save your eggshells after Sunday's omelet and sprinkle them near vulnerable plants to protect from insects and fertilize the soil. A garbage double-whammy!

Homemade Remedies

Resourceful gardeners don't dash out to the garden centre or home improvement store every time there's a problem in the garden. Everyday items you have in your house right now are inexpensive, safe, and often effective anti-critter treatments.

Baking soda: This is one effective homemade fungicide. Combine 5 mL (1 teaspoon) of baking soda with 1 L (4 cups) of water and a few drops of plain dish soap. Spray plants liberally. Works for: fungal diseases, including powdery mildew, tomato blight, rust and black spot; also repels cabbage worms.

Eggshells: If you crush them and place them around the base of plants, eggshells transform into miniature deadly knives to many insects, killing them. As a bonus, calcium from shells helps reduce blossom-end rot in tomatoes. Works for: soft-bodied insects like earwigs, slugs, and cutworms.

Salt: A dash of salt on a slug is a tried-and-true method of drawing moisture out of this pest and spelling its end. Moisten your hands or gloves with saline solution while on a slug hunt and this pest won't crawl on you!

Newspaper: Along with its ability to act as an inexpensive weed barrier under mulch, newspaper can be rigged into a very effective earwig trap. Roll one section of a newspaper up tightly and secure with an elastic or some string. Lightly moisten it and lay it under the foliage of your food-growing plants. Within three to four nights, earwigs will have set up house inside the roll to hide from the sun. Just pick up the roll and toss it, and you've rid yourself of a sizable population of bugs.

Grapefruit: After eating your half grapefruit for breakfast, place the rind upside down in the garden to trap slugs. Either create a small hole in the rind, or prop it up at a slight angle so the wee critters can get inside—but will be too busy munching on the citrus or sheltering from the sun to get out again. Harvest your slugs daily, discard both the bugs and the rinds, and start again the next day. Try making traps with orange or melon halves or quarters too.

Garlic: This cooking staple does a whole lot more than repel vampires. Purée 1 whole garlic bulb using a garlic press or blender and steep this in 500 mL (2 cups) of water for a couple of days. Strain the bits out and mix the garlic solution into 4 L (1 gallon) of water—or aim for a ratio of 125 mL (½ cup) to 1 L (4 cups) of water. Spray the undersides and top of leaves to repel little critters. You can also spray it on your own person to repel mosquitoes! (I wouldn't do this on a first date.) It works on bugs such as aphids, whiteflies, spider mites, and even mosquitoes.

Your recycling can help in the garden too! This rolled-up newspaper is a deadly trap for earwigs.

Insects

What's bugging you? If it's bugs, you might have to deal. Insects are a natural and normal part of the food garden. Some bugs like bees are good for your crops—and the environment. Others can destroy your gorgeous plants in just a few hours.

With most of the bugs below, you can prevent and treat with regular use of insecticidal soap. And you can monitor and reduce with yellow sticky strips. Any time you find offenders, remove them from the area right away and discard them carefully or they'll come back! Here are the most common bugs you'll find in Canada and what you can do about them—or why you should leave them be!

Top Bad Bugs

Aphids: These little tubular creatures can camouflage themselves by turning green, black, grey, brown, and reddish brown. Aphids are suckers, literally sucking the life out of tender shoots. You will often spot aphids on the newest growth of a plant. The obvious sign of an aphid infestation is stunted or weakened growth. Aphids leave behind a sticky substance after eating—a substance enjoyed by ants, so if you have ants on your plants, you probably have aphids. This sticky substance is called "honeydew," and it also attracts sooty mould (which looks like a blackish powder). Sooty mould further inhibits the growth of plants. Those plants at risk include vegetables, most fruits, and herbs. Treatment:

- As soon as you see aphids, blast them with a hose to try to wash them off.
- Attract or purchase ladybugs, lacewings, or parasitic wasps. They'll eat the aphids.

Beetles (Colorado potato beetles, Japanese beetles, June bugs): Coming in many shapes and sizes, beetles are sneaky and very aggressive. They appear and disappear within days and can destroy entire gardens. The yellow-orange Colorado potato beetle has 10 black stripes on its wings, and metallic blue-green bodies are the marker for June and Japanese beetles: both these beetles are the adult form of grubs. Beetles are very difficult to treat because very little gets through their hard-shell bodies. Plants at risk include almost everything, particularly potatoes, tomatoes, eggplant, and small fruit shrubs. Treatment:

- Pick and squish adult beetles.
- Shake beetles from plants.
- Use pheromone traps purchased from a garden centre. Place them away from infected areas and beloved plants—they work so well you can actually draw more beetles to your garden!
- Treat lawn and garden areas with nematodes, which are parasitic insects that infect grubs and kill them. Nematodes only work in early summer, and you have to water the garden, apply them, and water again.

Cabbage moths/cabbage loopers: They are also known as the white cabbage butterfly. Look for a small, white butterfly—females have two spots on each front wing; the male only has one. They're harmless as butterflies, but adult females will lay eggs on the undersides of leaves and within four days caterpillars emerge. These little guys will eat outer leaves first and then embed themselves in the heads of plants next. Caterpillars live for about 20 days—that's almost three weeks of feasting. Plants at risk include anything from the cabbage family: cabbage, cauliflower, kale, collards, Brussels sprouts, and broccoli. Treatment:

- Use floating row covers. These are bedsheets, pieces of cloth, or frost blankets draped over high stakes so they float over the garden, allowing air flow and only slightly reducing light exposure. They prevent butterflies from landing on plants and laying eggs.
- Hand removal. Get picking and squishing. Unfortunately, it's hard to spot cabbage butterflies and caterpillars, especially if the larva has begun to eat the inner parts of a cabbage or the inner florets of broccoli.
- Put your kids to work: give them a small net and have them catch as many cabbage moths as possible. (A fun project, but not a method guaranteeing complete control.)
- Attract natural predators of this moth such as birds and parasitic wasps.

Caterpillars: There are many different types—including those that turn into cabbage moths. They are heavy feeders and strip and chew leaves of your food plants. Most caterpillars leave a trail of green bumps—their waste—behind. Plants at risk include most vegetables, fruits, and herbs. Treatment:

- Pick and squish immediately.
- Apply BTK (see page 135).
- Put together floating row covers to limit an infestation by preventing adults (butterflies) from laying eggs. (See cabbage moths opposite.)
- Lure in their natural predators such as birds and wasps.

Cabbage moths can wreak havoc on all members of the brassica family. Your best defence? Pick and squish.

Cutworms: These are another type of caterpillar and are actually the larvae of several types of moths. These fleshy creatures come in different colours—brown, pink, tan, and black—and some are solid, while others are striped or even spotted. If you touch a cutworm, it will curl up in a "c." But the true way to know if you have this pest is by the damage left behind: Plants appear cut at the stem. Cutworms often target small, new plants in early spring to mid. Although cutworms are active in summer, you often don't see much damage from them this time of year. Plants at risk include young plants and newly planted vegetables. Treatment:

- Block this critter from easy access to your plants by placing cutworm collars around the base of small plants. You can buy the collars or make them yourself from toilet paper rolls or by cutting out the top and bottom of plastic containers or pop cans. One end should be pushed into the soil and the upper foliage of the plant should emerge above the collar.
- Hand-pick cutworms from the surface of your soil in early morning.
- Place crushed eggshells, crushed shells, or purchased diatomaceous earth around the stems of plants to cut and kill the cutworms.

The swift work of an apple maggot.

Potato bugs: These greenish-blue beetles are quite the pest. They've got a hard shell and are really hard to get rid of. They adore potatoes and tomatoes, and I've seen them nibble on basil too. Treatment:

- Pick and squish.
- Use floating row covers to prevent potato bugs from landing on potato plants.
- Buy pheromone traps designed for potato bugs to lure them away from your crops.

Potato bugs are tiny and voracious. Pick and squish!

Scales: These plant-sucking, hard-shelled insects only go for plants with woody stems, such as fruit trees, currants, raspberries, and grapes. There are numerous species, such as Oystershell scale, Lecanium scale, and San Jose scale, and they are hard to spot, but you might see them as little warts or brownish-black bumps on stems of your trees or shrubs. They injure plants by feeding on the sap, and this stunts growth. Signs of an infestation include yellowing leaves, sticky residue on a plant's foliage, and halted growth. Plants at risk include fruit trees and shrubs. Treatment:

- Attract or bring in scale's predators: ladybugs (ladybird beetle) and parasitic wasps.
- Water and fertilize your impacted plants—scale thrives on plants under stress and may leave healthy gardens alone.
- Reduce their spread by pruning away any heavily infested parts of the plant.
- Rub off scale bumps by hand or with a toothbrush.
- Smother scales by using horticultural oil purchased at a garden centre. You need to apply oil several times to drown scales; be careful not to overdo it and harm your tree or shrub.

Slugs and snails: The only difference between these common and very destructive garden pests is the snail's external shell. Both slugs and snails are hermaphrodites, meaning they can fertilize their eggs on their own, without having a partner; they breed at a rapid rate. Both leave behind a so-called slime trail, which is the mucus that helps them move along the ground. They're most active at night; in the daytime, they hide in cool, shady places and feed on living plants and decaying plant material. When they chew, they leave irregularly shaped holes. They love to munch on the tender growth of young plants. While they generally stay away from trees and shrubs, they adore ripe fruits like strawberries that are close to the ground. Plants at risk include young plants, vegetables, ripe fruit, leafy greens, and herbs. Treatment:

- Make your garden inhospitable. Water in the morning so your garden stays dry at night. Clean up plant debris and place crushed shells (egg, oyster shells, mussel shells, shellfish) around the base of plants. Get rid of places that offer cool shelter during the day such as boards, bricks, and leaves growing close to the ground.
- Water right and use drip irrigation to minimize moisture on foliage.

Given half the chance, this little slug and his friends will devour your entire garden!

- Hand-pick slugs and snails from your garden. Draw them out by watering late in the day; pluck them up and right away place them in a bucket of soapy water, then discard in the garbage.
- Salt them. A dash of salt on a slug in the garden will dehydrate and kill the pest. A classic British garden activity is salting slugs with friends, glasses of wine in hand.
- Trap them by setting up hiding places such as overturned pots, boards, or buckets. Lure them into your trap with beer and then toss them. Or buy slug and snail baits at a garden centre. These are simply pellets that you scatter in your garden. The critters eat them up and die. Look for baits that are safe for children and pets.
- Copper to the rescue! Copper reacts to the mucus secreted by slugs—some say it shocks them. That's why many gardeners suggest you place pennies around your plots. Sadly, it won't work: pennies, what few we have left, contain no copper now. You can buy copper tape at garden centres; lay it around your garden.

Spider mites: These tiny creatures are arachnids closely related to ticks and spiders. Spider mite damage initially appears as light dots on leaves. Eventually, the leaves will turn yellow and begin to fall off the plant. This critter also leaves behind a fine, silken web. Since spider mites are so difficult to see, try holding a white piece of paper underneath a concerning branch and shake. If you see tiny specks scurry across the paper, you have mites. Yellow sticky strips also help with identification. Plants at risk include asparagus, beans, peas, zucchini, melons, cucumbers, squash, tomatoes, and strawberries. Treatment:

- Keep plants healthy by watering properly and fertilizing: spider mites feed on plants under stress.
- Wash mites off. Wash both the top and underside of leaves to break up webs and get the mites off your plants.
- Be nice to ladybugs. They eat mites.

Thrips: These little black bugs scurry on the undersides of leaves, embed themselves in flowers, and leave tiny black sooty spots behind (these are fecal spots). Thrips are tiny, measuring just 5 mm (1/5 inch) long. As with mites, seeing thrips is hard,

Look closely and you can see aphids in action—and the stunted growth they've caused in this kale.

so you can test for them using yellow sticky strips, or by placing a white piece of paper under your plant and shaking. For flowering plants, you can remove a bloom and do the test on it. Thrips rarely kill a plant, but they will impact their growth. An affected plant will appear brown and dry or develop a mottled, silver colour. Thrips are difficult to control. I can't tell you how many times my family greenhouses have dumped several flats of plants just trying to limit the spread to other crops. Plants at risk include small fruits, vegetables, tomatoes, and herbs. Treatment:

- Remove sections of infected plants and place them in a bucket of bleach and water right away—thrips can jump off plants and spread if you don't.
- Encourage green lacewings, ladybugs, and praying mantises, all of which love a healthy diet of thrips.
- Remove weeds, keep garden clean, and ensure all your plants are healthy. A messy garden full of plants under stress is a haven for thrips.

Tomato hornworms: These are one funky caterpillar! The larva looks almost prehistoric. It's green with a spiky tail and horn and is about 10 cm (4 inches) long. This beast doesn't just look

Anti-Bug Flowers

Nasturtiums are annual flowering plants. While both the flowers and foliage are edible and you can use nasturtiums in salads, I plant them as a sacrifice. Many insects like to eat nasturtiums and chomping on this pretty plant will keep them busy and away from your food garden. In the world of battling bugs, sometimes you just need to give them something to eat!

scary—it does a frightening amount of damage, devouring several tomato plants in just a few days; some will even chew into tomatoes too. From their larva stage, tomato hornworms grow into greyish-brown moths about 10 to 12 cm (4 to 5 inches) in size with orange markings. At this stage, they can lay greenish-yellow eggs on the underside of a tomato plant's foliage. Plants at risk include tomatoes, potatoes, peppers, and eggplant. Treatment:

- Pick, then place hornworms in a bucket of soapy water right away and discard them.
- After harvest, till the area. Turning up the soil will destroy any pupae, reducing next season's population of hornworms.
- If you see white eggs on your hornworms, that's a good sign. These are the eggs of parasitic wasps, which will hatch and get rid of hornworms for you.

Whiteflies: If you see a cloud of white insects above your tomato plants, you have whiteflies. These pinhead-size insects multiply rapidly and do not immediately kill plants. They suck on sap and will gather on the underside of leaves in areas of tender growth where the sap is the tastiest. After feeding, whiteflies excrete honeydew, which causes yellowing and eventual death of leaves. Plants at risk include tomatoes, peppers, eggplants, cucumbers, zucchini, and potatoes. Treatment:

- Tear out heavily infested plants—whiteflies are very difficult to control.
- Apply insecticidal soap, but understand that this will only help reduce the population, not eliminate it.
- Vacuum off the plants. It sounds ridiculous, but this will help get rid of them.

Good Bugs

Not all insects will eat your food plants for lunch. Some are pretty amazing creatures that will get rid of other bugs or nasty diseases in your quest to create garden magic. The key to low-maintenance gardening is to let the good bugs take care of the bad so we can kick back and enjoy Mother Nature.

Encouraging the good bugs to do work for us is about using a few techniques to attract them to the food garden. Or, if these helpful critters just aren't around, you can actually buy them. Many are for sale at your garden centre and if not, staff there should be able to help you find out where to get them. Here are some helpful bugs that some gardens just can't do without:

Green lacewings: In their larval form, green lacewings—also known as aphid lions—consume most soft-bodied insects, including aphids, scale, thrips, spider mites, whiteflies, and more. How to attract: They can be purchased; green lacewing lures are available too.

Ladybugs (ladybeetles): The best-known good guy of the garden. Ladybugs love aphids, asparagus beetles, Colorado potato beetles, thrips, mites, and more. Believe it or not, over a lifetime a ladybug can eat up to 5,000 aphids. Don't go too far. If you attract too many and there's not enough food, they'll leave. How to attract: They're available for sale at most garden supply stores. You can also buy ladybug lures.

Ladybugs love to eat the bugs you hate.

Parasitic wasps (trichogramma, brachonids, chalcids, ichneumons): These little creatures infect other unwanted ones like hornworms, cutworms, cabbage worms, and various borers. They lay eggs beside the eggs of garden pests and then the newborn wasps feed on the embryos of the hosts. How to attract: Plant carrots, celery, parsley, or purchase parasitic wasps at a garden supply store.

Praying mantises: Straight out of Jurassic Park. These bugs are not as big as dinosaurs, but they do look like they came from the same era. Praying mantises eat almost any garden pest—good or bad. If something moves and it's an insect, a praying mantis will have it for lunch. How to attract: Buy eggs online or at garden stores, and just place them in the garden. They hatch and quickly grow into adult size. If you want bees and butterflies to stick around, know they might get eaten too.

Hoverflies: These masterful aviators fly through the garden with ease. Adult hoverflies feed on nectar, but their larvae adore most soft-bodied bugs such as aphids, whiteflies, and mites. How to attract: Provide adults with lots of nectar via plants like alyssum, chives (they love the flowers), and oregano, and hoverflies will stick around and have babies.

Bees: While bees do not feed on any unwanted creatures in the food-growing garden, they are your friends. Yields for many plants are dependent on the work bees do to help pollinate fruit and flowers. Attract bees with sunflowers and water such as a bird bath or water feature.

Bees are a sign of a healthy garden—they're working hard for your harvest.

Diseases

There are pests you can see and pluck off your plants, but sometimes the most dangerous critters come in microscopic sizes. Diseases range from slow-moving problems that discolour a few leaves and might stunt plant size a little to illnesses that will take a crop down in its tracks and infect the plot for years.

Top Food Plant Diseases

Mildew: Both downy mildew and powdery mildew can infect your food plants; both appear as yellow or brown spots on the upper side of leaves. Powdery mildew will also cover leaf undersides with white, powdery fungal structures, while downy turns undersides white to purplish. With both, leaves may start to curl or turn brown and can fall off the plant. Prevent mildew by making sure you leave lots of space between plants, practising crop rotation, limiting overhead watering, and purchasing plant varieties that resist mildew. Plants at risk include cucumbers, squash, melons, and onions. Treatment:

- Once infected, there are no quick fixes—just discard infected plants to curb the spread.

Blight: Of the two types—early blight and late blight—late is the more common and the biggest threat. An infection begins with water spots appearing on leaves and the areas surrounding the spots turning yellow, then brown; eventually, the entire leaf goes brittle. On potato and tomato plants, you'll often see black lesions on the leaves. The fruit can also be affected. You'll see blotches and then the fruit becomes brown, sunken, and dry. Late blight often appears after a long stretch of hot, humid, wet weather in late summer.

Plants at risk include beans, peas, cucumbers, melons, peppers, potatoes, tomatoes. Treatment:

- Limit overhead watering: the drier the foliage, the less chance of blight.
- Limit spread by discarding infected plants and rotating crops.

Keeping a close eye on your plants (opposite) is the only way to catch diseases like powdery mildew (top left) and rust (top right) before they spread.

Leaf spot: One version, often called "black spot," starts as tiny dots that turn into large black ones. Another, nicknamed "white spot," begins as white dots that turn light tan and then morph into larger white lesions. Neither type will kill the plant, but both will impede health and yields.

Plants at risk include tomatoes, parsley, and blackberries for black spot, and kale, cabbage, cauliflower, and Brussels sprouts for white spot. Treatment:

- Apply a fungicide designed to fight leaf spot. Or try baking soda.

Rust: This appears as small, red to reddish-brown dots or bumps on the undersides of leaves. Rust won't kill your plants, but it will stunt their growth. Plants at risk include beans, asparagus, and corn. Treatment:

- Rust thrives in a wet environment, so limit overhead watering and avoid overwatering.
- Make sure plants have air circulation between them.

- If you see rust, immediately remove infected leaves and dispose of them—do not compost. Wash your hands before touching other plants.

Blossom-end rot: If you've grown tomatoes or peppers for a few seasons, you most likely have experienced blossom-end rot. It first emerges as water-soaked spots on the ends of green or ripening fruit. The spots enlarge and then become depressed and black. Plants at risk include tomatoes and peppers. Once blossom-end rot appears, it is too late! The cause can be inconsistent watering or a calcium deficiency in the soil. To limit or prevent blossom-end rot next year, improve calcium levels by using a calcium-enriched fertilizer or placing a generous handful of crushed eggshells in the planting hole at the start of the season. Treatment:

- Once you spot it, there's nothing to do to save that tomato or pepper—just pick it and discard it so your plant doesn't waste energy growing it further.
- During the growing season, do not allow plants to dry out; water them consistently and use mulch. Do not overfertilize with nitrogen.

Blossom-end rot is a disease prevented only by proper soil nutrition and watering.

Critters

Some critters are furry, while others are covered with feathers, but they all threaten our food-growing garden. Larger creatures that visit yards and patios may endear themselves to you at first. But once they start munching, doing more damage in a shorter time than any tiny or microscopic predator, they suddenly don't seem so sweet.

Critter Deterrents

Sadly, many of the clever natural, homemade concoctions that keep bugs and diseases off your plants won't do much when it comes to larger-scale critters. These guys have a mind of their own. But I do have a general list of approaches to keep your yard or patio a place that bigger pests won't want to visit.

The key is to play with the senses of furry beings and make your yard unwelcoming. Critters will show up if your garden plots smell great, taste great, look great, or feel great. But if just one of these senses is offended, they might pass your garden plots by and go have lunch elsewhere:

Smell: Put the smell of fear in their noses. Most critters are sensitive to odours and easily frightened away by smells of their predators. You can buy urine of predators such as coyotes at sporting goods stores. Gross, but it often works.

Sight: A healthy, happy vegetable garden looks delicious to hungry, furry, or feathered friends. The sight of a predator, even if it's a fake predator, may send them walking (or flying). That's why gardeners perch fake owls in the garden and indeed why scarecrows were invented.

Sound: A quiet, calm space is a welcoming place. To send visitors packing, you need to disturb the serenity. A radio set to play an all-talk station at dusk and dawn may bother deer and rabbits, which love silence. Or create vibrations with a garden whirligig, miniature windmill, even a wine bottle buried open-end up in the ground (the wind will create vibrations as it passes over the bottle opening). Underground creatures such as mice, moles, and voles really don't like such vibrations.

Taste: In the eyes of "the unwanted," your garden is basically a buffet. But if even a nibble tastes bad, furry creatures will move on. Use garden centre products that make your plant's leaves taste bad. Or plant crops such as leafy greens at a distance from your "real" crops to distract nibblers from the larger feast. Remember, sharing is caring.

Touch: Rich garden soil is great for the garden and wonderful to walk on. Coarse mulch (crushed bricks, river stone) looks great, reduces weeds, retains water, and feels awful on small paws, so it keeps cats and other digging critters out of the garden.

Adapt: An unpleasant smell, a scary sight, a disturbing sound, distasteful leaf, or uncomfortable walking space will keep the unwanted away. However, nature's creatures adapt. If you don't switch up deterrents constantly, your critters will get used to the discomfort, return, and start snacking. The key to critter control is to always keep them guessing with new and clever ideas.

Chicken wire is porous enough to let seedlings grow through, but tough enough to stop pests from digging.

Unwanted Garden Critters

Rabbits: These big-eared animals can quickly destroy your crops. Their food of choice is leafy greens, but they will eat whatever is available. They will chomp a stem, chew the flowers of a zucchini plant, or eat half a cabbage before moving onto the next treat. In the winter, rabbits will gnaw at fruit tree bark and cause permanent damage. If you come out into your garden in the morning and it looks like someone took pruners to plants, you have rabbits. To confirm, look for rabbit tracks or dark brown, pellet-size droppings. To help control rabbits:

- Build a fence. It does not have to be tall—just 60 to 120 cm (24 to 48 inches)—but it must be buried 35 to 45 cm (14 to 18 inches) or these critters will just dig under it.

Hiding in these raspberries is a rabbit at the garden buffet!

- Rabbits are terrified of coyotes, foxes, owls, and dogs. Place a plastic owl in your garden and move it often. Dog hair and coyote urine work well too.
- Blood meal, cayenne pepper, and a whole host of anti-rabbit repellants for sale at garden stores might work—but not always. Such products have to be reapplied after rain.
- Trap them yourself for humane removal, or call in a professional.
- A small plot of leafy greens such as lettuce, kale, or even cabbage planted just outside the garden can keep rabbits busy. I often say if you can't beat them, feed them.

Deer: These four-legged furry friends are timid by nature but can become aggressive. Once they get comfortable somewhere, they keep coming back night after night—and morning after morning, since they feed dawn and dusk. Entire crops can be destroyed seemingly in minutes. In fact, an adult deer can consume as much as 4.5 kg (10 pounds) of greenery in one day. To help control them:

- Build a fence—but go tall: a white-tailed deer can jump over 2 m (6 feet) in height. An ideal deer fence should be a minimum of 1.8 m (close to 6 feet) high, and slightly angled at 45 degrees.
- Scare them using radios, strobe lights, even propane gas exploders—seriously! More sensibly, try a sprinkler set on a motion detector, or an alarm clock set to go off at dawn during feeding time.
- Smell-sensitive deer can be deterred by bars of soap inside nylon stocking hung off branches, dog hair placed just outside the garden, or droplets of coyote or fox urine planted around the yard. Some gardeners will even urinate around their garden (the neighbours will think you are crazy). Keep

mixing it up. Deer are smart and get wise to tricks over time.

- Liquid and granular repellants on the market focus on either offering an unpleasant smell or taste. The smelly ones contain high concentrations of egg solids or fatty acids. For bad taste, products often contain capsaicin. One of my favourite products to protect fruit trees from deer damage in winter is Skoot. Apply on fruit trees in the late fall and the residue leaves them bad tasting all winter long.

Squirrels and chipmunks: I often joke that squirrels and chipmunks must be hired by garden centres to destroy crops and help sell more plants. Really, these guys are frustrating. Many don't even eat plants but seem to be content tearing them out of pots or out of the ground. To help control them:

- If these critters get enough of their main diet— seeds, berries, nuts, and leaves—they may leave your garden alone, so put up a feeder. They also need water and will dive into a tomato or pumpkin just for the moisture, so installing a bird bath or water feature helps them stay hydrated. I say give them what they need and they will leave your good crops alone.
- Pelletized hen manure turns these critters off, so top-dress your yard. As an upside, hen manure is a great overall fertilizer. Other granular repellants such as blood meal and capsicum might also keep them away.
- Contain your crops with a chicken wire cage—a fence isn't enough; you need to have a roof or squirrels and chipmunks will climb over and get in.
- Get a cat. Feline friends send these critters running.
- Urine or hair from predators such as dogs and humans are worth a try.

Raccoons: Raccoons think with their stomachs and will eat anything and everything, but they particularly go for insects, worms, frogs, nuts, and fruit. Raccoons can cause major damage in yards by turning over containers, hollowing out melons, and stripping ears of corn right off the stalks. To help control them:

- Avoid growing corn! Corn is a fan favourite for these masked bandits and will just attract them.
- Trapping on your own or hiring a professional is often just a temporary solution. Raccoons are territorial. When one moves out of an area, another one will move in.
- A sprinkler on a motion sensor will scare some raccoons away. But if food sources are limited, nothing—water, lights, sounds, or smells—will keep them away.
- Cage in your garden the way you do for squirrels and chipmunks. But be warned—raccoons have been known to tear down cages, rip apart fences, and unlatch garden gates. If they want your crops, they'll probably get them.

Groundhogs (woodchucks): These plant eaters can go through up to 1 kg (2 pounds) of vegetation a day. If you come across a chomped cucumber, kale cut off at the stem, or a mangled zucchini, these may be signs a groundhog is visiting your garden. To help control them:

- Build a fence buried 30 cm (1 foot) into the ground. It should be about 120 cm (4 feet) high. Chicken wire or wire mesh is best.
- Groundhogs are easy to lure into a trap—they like apple slices—and relocate to a new home. They are best caught during the day; put traps away

at night to avoid catching a raccoon or skunk. Relocating any animal is touchy, and I recommend getting professional help to make sure you're doing it properly.

- If you discover a groundhog hole, cover it. The bigger a nuisance you can be, the greater the chance the groundhog will move on.

Birds: Like walking critters, feathered friends get hungry too, and they'll threaten your grapes, strawberries, apples, pears, raspberries, even corn. Everything from blackbirds, crows, grackles, orioles, robins, and starlings to woodpeckers are destructive. To help control them:

- Frighten birds with traditional scarecrows or aluminum plates hung from trees; try streamers, flash tape, and scary-eye balloons, which you can buy from garden centres. Plastic owls, falcons, and other birds of prey perched high above the garden might work too. Check out the supply of other bird-scaring devices at your garden centre.
- Cover berries and fruit crops with plastic netting. Birds fear getting caught in the netting and will stay away.
- You can purchase electronic scaring devices that bother birds. But these can get pricey.

Cats: Felines consider yards their personal bathroom and will not just pee and poo near your crops—adding potentially dangerous bacteria to the soil—but often dig to bury their waste. To help control them:

- Cats are very sensitive to textures, so make your soil no fun to walk. Scatter crushed eggshells or diatomaceous earth near food plants. Cats also dislike citrus, so lemon, lime, and orange peels in the garden might keep them away.
- Snakes freak cats out, so place plastic snakes from the dollar store around the yard.
- A water gun at the ready or hose on a motion sensor can spray them away from your crops.
- Plant rue, a stinky inedible herb that cats despise.

Traps seem like an easy and humane solution—until you have a scared animal in one and nowhere to take them. Work with professionals when using traps.

Welcome Critters

Toads: Every garden should make room for a toad abode. Toads eat insects—lots of them. Toads enjoy places where they can hide, so a toad abode can simply be a clay pot turned on its side and partially buried, or an abode built from a flat rock or board angled over some loose soil to create a cave-like cavern underneath.

Snakes: Most snakes in Canada are harmless to humans but a menace to garden pests such as mice, moles, and voles. (They also eat toads and frogs, which you might want to attract, so that's a downside.) Snakes love rocks. They can hide under them or lie on top of them to sun themselves.

Marigolds and Critters

Marigolds are good for the food-growing garden, but they may be a little overhyped! It's been said that a border of these pretty, fragrant plants will keep insects and furry friends at bay. True, they do emit a strong perfume that may mask the smell of food-growing plants and could repel pests such as beetles. But I've also seen many a garden planted with marigolds suffer infestations. I've even seen rabbits feast on the marigolds themselves.

Spiders: These arachnids eat bugs. In fact, having a lot of spiders indicates you have a lot of bugs. Don't kill garden spiders. Just be happy if they are present—they're working hard for the health of your garden.

Wind and Elements

I know, wind, rain, and hail are not living beasts that will chew your food plants. But like pests, they can have a go at your garden and ruin it.

A windy location, over time, can really impact plant growth and yields. Wind dries out soil, making moisture retention a problem. When plants get pushed around by wind consistently, it diminishes the ability of their roots to absorb moisture and nutrients from the soil. Here's how to protect your windy plots:

Build a windscreen: A fence or a row of evergreen trees or shrubs will protect a garden year-round from the ill effects of wind. Place your screen to nip prevailing winds. For much of Canada, that means placing barriers to the west of your plot to catch westerlies. Some locations have different wind patterns and you might even have a wind tunnel caused by buildings—track the wind to find out.

Grow shorter: Forget pole beans or corn. Go for bush beans, kale, cabbage, broccoli, radishes, carrots, and beets. These low-growing root vegetable crops aren't pushed around a lot by wind. Avoid crops such as large leaf basil, peppers, squash, and zucchini—they need lots of water or can be damaged by ongoing wind.

Mulch: Putting down a layer of mulch helps the soil and plants retain moisture.

Water: Plants in windy spots use up moisture faster, so water them more than the rest of your garden.

As for a violent storm with hail, it can destroy your garden and there's little you can do about it. If the forecast threatens hail, take your containers into the garage, or place under a covered patio. Extreme high winds and violent rain, either from a big storm or even a hurricane, will also damage your garden, and there's pretty well nothing you can do to protect your in-ground crops. Seek cover for yourself and cross your fingers!

SOS: Signs Your Plants Are in Trouble

Don't be sad, but when you garden, plants may die. No matter how prepared you are, how good your soil is, or how much money you invested in growing your own food, you are working with living things. There is always a chance they may get sick, destroyed, or eaten. Sometimes, plants die for no reason you can identify. But most of the time, there is a reason and you can spot the early-warning signs of looming serious problems. The only way to nip problems in the bud (garden humour here) is to hang out in your garden, both morning and night, and inspect your plants and yard. Confiscate discoloured or chewed leaves, sealed in plastic bags so they won't infect other plants, and take photos. Then look to my troubleshooting chart to figure out exactly what's going on in your food plot. If you suspect a disease has been at your plants, discard any infected bits, throw them in the garbage—not the composter—and wash your hands well.

Symptom	Possible Causes	Solutions
Seedlings do not emerge	Planted too deep Soil or weather too cold Seedlings too wet or too dry Seed is old/damaged Birds ate the seed Seed is slow to germinate	Wait or start over
Seedlings fall over	They have damping off Are too wet or too dry	Start over Adjust watering
Seedlings chewed at stems	Cutworms Rabbits Chipmunks	Cutworm collars Repellants
Spindly, weak plants	Not enough light Overcrowded Poor soil	Move to sunny location Thin existing plants Improve soil
Plants are stunted or slow growing	Poor soil Cold weather or soil Too wet Not enough sun Seeds/seedlings were poor quality	Improve soil Adjust watering Start over with healthy seeds/seedlings

Symptom	Possible Causes	Solutions
Leaves discoloured	Virus Wilt (fungal disease) Nutrient deficiency Too much/not enough sun	Improve soil Fertilize Move to a sunny or shady spot
Leaves turned black	Frost damage Mould Fire blight Fertilizer burn	Replace frost-damaged plants Thin or prune to improve air circulation Remove plants infected with fire blight Remove leaves damaged by fertilizer
Dark spots on leaves	Scab, on fruit trees Black spot	If available, treat with a fungicide Improve air circulation Treat fruit trees with dormant spray in early spring to prevent (dormant spray is sold in a kit)
Leaves grey or white/powdery coating	Powdery mildew Mildew	Improve air circulation
Leaves yellow with webbing	Spider mites	Spray with insecticidal soap
Leaf tips burned	Frost damage Fertilizer burn Too dry	Pinch off badly damaged leaves Improve moisture
Leaf tip curl	Too dry	Increase watering
Leaf curl	Wilt (fungal disease) Aphids Spittlebugs Leaf rollers Too dry	Wash plant with high-pressure water Improve watering Apply insecticidal soap Remove damaged leaves Improve air circulation

Symptom	Possible Causes	Solutions
Leaves with holes	Insect infestation Hail Wind damage	Monitor for type of insect and treat Water and feed
Leaves with holes and greenish droppings	Caterpillars	Hand-remove Treat
Leaves stripped	Slugs Beetles Hail	Reduce watering at night Monitor for slugs and treat
Sticky coating on leaves	Scale	Pick off Treat with insecticide if available Discard plant
Wilted plant	Too wet or too dry Wilt (fungal disease) Frost damage	Adjust watering and/or improve drainage Discard damaged sections
Plants chewed/eliminated	Rabbits Deer Squirrels Chipmunks	Repel, repel, repel If you can't beat them, feed them with a crop of greens
No flowers	Late frost Lack of light Wrong soil type Improper pruning	Protect against frost Transplant/move into sun Amend soil pH Determine best pruning schedule
No fruit	Frost damage Lack of pollinating insects Lack of pollination partner Improper fertilizing Not enough sun	Attract pollinators or pollinate by yourself Plant a partner Adjust fertilizer Transplant/move into sun

Symptom	Possible Causes	Solutions
Poor fruit yield	Poor soil Inconsistent watering Cold at time of planting (peppers)	Improve soil quality Fertilize Improve watering Next time plant in warm soil
Fruit drop before maturing	Disease Insect damage	No solution for current year For next year prevent via cleaning up and discarding all leaves Spray next season if chemicals are available
Fruit distorted and scarred	Disease Fruit maggots	Same as above
Scarring on bottom of tomatoes	Blossom-end rot Inconsistent watering	Improve calcium in the soil via fertilizing Discard infected fruits Improve watering
Poor growth and abnormally large roots with cabbage, collards, cauliflower, broccoli	Club root	Discard plants Do not plant these same varieties in the same spot for up to five years
Holes in leaves of cabbage, collards, cauliflower broccoli, Brussels sprouts, and white moths flying around	Cabbage moth larvae	Hand-remove Treat with BTK (Bacillus thuringiensis) Where available use pesticides as a last resort

Chapter 8

Eating Time:
The Harvest

You made it! You have planned, planted, nurtured, and protected your garden. Now it's time to enjoy. Once early summer hits, the harvest of your crops should be in full swing. Each and every week something new will be ready for picking. Check out your garden every day to see what's ready, what's going to be ripe very soon, and what you should photograph and brag about to friends and co-workers. And walk through your garden regularly to note which spaces are available for a new, quick-growing crop.

Harvest time isn't the time to give up on weeding and watering, or even protecting your plants from insects and critters. In fact, it's more important than ever to keep up the overall health and tidiness of your garden—you want to feast on the fruits of your labour, and so do pests of various sizes. Your goal now is not just to pick your crops but to keep the harvest rolling smoothly—ideally, until the snow flies.

Did you know you can harvest your carrots throughout the growing season? Pluck them early for sweet baby carrots or leave them to get a bit bigger, like these ones.

Harvesting Basics

Knowing when to harvest is a key step toward garden glory and a tasty meal. Just a few days can be the difference between a tender bean and a tough one. You don't want to waste your efforts and get the picking wrong! Often, new gardeners miss the mark and harvest either too early or too late.

When to Pick

Different plant types offer up different signs telling you it's time for harvesting. Leafy greens are ready pretty much as soon as they shoot leaves. The risk here is waiting too long—leafy greens bolt *after* their best eating time, and once they've grown tall and produced seeds, they taste bitter and are more or less done. Onions, garlic, and potatoes die back when they are ready to harvest. I grew up close to onion fields and I always knew the end of summer was near when the tops of onions fell over. Apples and tomatoes will loosen their hold on their fruits when they're ready to go, even letting them drop to the ground.

And for many crops there is no ripe or wrong (that's plant humour) time to pick. You can pull carrots early and get sweet baby carrots. A red pepper that is still green may not be full-size, but it will still taste great! Bean pods are tastiest early on, but if the bean seeds are what you're after, you wait for maturity.

For some garden plants, harvesting isn't a one-off. Zucchini, beans, peas, cucumbers, and some tomato varieties are repeat producers. Regular harvesting promotes new growth, more yields, and often a healthier plant. Swiss chard is a great example of a crop that bounces back after every cutting. The more you cut, the more it produces.

To help you with the timing so you'll get your harvesting right, I've broken down your food-growing garden into categories: leafy greens, root vegetables, berries, fruits, and herbs. (The Food to Grow Food Guide starting on page 188 also lists harvest information for individual plants.)

Be Flexible

Your crops will not always be on schedule. Seed packets, plant tags, websites, and garden books, including this one, will tell you the days from planting to maturity for both seeds and plants. These are guidelines only and shouldn't be seen as gospel. Lack of sunlight, extended periods of cool weather, drought, and insects, among other things, could increase the days to maturity. The more sun, heat, and adequate moisture your plants get through the growing season, the sooner they will be ready to pluck.

How to Pick

Take it easy! When you remove a tomato, bean, or berry, your goal is to be as gentle as possible and avoid harming the plant. For fruits (including tomatoes), simply spin the fruit until it breaks free. For foods that require a bit more effort, use a sharp knife and cut as close to the food as possible.

When you pick, as always keep it clean. Wash your hands after touching plants and wash your knife too. If you've got a disease anywhere in your garden, be extra clean and wash your tools with bleach to prevent any disease from spreading.

Best Time of Day

Just like watering and most gardening tasks, harvesting is best done in the morning. Your food plants are still moist with dew after sunrise, which gives them maximum taste, and the moisture helps

Reach for them apples! I'm going to be gentle and twist off some ripe fruit without harming the tree.

with freshness so they'll store longer. Picking in the heat of the sun is harder on the plant, and the food you've picked is now drier, so it may have a bit less flavour and not keep as long.

Yes, morning is best, but let's be realistic. Most people with backyard or patio gardens harvest peppers, herbs, and berries while they're making meals and want to add an ingredient and some flavour. (I already told you I keep my herb plants near my barbecue. Do you think I get up early in the morning and cut basil and sage for my dinner? No! I clip as I grill, in the evening.) Harvest on your own terms. It's your garden.

Leafy Greens

Harvesting

One reason leafy greens are so great to grow is they are ready to pluck just weeks from planting, and they keep on giving. By picking outer leaves when they reach a moderate size, you actually help extend the harvest.

Be warned—you can wait too long. If you let lettuces such as leaf lettuce, Boston lettuce, and mesclun mix fully mature, they'll bolt, sending up large seed spikes. By this point, the leaves lose their tenderness and turn bitter—you won't want to eat them. The one exception is iceberg (head) lettuce, which is best when the heads are firm and the size of a small ball.

Similarly, cooking greens such as spinach and Swiss chard taste the best when leaves are young or mid-size. If you let leaves linger, they'll develop more fibres and even cooking won't tenderize them. So, rule of thumb with greens: Check them daily

and harvest them constantly. As with most crops, leafy greens love to be harvested in the morning. When you plan to store leafy greens, avoid plucking them if they're wet or during the heat of the afternoon sun, as they won't keep very long.

Storing

Since fresh is best, the ideal way to enjoy leafy greens is by picking what you'll eat that day. If you happen to harvest too much or are plucking to share with others, follow these steps to cleaning and storing them so they'll keep:

1. After harvesting, trim your greens by removing any damaged leaves or stems and any pieces you will not use such as thick stalks and ends.
2. Fill the kitchen sink with tepid water, remove leaves from stems, and place greens in water. Agitate them with your hand to remove any dirt or sand.
3. Remove the greens from the water and spin in a salad spinner, or pat dry with a paper towel.
4. Chop only those greens you will use right away— they will brown on the edges before long. Place those greens in a sealed container or bag and refrigerate. For any unchopped greens you want to store longer, spread a thin layer across a clean tea towel or some paper towel. Fold the towel and add more layers of greens. Roll the towel up, secure with a rubber band, and put it in the refrigerator. Greens will keep this way for five to seven days.

Greens just keep on giving: Harvest the outer leaves of your lettuce plants and more will grow back. It's like magic!

Root Vegetables

Harvesting

There's a wide range of rules for harvesting root vegetables. Radishes taste best when pulled early and the bulb is just 2 to 3 cm (about 1 inch). Some onions can be harvested almost any time for their greens, or you can wait and harvest the bulb in late summer. Beets give you two harvests. Pluck the foliage (the greens) first and the roots later. To harvest beet greens, cut them, leaving 5 cm (2 inches) of greens still sticking out of the ground; the beet below will be fine. The beet itself can also be plucked at several stages of maturity—the smaller the root, the more tender the texture.

Pull potatoes and sweet potatoes before hard frost, but wait after a frost to dig your parsnips up.

To harvest carrots, parsnips, beets, or onions, I recommend using a garden fork, which helps to gently loosen them from the ground. Remove all excess soil by shaking or rubbing it off. Do not wash your root vegetables until you're ready to use them.

Technically speaking, potatoes are not true root crops—they're tubers!—but they are harvested and stored much in the same way. Similar to garlic and

onions, potatoes are ready and ripe when foliage dies. The exception are new (also called "early") potatoes. You can actually harvest some of these early in the season; the plant will keep on growing and give you more, larger, potatoes later in the season if you do it right. Try this: Very gently dig up the plant, pluck some of the little potatoes off the root, put the plant back in the ground, and tamp down the soil around it. You risk losing the entire plant so be cautious. Experiment with a few plants and never remove a potato plant in the heat of the day, when it will stress the plant. Keep your eye on the replaced plant and water it often until it settles again.

Storing

If stored properly, root vegetables can last months. To prepare them for storage, trim all foliage/tops, leaving a 2 cm (1 inch) stub. Do not cut the root flesh or the root tips. Avoid breaking the skin in any way—once you break the skin, the root can start to rot.

Most root vegetables last longest when stored in slightly moist conditions and temperatures just above the freezing mark (1 to 5°C/34 to 41°F). That means the fridge. Keep your root veggies away from fruits, particularly apples and pears, which give off ethylene gas and accelerate ripening (that's why your fridge has two crisper drawers). Things will probably become overcrowded after the frost and your entire root harvest is vying for refrigerator space. The solution: storing in sand in a box.

The box method: To store your root vegetables successfully without clogging a crisper drawer, first harvest the vegetables and let them sit at room temperature for a few days. This will help the skin toughen up a little—they'll need a little armour during storage to keep the flesh inside fresh and protected. Do not wash your roots—just brush off any dirt. Then line a cardboard, wooden, or plastic bin with slightly moist sand. Why sand? It helps regulate humidity and keeps excess moisture away from your food. Spread a layer of root vegetables over the sand base. The roots can touch each other, but the more space between them, the lower the risk of rot. (FYI: Carrots and parsnips store best when standing upright, just as they grew in the ground.) Cover the vegetables with 1 to 3 cm (about ⅓ to 1 inch) of sand and continue to layer root vegetables and sand until the box is almost full. Cover the final layer with 5 to 10 cm (2 to 4 inches) of sand. Store in a cool, frost-free location, such as a cold cellar, basement, or insulated garage. The colder the location, the more sand you should place between the layers. Check on your vegetables regularly, looking for signs of rot. If a vegetable goes bad, discard it right away. Your sandy box should keep for the winter. This storage trick works best with carrots, parsnips, potatoes, turnips, beets, onions, leeks, and shallots.

Pick your potatoes before the frost hits. If you can't cook them all up in a few days, store them in the fridge or even in a box covered with sand in a cool, dry place—they'll keep for months.

Berries

Harvesting

There is nothing like berry season. I have so many happy memories of berry picking as a child, and I take my children out every spring and summer. So few berries make it into the basket and so many end up in our mouths and on our shirts. Tip: Never wear white when berry picking!

A ripe berry tastes the best and won't store for long. Determine if berries are ready with your eyes, nose, and mouth. If a berry is fully coloured and appears plump and full, it should be ready. Follow your nose: The smell of the berry will intensify when it's ready to eat. Finally, taste your crop. A ripe berry should be flavourful, sweet, and firm. If it's soft and soggy, you've waited too long.

Strawberries: Pick when fully coloured and keep the cap and stem attached.

Raspberries: Harvest when they easily pull away from the cap. Once you get a few, you'll find the rest will soon follow. Visit your raspberries daily and you'll probably come away with a handful.

Blueberries: Your taste buds are the best guide since blueberries can be blue before they are fully ripe.

Blackberries: A glossy blackberry is an unripe berry. The less shine, the more ripe a blackberry.

Storing

Never wash a berry until you are ready to eat it, because a washed berry won't last long in storage.

On average, fresh berries will stay delicious for between three and seven days in a refrigerator. Before you store them, remove any crushed or spoiled fruits from the batch. Store them in plastic bags or sealed containers and rinse well before eating or cooking.

Freezing: Too many berries? You really have two options: jar or freeze. I'm a big fan of smoothies and frozen, homegrown berries. Follow these steps to freezer success:

1. Wash berries and drain.
2. Remove caps or stems.
3. Dry gently with a towel—this prevents ice buildup on the fruit.
4. Place on a cookie sheet in a single layer.
5. Put into the freezer overnight.
6. Transfer your frozen gems into a sealable freezer bag; remove any air before closing it up. These should last for three to five months in your freezer.

Eat up your luscious, ripe berries in a week or less or you'll need to freeze them or make jam. Hold off on washing fresh berries until just before you eat, preserve, or freeze them.

Fruit from
Fruit Trees or Shrubs

Harvesting

Many of the rules for berry picking apply to plucking fruits from fruit trees. You want to harvest when fruits are at their peak, as picking at maturity gives you maximum freshness and nutritional value. But maturity is different for different fruits. When apples begin to drop unblemished, they're ready. With apricots, look for firmness; the fruit should be slightly soft and should easily separate from the stem. Size is an indicator of ripeness for cherries and peaches; both increase in size until fully ripe. Pears can ripen on the tree, but they'll store longer if you harvest them early when they're full size and let them ripen indoors. Colour tells the ripeness story with plums; sugars increase as they mature, triggering a dramatic change in colour.

Storing

Keeping your fruits fresh once they're off the tree or shrub can be a challenge. While apples can last months if stored properly, apricots and cherries go from fab to compost within a few days. Also, most fruits off-gas ethylene and will cause your vegetables to ripen and rot quickly, so keep them separate.

To keep fruit fresh for as long as possible, you might be tempted to pop them all in the fridge. But that can make some fruits lose flavour.

Refrigerator fruits: Cherries, berries, grapes, rhubarb.

Room temperature fruits: Apples, apricots, nectarines, pears, plums, peaches.

Of course, if these fruits start to soften, are on the cusp of going bad, and you notice as you're dashing out the door, by all means toss them in the fridge. They'll lose some flavour, but that's better that losing the whole fruit.

Pick your tree fruit when all is ripe and ready. Peaches are good to pluck when they grow in size. Apples will start dropping to the ground.

Herbs

Harvesting

Herbs loved to be harvested. The more you cut, the more they will grow. Even early in the season, clipping off recently matured parts of an herb plant stimulates it to create more healthy growth. If you don't harvest your herbs, you run the risk of them bolting, which can ruin the flavour—so cut even if you're not using them.

One exception: If you're pickling this year and want to collect the dill seeds from your dill plants,

feel free to stop harvesting them and let them bolt. When the seed heads turn, remove them and place them in a paper bag for a few days so they dry out. Your seeds will naturally separate from the seed head.

To harvest most herbs, use a sharp knife, scissors, or pruning shears. Cut stalks just above a pair of leaves and never cut more than one-third of a stem's length. With chives and lavender, you can cut just above ground level.

Storing

Fresh herbs pack the most culinary punch. During the growing season, harvest what you need. If you overpick, remove bottom leaves and place remaining stems in a glass of water on the counter. Use these up in three to five days.

Freezing

Flavour cubes: Rinse your herbs in cold water, shake off excess moisture, and pat dry with a towel. Chop coarsely. Place the herbs in ice-cube trays, filling them to about two-thirds. (You can actually buy special herb cube trays, which are small. The smaller the better for herb cubes. Or underfill the regular ice-cube trays.) Pour in a little water and freeze overnight. Transfer herbs into a sealable freezer bag, where they'll keep for two to three months.

Drying

Drying works for all leafy herbs. No matter how you dry your herbs, when leaves are fully dry, remove the stems and place the herbs in sealed containers

If you cut a herb's stalk just above a pair of leaves, leaving at least two-thirds of the plant behind, the plant will keep on growing, offering up an ongoing harvest all season.

with tightly fitting lids. Store in a cool, dry place. Dried herbs should keep for about a year.

Old-school drying: Harvest and dry your herbs, but don't wash them. Tie the stems into small bundles using twine or twist ties. Hang the bundles upside down in a warm, dry, dark location with good air flow. They should dry out in two to three weeks.

Air-drying on screens: Spread herbs loosely on an old, clean window screen. Place the screen in a dry, warm, and dark location with good air circulation. Either use two screens to sandwich the herbs, and flip the screens often, or manually turn over all your herbs until they are dry.

Microwave drying: Lay a single layer of herbs between two sheets of paper towel and microwave on high power for one to two minutes. Cool. Leaves should be brittle. Sage may need to be air-dried first before microwaving.

Other options: Oven or dehydrator. Place a single layer on a cookie sheet and bake at the lowest oven setting until brittle. When using a dehydrator, follow the manufacturer's directions.

Just Eat

The best thing about food gardening is you can taste the rewards. Have your friends over, make a huge salad, adorn everything with fresh herbs, and bask in their compliments and the healthy deliciousness of all your hard work. When you are full of tummy and full of pride, those hours spent weeding and pondering rabbits seem very much worth it.

So Rotten: Setting Up a Composter

Food-growing gardens produce a lot of food, yes, but they also produce what gardeners call "green waste": leaves, spent plants, and overripened fruit. You can turn this waste into gardening gold in a composter. Then you can use the compost to amend and feed your garden soil. Composting is the ultimate way to be an environmentally responsible gardener. It repurposes waste and you become more self-sufficient. (You also save money, over time, on buying soil amendments.)

There are many types of composters and many factors you need to consider before setting one up:

Location: People love to hide their composters and compost piles. (They're not always pretty.) But hidden often means in a dark, shady corner of the garden. Won't work well. Composters need full sun, as the heat from the rays is what breaks down materials. The more sun and the more heat, the more effective your composter will be.

Size: The bigger the pile, the better the compost. A good-size composter should measure at least 135 by 135 cm (4 by 4 feet).

Composter Types

Compost pile: A composter can be as simple as garden and kitchen waste combined in a heap in a sunny location.

Wooden composter: Just build your own using a safe, non-treated wood such as cedar. The trick is having one side removable so you can access your compost to turn it, and remove the compost when it's done. The side slats must be evenly spaced apart to allow air flow—air is what does half the work in a composter.

You will need:
- 4 cedar posts (minimum 5 by 5 cm/2 by 2 inches) all cut to 1 m (3 feet) or your required height
- Cedar 1-by-6 planks (cut to 1 m/3 foot lengths if you're making a 1 m/3 foot square bin)
- 16 m (48 feet) of roof tiling cedar batten
- A box of nails or screws (galvanized for longer life)
- Hammer (if using nails) or drill with screwdriver attachment (if using screws)
- 4 m (12 feet) cedar batten (2.5 by 2.5 cm/ 1 by 1 inch) for lid
- 1 by 1 m (3 by 3 foot) wire welding mesh

Steps:
1. Cut the roof tiling cedar batten into 1 m (3 foot) lengths and fix to the posts using nails or screws.
2. Position the batten so that the two lengths run parallel to each other with a gap in between large enough to slide in your 1 m (3 foot) cedar planks.
3. Slide in the planks and secure the bottom plank with a screw or nail through the batten and plank. This will stop the composter from falling apart when you move it.
4. Repeat this process for the other three posts to build a four-sided square box. You may wish to secure the top planks on three sides of your compost box to increase stability. Leave the fourth side unsecured so you can gain easy access and turn the compost.
5. Place the welding mesh flat on the ground. Put the compost box on top of it. Attach it to the sides of the composter with fencing tacks for added security.
6. To build the lid, measure the inside of the compost box and construct a square frame from the 2.5 by 2.5 cm (1 by 1 inch) batten and the cedar planks. The lid should fit snugly inside the compost box.
7. Start to fill with waste. Remove the unsecured side every month or so and turn the material.

Pallet compost bin: Wood pallets used for shipping can be rejigged into composters with a minimum of work. You can buy them from garden centres, home supply stores, and farm supply stores, and sometimes, when you ask nicely, you can get them free! Choose your pallets from the same manufacturer so they're exactly the same size, and go for those made out of rot-resistant wood such as oak or cedar. Avoid pallets made from pine or pressure-treated wood.

You will need:

- 7 non-treated pallets of equal size
- Ten 2-by-2 patio slabs
- A box of 3-inch galvanized deck screws

Steps:

1. Select or create a level surface in full sun. Ten 2-by-2 patio slabs create the ideal base.
2. Attach the outer side wall of one pallet to another pallet to create the back of the first bin. Screw together.
3. To the rear pallet, attach another parallel to the side wall to create an inner wall. This will serve as a divider. Attach with several screws so it's secure.
4. To the dividing pallet, add another rear-wall pallet; screw together. Continue for the next two sections,

using the four remaining pallets to complete. *Voilà*—you have a composter with three bins, which allows you to make and store compost, plus store compostable materials.

Wire-mesh compost bins: Heavy-gauge galvanized mesh is an ideal material for building compost bins, as air flows through it. And it's cheap. I don't find it the easiest to work with—edges can be sharp and I've ripped numerous pairs of jeans walking by both benches and bins made from this. But they're pretty easy to put together. You just rig up a bin using four wooden posts and nailing the mesh to them, creating a see-through bin. Look online for more elaborate instructions.

Store-bought bins: Commercially made compost bins are available in numerous shapes and sizes: Some tumble (have a handle you can use to turn them) and some are just a box of wood—you get the picture. Just remember that bigger is better. All too frequently, compact store-bought composters look good, but they don't create enough compost and often can't even deal with the green waste your garden and home produce.

Composting 101

Here's how to create the right mix:

- Choose your compost container based on what you like, your handy skills, and the plant matter—grass, leaves, and kitchen scraps excluding meat, poultry, or dairy—you have. But go as big as you can.
- Locate the bin or pile in full sun.
- Know your terms: Brown materials generate carbon, and they include shredded newspaper, disease-free dried leaves, twigs, shredded tree bark, cardboard, paper bags or towels, egg cartons, and/or wood chips. Green material brings nitrogen to the mix. This term covers garden waste, grass clippings, flowers, fruit and vegetable scraps, coffee grounds, and tea bags.
- Diversity is good. A mixture of different kinds of brown and green materials makes for better compost.
- Avoid contaminants. Never put diseased or bug-infested plants in your bin. Place them in the garbage or safely burn them.
- Start your bin by piling a thin layer of small branches or woody stems; this improves air flow. The next layer is brown and green materials at a ratio of 30 parts brown to 1 part green. Keep adding material on top of this base regularly, but you can do green and brown in more or less equal parts now.

Three-Bin Benefits

The ideal compost set-up has three bins. Here's why. In one, you are making compost. When it's done, you can transfer it to a second bin and use it at your leisure, while still making more in bin one. And in the third bin, you can stash things like brown materials when you have too much (such as in the fall). It's the most efficient way to compost. Pallet bins are the easiest three-bin composters to build. Look online for instruction on how to build them from scratch, or buy a kit.

Chapter 9

Nighty-Night: Winding Down

Brightly coloured leaves drifting through the air. Frost in the forecast. Not being able to think of a single new thing to do with zucchini. Sure signs that the garden season is winding down. Even if you've brought in most of your harvest—perhaps you have some root vegetables still happy to go a little longer—the outdoor work lingers. Time to take the quieter fall days to wrap up this growing season and prepare for next. There's tidying, improving, protecting, even planting to do as the leaves turn and the garden closes down. It's not a lot of work, and it can be relaxing after a fine meal of your harvest crops. But wrap up your garden properly this year to be sure that next growing season you'll have a little less work, a plan already under way, and the best start possible.

Preparing for Frost

Just like in the spring, keep your eye on the forecast this time of year. When it calls for 5°C (41°F) or cooler under clear skies and light winds overnight, expect frost to hit your plots. You need to take action.

If you have fruits and vegetables still on your plants, pick them right away to eat or to store for later. (See chapter 8 for harvest and storage tricks.) If you insist your peppers, tomatoes, or greens hold on a bit longer, cover them over for the early frosts. But once it gets really cold and hard frosts set in, you must bring in your harvest or risk losing it.

Root crops such as carrots, parsnips, turnips, and beets can handle a light frost, as can vegetables from the cabbage family such as broccoli, cauliflower, and Brussels sprouts. Some gardeners say a little frost makes these vegetables sweeter. Cover the soil well with mulch to keep it moist and warm, and continue harvesting your root vegetables into the fall and early winter. You might want to add some tall stakes to mark their whereabouts in case of an early snowfall. How do you know it's over for these late harvesters? The tops will show signs of frost damage. Once the weather goes below −5°C (23°F) on a consistent basis, the ground will freeze and you are done.

Cold Frames

If some of your more tender crops are not ripe yet and frost is imminent, consider covering them with a cold frame of some kind. It can be as simple as a rigged-up faux greenhouse using old windows. You may get a few more weeks out of the growing season. (See more on page 88 in chapter 4.)

Planting in Fall

Wait, don't you plant in the spring? In fact, some crops do well with a late-fall planting.

Garlic: This grows beautifully when planted in the fall and harvested the next growing season. Garlic takes a long time to mature, and without winter giving it a head start, it might never reach harvest in Canada. About three weeks before you expect the ground to freeze—which it does after repetitive nights below −5°C (23°F)—plant seed garlic in the ground. You buy this at the garden centre in a netted bag just like bulbs (and you plant them in the fall like bulbs). These look like heads of garlic, but you want to plant them clove by clove in the ground at a distance and depth recommended on the label.

Over the next few weeks, your garlic will germinate and develop tiny roots but ideally, not grow upward and break the surface of the soil. If you cover the bed with 7 to 12 cm (3 to 5 inches) of clean straw, that will keep your garlic somewhat warm and protected while it goes dormant over the winter. As soon as spring warmth hits, it'll start growing again and you'll have garlic that summer.

Cover crops: If you've got a windy in-ground garden that's getting eroded, or your soil amendments and improvements just aren't cutting it, consider putting in a cover crop. This is a winter crop such as winter rye or wheat that you don't eat or even harvest; you just use it for the nutrients it adds to the soil. (For more on how to plant a cover crop, see page 86 in chapter 4.)

Tidying Up

Keep it lean and clean when it comes to fall. Once most of the harvest is in, your mission is to tidy up your yard and patio in advance of winter snow. Do it now and you'll have a better, more relaxing, start to the growing season next spring. My garden cleanup to-do list looks long, but trust me, it takes no time at all. Get the kids out there helping. They love fall cleanup—particularly when it ends with them diving into a pile of leaves.

- If you have a garden composter, empty it of its rich, ready-to-go compost and use it as a soil improver (see page 31). You want to do this before you start adding fall cleanup materials, which won't turn into useful compost until spring.

- Pull out all vines and plants that are now dying off. You can start this before the first frost as plants begin to fade. For certain, after a hard frost remove all plants and overripe or damaged fruits and vegetables. Healthy plants can be put in the compost pile.

- Take extra care with any part of your garden that had bugs or disease. Pull these sections out and either burn them or throw them in the garbage. A trace of a mould or an egg can often endure the winter and reinfect some or all of your garden next year.

- Collect all stakes, trellises, and tomato cages. Hose them down, dry them off, and store them neatly in the garage or shed.

- Empty small pots and any containers that contained diseased plants. Hose them out and store upside down to avoid cracking. Clay and ceramic pots should be brought indoors. If a container housed a healthy plant, and you'd like to reuse the soil next year, empty the top third, give the pot a quick wipe, and store.

- For any perennials in pots that you plan to overwinter, such as mint or chives, take them into a warm garage or bury the pot in the ground.

- Drain and store hoses. Collect all nozzles and sprayers and store. Turn off your outdoor water outlet.

- Clean all garden tools (with bleach if your plants had a disease) and oil them to prevent rusting.

- Once the work is done, cover your compost pile with black plastic to attract heat. Weigh the plastic down with old pots or bricks. That'll keep it cooking all winter long and you'll have compost again in spring.

Improving Soil

Now that we have reaped the harvest from the garden, it may be necessary to add nutrients back into the soil. You can enrich the soil in the spring, but fall is better: The freezing and the thawing through the winter help everything break down and work into the soil. Plus, it's just a quieter time in the garden.

Amending

If your crops struggled during the growing season, you may want to get back to thinking about soil again. Was drainage a problem? Maybe the pH was off? You can do a soil test to find out if your soil needs some more help via amendments. Go ahead and add them now; then the work is done in advance of spring. (Have a look back at page 29 in chapter 2 for a reminder of how to amend clay, sand, silt, and acidic or alkaline soil.)

Improving

No matter how amazingly well your crops did, you'll want to help the soil out again next year. In the fall, a quick top dressing of an enriching material is all you need. Put down a 5 to 8 cm (2 to 3 inch) layer of compost, manure, triple mix, or organic material such as leaves or garden debris. Dig this into the soil to a depth of 20 to 30 cm (8 to 12 inches). It's a good idea to mulch on top using straw or hay to prevent the soil from blowing away and help it retain moisture.

While compost or organic materials do feed the soil and will feed any perennials, they're not strong feeders that will get your garden growing right away. You want to avoid chemical fertilizers

that stimulate new growth this time of year. First of all, such products will be gone by the next growing season. But also, we don't want the kind of fast top growth that fertilizers encourage. Anything that is overwintering in the garden needs to focus on having strong roots, going quiet and dormant, and staying as warm and as protected as possible.

Protecting Perennials

Your perennials will happily go dormant over the winter and return again next spring. They're more likely to come back to you on happy terms if you give them a little loving before the snow flies.

Herbs

Sage, thyme, oregano, mint, marjoram, and chives will grow again year after year. Parsley is a biennial that may come back (don't count on it). All you need to do is cut it back. That's easy. Just keep harvesting it until the frost cuts you off. I love having sage and parsley in the fall to use for our Thanksgiving turkey. One mild early winter, I even got to use my herbs at Christmas.

To further encourage herbs to return healthy, water the soil well before the cold weather sets in and mulch around them. This will help them retain moisture and protect them from the severe cold. Perennial herbs in pots can make it through the winter outside, but you need to protect their roots. If they're in a large pot—or a raised bed or trough—they should be fine. Smaller potted herbs should be sunk into the ground or moved into a partially heated shed or garage. Or just move the container closer to the foundation of the house and cover the soil with a thick layer of mulch or hay.

Berries

Berry bushes are perennial and will come back with a sweet, ample harvest next year if you put them to bed just right.

Raspberries and blackberries: These plants grow canes that produce leaves the first year, followed by both leaves and berries the second, after which the canes die. Any cane that produced this year should be cut all the way back so the shrub can create new canes. First-year canes can be left alone, but they should be thinned so each one has about 15 square cm (36 square inches) to itself for next year. After cutting and thinning, water your canes deeply, put down a layer of compost and mulch about 5 to 8 cm (2 to 3 inches) thick.

Blueberries, currants, and gooseberries: Prune them back in the fall to no more than a third of the whole plant so winter snow, freezing rain, and wind won't damage them. Mulch, and they'll go for a nap.

Strawberries: This delicate grower needs to be protected from winter damage to the crown of the plant. Once the cooler days of fall arrive, cover your strawberry plants with several inches of straw. Do you have container-grown strawberries? They can overwinter in the container, but the roots need to be protected, so move the pot into a garage, shed, or under a porch. Or plant the entire pot in the ground.

Grapes: Grapevines will survive winter provided they are in a dormant state before the harshest weather arrives. To speed dormancy, quit watering for a few days after the last harvest; the vines will drop their leaves and start going dormant. At this point, water well and mound about 12 cm (5 inches) of hay or straw around the base of the vine. In extremely cold parts of Canada, you may need to pull the vines off their supports and protect them with a heavy layer of straw or hay.

It's tempting to ignore rotting apples at the end of the season, but cleaning them up ensures a healthy harvest next year.

Fruit Trees

I know I'm going to sound like such a neat freak again, but when it comes to your fruit trees like that backyard apple everyone loves, cleanliness around the base is really important as you head into winter.

Long grass, fallen leaves, and rotting fruit offer an ideal environment for rodents, insects, and disease. Rake up those fallen leaves, pick up the rotting fruit, and add it to the compost pile; burn or put infested leaves in the garbage. Cut long grass at the base of trees to prevent mice from nesting and feeding there. After your tidy-up, water the tree thoroughly and mulch the area.

Along with tidying, you might want to take some steps to protect your trees from pests and the elements. Consider installing plastic tree guards at the base of trees to protect the bark from rodents, rabbits, and deer, which love to snack on it—pests really love young, soft bark.

On top of the mulch you put around the tree, you can sprinkle deer or rabbit repellant if these pests might come by for a meal. Insects like cankerworm and tent caterpillars can be treated in fall for the next season with an application of Tanglefoot, a sticky substance that stops these insects in their tracks on their way up the tree to feed or lay eggs. This product cannot be applied directly on the bark; instead, wrap the trunk with a band of plastic wrap, filling any gaps underneath with cotton balls. Then apply Tanglefoot to the wrap using a stick or disposable spatula.

The elements are rough on fruit trees over the winter, especially young ones. Make sure all your young trees are staked to keep them upright in winter winds. Young trees are also at risk for something called "sunscald." This is damage done to the bark by the sun and fluctuating temperatures. You can wrap your fruit trees with paper or paint them with watered-down latex paint for protection.

Pulling Plants Inside

Some food plants just don't like winter, and if we want to keep them alive—even for a little while—we need to get them out of the frost and snow. Before you bring any outdoor plant inside, inspect it for bugs and give it a quick spray with an insecticidal soap just in case.

Herbs

Annual herbs, once the frost hits, are gone forever. Many cooks like to keep them growing inside. There are two ways to do this. If your herb is in a pot, bring the pot inside. But take it easy—you need to do a kind of reverse hardening off. Before the first frost, move your pot to a shady outdoor location; then gradually bring it inside for increasingly longer visits. It has to get used to the light and the moisture levels inside the house. Put herbs on a sunny windowsill where they will get six hours of sun a day, or place under artificial lights. You should get at least another month of growth.

Or it might be easier to take a cutting, particularly with in-ground growing herbs. Just snip off a strong stem and place it in a pot filled with potting soil. Give it lots of light and moisture and see if it takes. This new plant will need some time to flourish, so do your clipping while the growing season is in full swing. By the time frost hits outside, you'll have new herbs inside.

If you've got the space, tote your herbs indoors. Many will keep growing in a sunny spot all winter long.

Tropical Fruits

If you've been experimenting with a lemon or orange tree in a pot on your patio, you'll have to bring this warm-weather gem inside before Jack Frost returns. Here are the steps to transporting the tropical world indoors:

1. Inspect your tree for insects and disease. Spray with insecticidal soap as a precaution. Prune the tree, removing no more than one-third of the plant.
2. Reverse harden off your tree by bringing it indoors gradually for an increasing number of hours each day.
3. Place in a south- or west-facing room that gets lots of light.
4. Encourage your tree to go into a dormant phase by reducing watering from mid-fall to late winter, and avoid giving it fertilizer this time of year.
5. In late winter to early spring, when the days grow longer, you can gradually increase watering and start feeding it again.
6. Next growing season, when there are no more frost warnings, you can take it back outside. Reverse the process and harden it off by getting it used to outside again. Let it bask in the sun all growing season long.

Reflect

Now that the work is done and the quiet days of late fall and winter are upon you, it's time to think back over the growing season and make some notes: What you liked about your food garden. What you enjoyed growing. What you ate and what you ended up tossing or giving away. How you coped with rabbits, watering, and insects, and what you wished you'd done differently. Ask your family what stuck with them through the growing season, and if they enjoyed all that kale or wanted more radishes. I'm hoping you took a few pictures to document your experiences.

Now create a folder, either old-school paper style or on your computer, or, if you're cool, in the cloud. Call this folder "Food to Grow Garden 2016." Next year's folder will be 2017 and so on. Gather up your garden plans, your multi-cropping notes, your photos, and your old plant tags and seed packets. These folders are your road map for following seasons. We forget, and all too often we repeat the same mistakes year after year. Be sure you have the right materials on hand to make next year an even better, more prosperous, gardening season.

Have a good winter and I'll see you again next year!

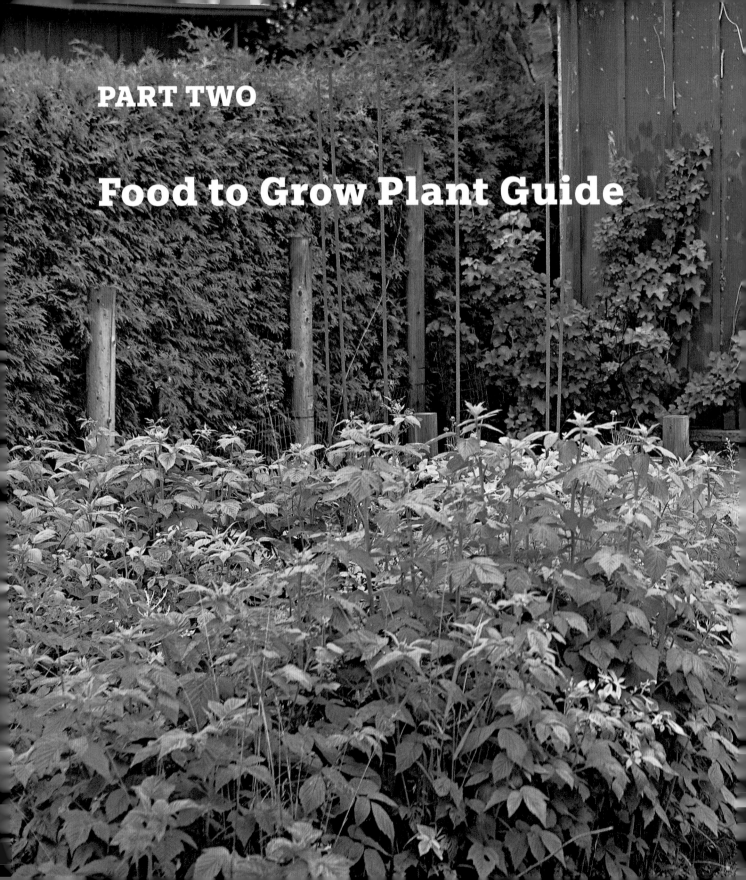

PART TWO

Food to Grow Plant Guide

Apple

WHAT IT IS: Fruit tree, perennial (zones 3–5)

HOW HARD TO GROW: Moderate

LIGHT NEEDS: Full sun

SOIL NEEDS: Well drained, fertile, pH 5.0–6.8

WATERING NEEDS: Deep, infrequent

DIMENSIONS: Height: 6 m+ (20 feet+); semi-dwarf 4.5 m (15 feet); dwarf 3 m (10 feet); width: 6 m+ (20 feet+); semi-dwarf 3.5 m (12 feet); dwarf 2.5 m (8 feet)

HOW FAR APART TO PLANT: 6 m (20 feet); semi-dwarf 4–5 m (16–18 feet); dwarf 2.5 m (8 feet)

CONTAINER SIZE: Container planting not recommended

HOW MANY TO PLANT: 2; each tree yields 500+; semi-dwarf, 350–500; dwarf, 250–400

WHEN TO SOW INDOORS: n/a

WHEN TO PLANT OUTDOORS: Early spring or late summer

READY TO EAT: Fruit in third or fourth season, late summer/fall

MULTI CROPPING: No, single crop

GROWS WELL WITH: Chive, garlic, leek, nasturtium, comfrey, tansy

DO NOT PLANT WITH: Potato, black walnut

FOOD TO GROW VARIETIES: Early: 'Crabapple', 'Honeycrisp', 'Liberty', 'Manchurian', 'Idared', 'McIntosh'. Mid: 'Akane', 'Gala', 'Red Delicious', 'Golden Delicious'. Late: 'York', 'Enterprise', 'Pristine', 'Northern Spy'

WHY TO GROW: You can go apple picking at a farm in the fall, or grow your own in your back or front yard. (Not in containers or very small spaces—sorry!) This incredibly versatile fruit is great cooked up in pies and other desserts. Or just eat apples on their own—take a bite! It's important to know that it takes two to tango with apples; they need a partner to pollinate. You can use two of the same variety, but you'll get the best yields by pairing with a compatible variety that blooms at the same time (see the list of recommended varieties at left and pair early, mid, and late bloomers with each other). Or buy a self-pollinating variety such as 'Golden Delicious' or 'Granny Smith'. Plant your pair under 30 m (10 feet) apart. Bees—which will do the pollinating—won't travel farther than this.

PLANTING: Look for a tree that has branches on all sides with no big branch gaps, and no damage on stems, branches, or leaves. Selection is best in early to mid-spring; apple trees thrive when they're planted in fall, but it's tricky to find good saplings this time of year. To plant, dig a hole two times the width of the root ball and one and a half times the depth. Mix in triple mix to amend the soil. If soil is low quality, remove all the soil and replace with triple mix. If you have clay soil, fill the bottom third of the hole with stones to help improve the drainage. Place the tree in the hole and tamp down until the root ball sits 5 cm (2 inches) above ground level. Fill in the hole and mound excess soil toward the root ball. Mulch around the base of the tree. Water frequently and deeply for the first two months after planting, then reduce watering to once a week. Stake against the prevailing wind; or, if in doubt, double-stake the tree until it's well established, which takes two to three seasons.

GROWING: Once the tree starts producing fruit in year three or four, feed with a top dressing of manure, water-based fertilizer, or granular fertilizer; or use fruit tree fertilizer spikes that offer continuous feeding. Thin newly grown apples when they are about the size of a dime so the remaining fruit are 10 to 15 cm (4 to 6 inches) apart and there's just one fruit per cluster. The first winter after planting, prune any branches that are inward growing or crossing and prune branches overall so there's lots of airflow, and of course get rid of any diseased or damaged bits. Prune annually with clean pruners.

PROTECTING: Growing the perfect apple isn't easy, as they are prey to many diseases and insects. Squirrels, mice, voles, deer, and rabbits like to munch on apple trees during the winter months. If rodents damage more than 50 per cent of the trunk, it can starve the tree and threaten its existence. If you want blemish-free apples, you may need to use chemical pesticides. To grow apples naturally, be extra clean, prune, and use natural control methods. Every spring, after the snow melts and before buds crack, treat your tree with a dormant spray. The horticultural oil and sulphur in this product will target overwintering diseases and insects. Apples can fall prey to apple scab. To prevent it, remove all leaves from under the tree as well as fallen fruit. Scab-resistant varieties include 'Liberty', 'Redfree', and 'Williams Pride'. To control apple maggot, an insect whose larvae tunnel into the flesh of apples, making them inedible, fasten plastic sandwich bags over the apples when they are small and green. The apples will develop, but the adult flies cannot lay eggs. To prevent water from collecting inside the bag, clip the lower corner. If you're spraying liquid insecticides or fungicides, apply after full bloom is over in late spring, spraying every 10 to 14 days until the harvest in late summer/early fall.

HARVESTING: The apple harvest is dependent on the weather and your apple variety. The base colour of apples will change and the inside flesh will lose its greenish tint and turn yellow or white. The flavour and texture will truly tell you when an apple is ripe. A ripe apple is crisp and juicy with a pleasing but not tart taste.

Yanking fruit off will disturb the tree and can cause other apples to fall and bruise. Instead, gently twist or turn the fruit until it comes off. If your apple is ripe, it should be easy to pick.

STORING: Keep your apples between 0 and 5°C (32 to 41°F) with humidity between 90 and 95 per cent. Crisper drawers, or a fruit cellar, are ideal. Apples will stay fresh for several months if stored properly.

Young fruit trees make for great critter snacks. Prevent damage by wrapping the base with a **tree guard**. You can purchase guards or make your own out of plastic 4-inch drainage pipe. Put the guard around the base of your tree in late fall and remove it every spring.

It's easy to get excited about picking apples when the trees are in bud at your local nursery, but think carefully about the variety you select—you want to make sure you'll end up with apples you want to eat. The great news? You can get saplings that have multiple varieties grafted onto the same tree—so you can choose a mix of eating and cooking apples, or even early and late varieties to extend the harvest.

Apricot

WHAT IT IS: Fruit tree, perennial (zones 4–9)

HOW HARD TO GROW: Moderate

LIGHT NEEDS: Full sun

SOIL NEEDS: Well drained, pH 5.5–6.5

WATERING NEEDS: Deep and frequent in spring

DIMENSIONS: Height: standard 4.5–6 m (20 + feet); semi-dwarf 2.5–3 m (15 + feet); dwarf 2 m (6–8 feet); width: all sizes are about as wide as they are tall

HOW FAR APART TO PLANT: 3.5–7.5 m (11–25 feet)

CONTAINER SIZE: Minimum depth: 60 cm (2 feet); diameter: 75 cm (2.5 feet)

HOW MANY TO PLANT: One tree will yield 5–10 kg (11–22 pounds) of fruit

WHEN TO SOW INDOORS: n/a

WHEN TO PLANT OUTDOORS: Spring or fall

READY TO EAT: Fruit in third season; late-summer harvest

MULTI CROPPING: No, single crop

GROWS WELL WITH: Pansy, basil

DO NOT PLANT WITH: Potato, tomato, eggplant, pepper

FOOD TO GROW VARIETIES: 'Hargrand', 'Wenatchee' (also called 'Moorpark'), 'Pui-sha-sin' (also called 'Chinese apricot')

WHY TO GROW: This attractive fruit tree starts the spring with a show of pink or white fragrant blooms. While these trees take three years to bear fruit, they eventually offer a bounty of fruit tastier than anything you can buy—apricots do not keep or travel well, so fresh from your yard is truly best. Apricot trees flourish in pretty much any soil type as long as there is good drainage, and they are fairly resistant to insects and disease. Since this is a self-fruitful tree and its blossoms can pollinate others on the tree, you don't need to plant a partner. The only real catch is that apricot trees bloom very early in spring, and if you select the wrong variety for your weather, you could get blooms before the last frost date and lose the fruit.

PLANTING: Plant your tree full sun. In colder climates plant on the north side of a building so the tree will stay cool early in the season and bloom late. To plant, dig a hole twice the width and depth of the root ball. Remove the sapling from its container and encourage the roots to spread outward by fraying them—snipping the roots with shears or scoring root ball with a knife before planting. Place the plant in the hole, making sure the root ball sits slightly above ground level. Water, pack the soil around the roots, and water again. I always recommend attaching a wooden stake about 20 cm (8 inches) from the trunk to keep the young tree upright and straight.

If your climate is much colder than your variety can tolerate, plant in a large container and winter in a shed or garage. To plant a dwarf or miniature variety in a container, drill draining holes in the bottom. If your winters are below −6°C (21°F), mount your container with castors so you can easily move the pot to shelter for the winter.

GROWING: Water the tree deeply and frequently while it's blooming and producing fruit. Put mulch—either sawdust or wood chips—around the base of the tree to keep weeds out and moisture in. The first early spring after planting, prune the tree to four well-spaced branches, and shorten each branch by a third. As the tree matures, prune in early spring to ensure each branch has good airflow, remove branches that grow inward, and cut away any small shoots along the trunk and at the base of the tree.

Fertilize only when the tree begins producing fruit. Give the tree a light feeding of manure or 10-10-10 fertilizer in the spring. When the tree starts bearing fruit, pluck any misshapen or discoloured fruit and generally thin out the fruit out so they will not touch each other when they ripen.

CHALLENGES: This tree's tendency to bloom early and get nipped by frost is its biggest challenge, so be sure to select the right variety for your zone (see page 396 for more on growing zones). Use a dormant oil spray in spring to prevent the development of disease and to treat any overwintering insects or diseases. Wrap the base of the tree with plastic guards as well to keep gnawing rodents

at bay. Peach tree borers will target apricot trees. They are nasty insects that bore right into the trunk and branches. There is little to be done when this happens other than to remove the affected branches. Brown rot shows up on ripened fruit as brown spots; they soon overtake the entire fruit. Remove any affected fruit immediately to prevent spread. Treat the tree with a fungicide right away and the following spring too.

HARVESTING: Pick your fruit when it's fully coloured and the skin gives slightly. Harvest early if you can—apricots keep ripening after harvest and will easily bruise if ripened too much on the tree.

STORAGE: Store apricots at room temperature, but once they are fully ripe, keep them refrigerated. Do not pile them on top of each other, as they bruise too easily (egg cartons make good storage containers). Apricots can be frozen for up to three months by cutting in two, removing the pit, and dipping the halves in an ascorbic acid solution to retain the colour. Packed in a sugary syrup, apricots can be kept in the freezer for a year. They can and dry well too.

Arugula

WHAT IT IS: Leafy green vegetable, annual

HOW HARD TO GROW: Easy

LIGHT NEEDS: Full sun to part shade

SOIL NEEDS: Well drained, moist, fertile, pH 6.0–7.0

WATERING NEEDS: Frequent

DIMENSIONS: Height: 30–60 cm (1–2 feet); width: 20–30 cm (8–12 inches)

HOW FAR APART TO PLANT: 15–30 cm (6–12 inches)

CONTAINER SIZE: Minimum depth: 15 cm (6 inches); diameter: 25 cm+ (10 inches+)

HOW MANY TO PLANT: 5 plants per person

WHEN TO SOW INDOORS: 2 weeks before last frost date

WHEN TO PLANT OUTDOORS: Early spring or late summer

READY TO EAT: 28–42 days

MULTI CROPPING: No, single crop

GROWS WELL WITH: Bush bean, beet, cucumber, carrot, spinach, onion, celery, potato, lettuce

DO NOT PLANT WITH: Strawberry, and avoid planting after cabbage crops

FOOD TO GROW VARIETIES: 'Roquette', 'Runway', 'Rocket'

WHY TO GROW: You can eat the foliage *and* the flowers as well as the seeds and the pod of this zesty green. Personally, I love it on a grilled panini. Arugula is hip these days because it's loaded with vitamins A, C, and K; it's also high in antioxidant phytochemicals called "indoles." New gardeners should love this crop. It's easy to grow right from seed, and it adores cool Canadian springs and falls—in fact, it can even tolerate a little frost.

PLANTING: Arugula can be sown indoors two weeks before the last frost date. But I don't see the benefit: Its seeds are quick to germinate, and within just five to seven days, they will be sprouting leaves. I recommend direct sowing in a sunny spot with well-drained soil in the spring when soil temperatures reach 10°C (50°F). Space in rows or in groupings, sowing seeds 1 cm (.5 inch) deep and 2 to 3 cm (1 inch) apart—you will thin them later. These small seeds will only require a light covering of soil to shield them from birds and hold in moisture until they germinate. For a continuous supply of arugula, stagger your plantings every two to three weeks. In spring and early fall, sow seeds in full sun, but in summer, sow in a partially shaded spot with good airflow. Your last crop of arugula should be sown one month before the last average frost date in your area.

GROWING: After your seeds germinate, and once leaves emerge, reduce watering and allow the seedlings to slightly dry out before watering again. When your seedlings have three leaves, thin them out so you have 10 to 15 cm (4 to 6 inches) between plants. After this stage and while you're harvesting arugula, it's okay to let the plant wilt slightly in between watering, but don't let it really dry out or it can bolt. If you're growing in containers, you can go as shallow as 15 cm (6 inches) for this compact green. But since the soil and plants in pots warm up rapidly, summer growing probably won't work out; just sow in early spring and late summer in containers.

CHALLENGES: Bolting! This fast-growing green can go from ready to pluck to a diminished green in a matter of days. Give your arugula adequate moisture and avoid growing in full sun in summer to prevent bolting—the process where arugula begins to set seed and becomes tough and quite bitter. Arugula's peppery flavour makes it an undesirable snack for bunnies, deer, mice, and most bugs, but cabbage worms, moths, and flea beetles will target it. Check the plants regularly, and if you get flea beetles, erect floating row covers. Be sure to remove them in early summer, as they can warm the soil and overheat your arugula.

HARVESTING: Start picking about 30 to 40 days after planting. Don't wait for leaves to get large, as they may be bitter by then. You can cut a few leaves and let the plant keep producing. But I like harvesting the entire plant when it's 10 to 12 cm (4 to 5 inches) high and relying on my next round of arugula, which will be ready to cut in a week or two, for my next meals.

STORAGE: If you store your arugula unwashed and kept dry in the refrigerator, it should last about a week. But it's best eaten fresh off the plant.

Asparagus

WHAT IT IS: Vegetable, perennial (zones 3–8)

HOW HARD TO GROW: Moderate

LIGHT NEEDS: Full sun

SOIL NEEDS: Well drained, fertile, pH 6.5–7.5

WATERING NEEDS: Frequent in spring

DIMENSIONS: Height: 90–180 cm (3–6 feet); width: 30–100 cm (1–3 feet)

HOW FAR APART TO PLANT: 30–45 cm (12–18 inches)

CONTAINER SIZE: Container planting not recommended

HOW MANY TO PLANT: Yields 1–1.5 kg (2–3 pounds) per plant

WHEN TO SOW INDOORS: Not recommended

WHEN TO PLANT OUTDOORS: Spring

READY TO EAT: Fruit in third year; early spring

MULTI CROPPING: No, single crop

GROWS WELL WITH: Aster family flowers, dill, cilantro, carrot, tomato, parsley, basil, comfrey, marigold

DO NOT PLANT WITH: Onion, garlic, potato

FOOD TO GROW VARIETIES: Zone 4: 'Viking', 'Guelph Millennium'. Zone 5: 'Jersey King', 'Purple Passion'

WHY TO GROW: It's a sure sign of spring when asparagus spears start shooting out of the garden. This perennial will produce for a very short time in early spring for several years. After that, when left alone, spears will grow tall, fern-like foliage and produce orange-red berries (except all-male varieties such as 'Jersey Knight' do not produce berries). Don't eat the berries: They're mildly toxic and will give you a tummy ache. When you plan your garden, remember just how tall these plants get, particularly by summer, so make sure they won't shade any other crop.

PLANTING: While you can grow asparagus from seed, why would you? When you plant from crowns (what we call their roots), it takes three seasons for a harvest. That's pretty long, so who wants to wait for seeds to germinate? Before planting, amend the area with two parts soil to one part manure. Traditionally, asparagus is planted in rows in trenches measuring 30 cm wide (1 foot), 30 cm (1 foot) deep and spaced 90 cm (3 feet) apart, but I recommend planting in individual mounds. Place 5 cm (2.5 inches) of soil at the bottom of the planting hole or trench, and place your crown—which looks like a spider with very long legs; the "body" of the spider should be at the top—in the hole and cover with 10 cm (4 inches) of soil. Every two weeks, add additional soil until the planting hole or trench is completely filled. Keep well watered.

GROWING: Do not harvest spears for the first two seasons so the plant can keep growing strong roots—your patience will be rewarded with healthy yields later on. Keep the area weed-free, as asparagus does not like to compete. Unless you're having a rainy autumn, give your asparagus a deep, heavy

watering in the fall before frost sets in. Otherwise, this low-maintenance plant just needs ample water and a side dressing of fertilizer in the spring and fall.

CHALLENGES: This plant has only one serious enemy: the asparagus beetle. But these critters are so slow moving you can easily pick and squish them, plus they easily fall victim to insecticidal soap.

HARVESTING: Starting in the third season, harvest your spears when their tips are tightly closed and stalks are 1 to 2 cm (.5 to 1 inch) in diameter and 15 to 20 cm (6 to 8 inches) tall. Asparagus can be harvested for up to six weeks after spears emerge. Harvest by snapping the spear off at the base. I always avoid cutting below soil level, as you can harm emerging spears. Stop harvesting in late spring and leave it be. You may want to cut back that tall, fern-like foliage, but resist until it turns brown in the late fall. Or leave it all winter; the dead growth will catch snow and allow it to collect around the base of asparagus crowns, insulating them for the winter and providing a source of moisture in the spring.

STORAGE: Asparagus will last in the fridge for three to five days unwashed. Wrap ends with dampened paper towels, cover with a plastic bag, and store standing upright. To store in the freezer, blanch a batch in boiling water for one to two minutes, immerse it in a bowl of ice water, drain and dry, and place in plastic bags and freeze; it'll last two months in the freezer.

Bean

WHAT IT IS: Fruit (really!), annual

HOW HARD TO GROW: Easy

LIGHT NEEDS: Full sun

SOIL: Well drained, pH 6.0–6.5

WATERING NEEDS: Deep, infrequent

DIMENSIONS: Height: bush 25–60 cm (10–24 inches); pole 1.5–2 m (5–6 feet); width: bush 30–60 cm (1–2 feet); pole 60 cm (2 feet)

HOW FAR APART TO PLANT: Bush 60 cm (2 feet); pole 15–30 cm (6–12 inches)

CONTAINER SIZE: Minimum depth for bush: 18 cm (7 inches); for pole: 23 cm (9 inches); diameter: 30 cm+ (12 inches+)

HOW MANY TO PLANT: 4–8 plants per person

WHEN TO SOW INDOORS: Not recommended

WHEN TO PLANT OUTDOORS: Mid-spring

READY TO EAT: 55–100 days

GROWS WELL WITH: Carrot, pea, corn, potato, strawberry

MULTI CROPPING: No, single crop

DO NOT PLANT WITH: Garlic, onion, shallot

FOOD TO GROW VARIETIES: Bush: 'Bush Kentucky Wonder', 'Harvester', 'Romano Bush', 'Blue Lake 47'. Pole: 'Scarlet Runner', 'Kentucky Wonder', 'Blue Lake'. Lima: 'Big Mama'

WHY TO GROW: Beans are such a great—and popular—backyard crop. They're easy growers and taste incredible picked and steamed up for dinner the same day. FYI—string beans, snap beans, and green beans are all names for the same thing. You can also grow shell beans: romano and lima. Before you grow, you have to make a decision about your growing type. Short on space? Pole beans—which grow on a vine—may be your best choice, since they take up less soil space and can look pretty as they climb up a trellis or arbour. Bush beans are more compact and great for small gardens and containers. Warning: Check the seed packets on your chosen beans for the maturity date and be sure you have enough frost-free days to get to harvest.

PLANTING: Beans love warm soil, so prep for a spring planting by covering your plot with some black plastic for a few weeks to toast things up. After the risk of frost has passed, sow your bean seeds 2.5 to 5 cm (1 to 2 inches) deep, keeping them well watered until they germinate. It won't take long. That's why there's no need to grow from seedlings for this easy crop. Seed bush beans in rows. Pole beans will require a support about of 2 m (6 feet) high of some kind such as a wall, fence, trellis, or obelisk.

GROWING: Bean plants have a very shallow root system, and their roots like it cool, so apply mulch after your seedlings emerge. The plants will lose their blooms if they get too hot or lack water, so water daily to at least 2.5 cm (1 inch) during blooming. Pole beans need extra TLC—you'll have to coax the vines onto their support by adjusting the vine and tying them on a regular basis. Since bean plants give nitrogen back to the soil, you don't really need to fertilize. But adding some compost or manure halfway through the growing season will keep pole beans producing well.

CHALLENGES: The tender leaves of this plant and mild flavour of the fruit itself make beans a favourite of many pests. Bean beetles munch on flowers, beans, and leaves; slugs chew holes in leaves close to the ground; and Japanese beetles and aphids will feed on bean plants. The four-legged variety of pests like deer, bunnies, and groundhogs can easily devour an entire plant, so consider a fence if these critters are nearby.

HARVESTING: Pick green beans once the pods seem slightly full and they snap when bent. Other beans can be left until the pods are quite swollen. Pick every three to four days to keep the plant producing. Leaving beans on the vine too long gives you a tougher, bitter bean and takes strength from the vine.

STORAGE: Fresh beans will keep in the refrigerator for five to six days. A bumper crop of green beans can be stored in the freezer by blanching in boiling water until the beans turn bright green (about three minutes), then cooling immediately in cold water and storing in freezer bags. To dry beans such as navy or romano, do it the way our ancestors did: leave the swollen pods right on the plant until the pods yellow and the beans become hard. In humid or rainy weather, cut the plant at the ground and hang it upside down in a dry spot until the beans harden. When dry, remove the pods and store the beans in a dark, dry place for up to 12 months.

Beet

WHAT IT IS: Root vegetable, annual

HOW HARD TO GROW: Moderate

LIGHT NEEDS: Full sun

SOIL NEEDS: Rich organic, well drained, light, pH 6.0–6.5

WATERING NEEDS: Average, about 2.5–4 cm (1–1.5 inches) per week

DIMENSIONS: Height: 20–30 cm (8–12 inches); width: 30 cm (12 inches)

HOW FAR APART TO PLANT: 5–8 cm (2–3 inches); rows: 45 cm (18 inches)

CONTAINER SIZE: Minimum depth: 20 cm (8 inches); diameter: 30 cm+ (12 inches+)

HOW MANY TO PLANT: 5–10 plants per person

WHEN TO SOW INDOORS: Not recommended

WHEN TO PLANT OUTDOORS: Up to one month before last frost date when soil reaches 10°C (50°F)

READY TO EAT: 50–60 days

MULTI CROPPING: No, single crop

GROWS WELL WITH: Bush bean, cabbage family, lettuce, onion; garlic is said to enhance flavour

DO NOT PLANT WITH: Pole bean (will stunt growth)

FOOD TO GROW VARIETIES: 'Early Wonder', 'Detroit Dark Red', 'Ruby Queen', 'Red Ace'

WHY TO GROW: So many reasons to grow beets! You can eat both the root and the leaves; they can withstand frost and freezing temperatures; and they contain vitamins and antioxidants that are said to clear the liver, prevent cancer, and protect your heart. Beets are also super-sexy: They contain boron, which is said to aid in the production of human sex hormones and increase endurance. Some varieties take a long time to harvest, but the ones I list at left are early beets you may be able to multi-crop in your Canadian garden.

PLANTING: Choose a location with full sun—although beets can tolerate a bit of shade. Clear the area fully; the roots of beets grow near the surface, so the soil needs to be soft and free of any rocks or other obstacles. Amend the soil by adding compost if the soil has a lot of clay. If you're growing in a container, make sure it has good drainage and is deep enough to accommodate the roots. Sow into the garden when soil has warmed to 10°C (50°F); sow seeds 2 cm (1 inch) deep. If you want an ongoing harvest—why wouldn't you?—stagger your sowing or planting 14 days apart, right up until the month before the last frost.

Water your seeds or seedlings daily until they germinate or plants are established. If you're growing from seed, you'll need to thin out plants, as one seed can create three or four plants. Thin until you have 5 to 8 cm (2 to 3 inches) between plants.

GROWING: Beets don't need a lot of water after the seedling is established. They will take moisture from the soil, and too much water can soften the root and leads to excessive upper growth. Allow nature to water your beets for you, and if you go through a dry spell, water them only every 10 days.

Be gentle with your beet plants—they can be damaged by weeding tools. Weed by hand and take it easy. Six weeks after your beet seeds germinate and break through the soil, give them a little feeding with a side dressing of compost, manure, or a granular fertilizer.

CHALLENGES: If you see beet leaves folded over and webbed, you're probably seeing the work of the beet webworm, a green pest that's about 5 cm (2 inches) long. Ideally, prevent getting this pest by having a weed-free garden. If you get it, encourage parasitic wasps and, as a last resort, treat with BTK (see page 135).

Holes in the leaves are probably caused by blister beetles. Tan spots on the leaves are the sign of the fungal disease leaf spot.

HARVESTING: Just eight weeks after sowing from seed, you can begin harvesting what will be baby beets that are perfect for salads and pickling. When the top of the root is about 2.5 cm (1 inch) in diameter, pick every other beet, or the ones that look big enough. Carefully dig under the root and lift the plant out of the ground by its leaves. Those plants left behind will grow faster now. Pick this next round at about 7.5 cm (3 inches) in diameter—any larger and they become woody. Twist the greens off the plant, to be enjoyed on their own. Don't cut too close to the base of the stem, as this will cause the juice to bleed out, which will affect the flavour and colour of the beet.

STORAGE: Just like other root vegetables, beets store well in a cool, dry spot or up to a week in the fridge. Keep longer by storing in sand (see page 167 in chapter 8 for instructions). Beets pickle well. You can also freeze them: Boil washed beets, keeping 5 cm (2 inches) of the stem intact and the skin on, for about 30 minutes. Cool immediately in ice water, drain, peel, and cut in 1 cm (½ inch) slices. Store in plastic bags in the freezer.

Blackberry

WHAT IT IS: Fruit vine, perennial (zones 5–10)

HOW HARD TO GROW: Easy (but needs extra attention to keep it under control)

LIGHT NEEDS: Full sun

SOIL NEEDS: Well drained, pH 6.2–6.8; will grow in poor soil

WATERING NEEDS: Frequent when fruit is forming

DIMENSIONS: Height: 1–3 m (3–8 feet); width: 1 m (3 feet)

HOW FAR APART TO PLANT: 1–3 m (3–8 feet)

CONTAINER SIZE: Minimum depth: 30 cm (12 inches); diameter: 30 cm (12 inches)

HOW MANY TO PLANT: Yields 4.5 kg (10 pounds) per plant

WHEN TO SOW INDOORS: n/a

WHEN TO PLANT OUTDOORS: Early spring or late summer

READY TO EAT: Depends on variety

MULTI CROPPING: No, single crop

GROWS WELL WITH: Garlic, chive, bee balm

DO NOT PLANT WITH: Tomato, pepper, eggplant, potato

FOOD TO GROW VARIETIES: Erect: 'Darrow', 'Cheyenne', 'Illini Hardy'. Semi-erect: 'Chester', 'Triple Crown'

WHY TO GROW: So easy to grow and so tasty. But blackberries—which are not actually a berry, FYI, but are actually something called an "aggregate fruit"—have a few quirks. They grow on thorny canes, but you can find thorn-less varieties. And they are almost too easy to grow—they can take over your yard if you're not careful! You need to prune them without fail. Before you plant, be certain you have time and space for blackberries! Either that or plant them in a container, which will keep them, well, contained. There are three types of blackberries: training, erect, and semi-erect. Training blackberries do not overwinter in cool climates and should be avoided. Erect blackberries produce fruit with large seeds on last year's growth with self-supporting canes, making them relatively low maintenance. Semi-erect require staking and produce high yields on thorn-less canes.

PLANTING: While blackberry shrubs will grow well if you plant in the fall, you'll find the best plant selection in early spring. For that spring planting, get your shrub into the ground as soon as the ground is soft and no longer frozen. There are really only two requirements for blackberries: loads of sun and well-drained soil, so avoid planting in clay with its problem drainage. Plant the shrub so the soil hits where the roots and the stem meet. Space at least 1 m (3 feet) from other blackberry shrubs and avoid planting close to raspberry canes, as they will compete with each other. Consider edging the area with stone or wood to contain roots and restrict the spread of your shrubs.

GROWING: Blackberries grow on their own in the wild and don't need a lot of help in your garden either. Shrubs will last 15 to 20 years if you feed them right. That just entails giving them a side dressing of manure every spring; I like using sheep manure. Then, it's really all about pruning to keep blackberries healthy and under control. For erect varieties, prune canes right after harvest. In spring, remove any dead or weak canes and keep the healthiest eight to 16. For semi-erect varieties, prune in early spring, removing canes that bore fruit last year— they will appear thicker than new growth—and dead ones too. The new growth canes will offer you fruit this year. Also offer these varieties a trellis or a fence early on, and train them to grow upward, securing them to your support with something like pantyhose, which won't cut their stems.

CHALLENGES: Aphids really love this shrub, so work hard to prevent them by spraying with insecticidal soap and introducing ladybugs to your garden. Other challenges include spider mites, beetles, rust, and blight. Few larger creatures go for blackberries if you are growing a thorny variety, but birds will stop by and eat some of your harvest. If you don't have enough to share, simply place some netting on your shrubs.

HARVESTING: Depending on the variety you choose to grow, you can have fruit in late spring all the way to early fall. Harvest your fruit when it's deep black; if the fruit is red or purple, it's not ripe. Look in between canes too, as berries sometimes hide in the foliage. Pick in the late morning after the dew has dried.

STORAGE: Do not wash your fruit until you are ready to eat or cook it. Store blackberries uncovered in the refrigerator and they should last a week, but you'll lose flavour on a daily basis. To freeze them, wash, drain, and freeze spread out in a single layer on a tray, then transfer them into a freezer bag.

Mulch is your friend. Spreading mulch on the exposed soil around your plants keeps the weeds away and holds moisture in. You need about 5 to 10 cm (2 to 4 inches) of mulch to really have an effect. Choose any mulch you like or see what I recommend for your particular crop. Overall, I like wheat straw mulch the best. It doesn't look as beautiful as some of the wooden mulches, but it's affordable and does the trick.

Blackcurrant

WHAT IT IS: Fruit, perennial (zone 2)

HOW HARD TO GROW: Easy

LIGHT NEEDS: Full sun

SOIL NEEDS: Loose, well drained, moisture retentive, pH 5.5–7.0

WATERING NEEDS: Moderate

DIMENSIONS: Height: 1.6 m (5 feet); width: 1.6 m (5 feet)

HOW FAR APART TO PLANT: 1–2 m (3–6 feet)

CONTAINER SIZE: Minimum depth: 60 cm (2 feet); diameter: 75 cm (2.5 feet)

HOW MANY TO PLANT: Yields 20–40 L (.5–1 bushel) per plant

WHEN TO SOW INDOORS: Not recommended

WHEN TO PLANT OUTDOORS: Early spring or late summer

READY TO EAT: Late summer

MULTI CROPPING: No, single crop

GROWS WELL WITH: Gooseberry

DO NOT PLANT WITH: White pine

FOOD TO GROW VARIETIES: 'Consort', 'Titania', 'Ben Sarek'

WHY TO GROW: This tangy berry, which is native to northern Europe and Asia, was once seen as a cure-all, particularly because it contains so much vitamin C. You can scarf a handful of raw berries, but they are most often enjoyed cooked, in jams and desserts. Be mindful if your property borders a forest, though. The shrub attracts white pine blister rust—the rust won't affect blackcurrants, but it will kill white pine trees. The disease has had a major impact on the commercial forestry industry in North America. Both 'Titania' and 'Consort' varieties are resistant to white pine blister rust. Since this perennial is hardy to zone 2, you can grow it in many parts of Canada.

PLANTING: Plant in the fall or early in the spring in a sunny spot ideally more than 1 km (.5 mile) from any white pine trees if you're not growing a resistant variety. Plant this berry in a container if you wish—but it should be a container that is able to winter outside without cracking. While these berries will grow in any soil, improve your plot with some compost to give you better yields. You have a couple of spacing options: Grow berries as individual shrubs 2 m (6 feet) apart, or aim for a hedge and space them just 1 m (3 feet) from each other. To plant your shrub, dig a hole one and a half times the depth and twice and width of the root ball or pot. When planting in a container, make sure your root ball sits 4 to 6 cm (2 to 3 inches) deeper than the container soil level so there's a space for water to collect. Once planted, severely prune the branches to the first two bud joints—those are the little knuckle-type bumps on the branch. Your cut-back shrub will better be able to establish its root system before growing any fruit.

GROWING: Feed your blackcurrants with a top dressing of manure in early spring. Pruning is essential: Blackcurrants bear fruit on the previous summer's new growth. So, right after harvest or in the late fall, completely cut away any branches that bore fruit. Also, trim any long stems that could be damaged by winter weather such as heavy wet snow or freezing rain. Again the next spring, remove any dead or diseased branches. While blackcurrants love moisture, you'll want to cut back on watering when harvest nears—it improves the flavour of the berries.

CHALLENGES: This berry can attract leaf midge, aphids, currant sawfly, currant fruit fly, earwigs, scale, and birds. It can fall victim to diseases such as powdery mildew and leaf spotting disease. Water the soil only and be sure your shrubs have good air circulation through smart planting and pruning. White pine blister rust shows up as orange-yellow spots in the spring, and leaves may curl up and die by summer. Trim away any infected areas and clean up afterward. Another major challenge is fruit drop, which is when your fruit just falls from the tree before ripening. Blackcurrants will do this when they haven't been pollinated properly. Encourage bees to your garden by planting bee-friendly perennials.

HARVESTING: Pick blackcurrants when they are dry and firm. Even if they seem ready, leave the berries on the stems for a few days more, as their flavour will improve. Berries on the higher stems will fall off on their own when they are ready for harvest.

STORAGE: Wash blackcurrants in cold water just prior to use. They can be stored on the countertop for a few days, or longer in the fridge. To freeze, spread clean, dry berries on a tray and pop it into the freezer for a couple of hours until the berries are slightly frozen, and then place them in a plastic bag.

To keep growing trees healthy, treat them with **dormant spray** every spring. It's made of horticultural oil and sulphur, which attack overwintering diseases and insects. Problems controlled by dormant sprays include mites, aphids, pear psylla, scale, and black spot.

Blueberry

WHAT IT IS: Fruit, perennial (zones 3–7)

HOW HARD TO GROW: Easy to moderate

LIGHT NEEDS: Full sun

SOIL NEEDS: Slightly acidic, sandy loam soils with high organic matter content, pH 4.5–5.5

WATERING NEEDS: Moderate

DIMENSIONS: Height: highbush 2 m (6 feet); half-high 45–90 cm (18–35 inches); lowbush 15–45 cm (6–18 inches); width varies

HOW FAR APART TO PLANT: Highbush 1.8 m (6 feet); half-high varies; lowbush 0.6 m (2 feet)

CONTAINER SIZE: Minimum depth: 60 cm (2 feet); diameter: 75 cm (2.6 feet)

HOW MANY TO PLANT: Yields 2.3–3.2 kg (5–7 pounds) per plant

WHEN TO SOW INDOORS: Not recommended

WHEN TO PLANT OUTDOORS: Fall

READY TO EAT: Fruit in year two, summer

MULTI CROPPING: No, single crop

GROWS WELL WITH: Rhododendron, heaths and heathers, thyme, yew, pine trees, bunchberry, raspberry, rhubarb, endive, parsley, radish, grape hyacinth

DO NOT PLANT WITH: Beet, cabbage, cauliflower, celery, carrot

FOOD TO GROW VARIETIES: 'Northcountry', 'Northland', 'Chippewa', 'North Blue'

WHY TO GROW: Blueberries are one of the few fruit species that are native to North America. They were collected by Native Americans, who considered the berry sacred because the blossom end is shaped like a five-pointed star. Blueberry shrubs can produce for up to 20 years, but they are very picky about where they grow. Be sure to choose the right site to get them started. When choosing a shrub, note there are three main species. The large highbush is the most popular variety but does best in warmer climates and produces very dark berries. Hybrid half-high makes less desirable fruit that's really best for jams—all the varieties I list at left are half-highs, as they do the best here in Canada. Lowbush are ideal for small spaces and cold climates but will actually spread underground. Of the varieties I list, I suggest you plant two different types to encourage cross-pollination and get the best yields.

PLANTING: Head for a sunny location in your garden that drains well. If your soil needs it, improve your site with some compost and some pine needles to increase the acidity. Dig a hole one and a half times the depth and twice the width of the root ball—you want the plant to sit slightly lower than it did in its pot. Mulch the area and water deeply. Blueberries won't produce fruit the first year; snip off any flowers so the plant can focus its energy on getting established. You won't need to prune for the first three years, except to remove dead or dying branches or low growth around the base.

GROWING: This fruit needs some specific care. That includes a weekly watering of 2 to 5 cm (1 to 2 inches), taking care not to drown your shrubs. Collect rainwater if you can, as it tends to be more acidic than tap. Weed gently so you don't disturb this plant's shallow roots. Rely on mulch to help you control weeds and retain moisture, and do not till or heavily work the soil around your shrubs. Also, never fertilize in the fall, as this will stimulate new growth that will be susceptible to winter damage. To get the best yields, encourage bees to come to your garden to pollinate your shrubs.

After the first three years, prune your blueberry plants at the end of winter or in the early spring, and eliminate about one-third to half of the wood growth on each plant. Take out branches older than five years, and wider than 5 cm (2 inches), and keep four to six of the youngest, strongest shoots.

CHALLENGES: Blueberries are one of the few plants that like acidic soil. (If you see yellow leaves after planting, your soil is likely too alkaline. See page 28 in chapter 2 for information about amending the pH of soil.) Blueberries can also grow slowly in poor soil. If your shrubs grow less than 30 cm (1 foot) in a year, use a natural fertilizer in the spring to give them a boost. Blueberry shrubs attract aphids and cherry and cranberry fruitworm moths. Adult moths will lay eggs during spring bloom and then the larvae feed on fruit—it will appear shrunken if they've been munching. To control this pest, apply insecticidal soap after the bloom. Cankers and grey mould (also known as botrytis) can impact blueberries. All you can do is prune out the infected stems and remove diseased leaves. You may also get some damage over the winter from critters such as chipmunks, rabbits, mice, and voles.

HARVESTING: Blueberries are ripe when they turn a dusty blue. Wait four to seven days longer for the best flavour. The berries on any one shrub should ripen at different times, and you should have fresh fruit for weeks.

STORAGE: Freeze berries spread out on trays. Once frozen, store them together in bags or containers.

If your plants are infected with a **bug** or **disease**, or are being eaten by a furry **critter**, see chapter 7 for information on preventing and treating these problems.

Broccoli

WHAT IT IS: Vegetable, annual

HOW HARD TO GROW: Moderate

LIGHT NEEDS: Full sun

SOIL NEEDS: Well drained, with good organic matter, pH 6.0–7.0

WATERING NEEDS: Regular

DIMENSIONS: Height: 0.5–2.5 m (1–8 feet); width: 45–60 cm (18–24 inches)

HOW FAR APART TO PLANT: 45 cm (18 inches)

CONTAINER SIZE: Minimum depth: 25 cm (10 inches); diameter: 30 cm (12 inches)

HOW MANY TO PLANT: Plant 3–5 plants per person

WHEN TO SOW INDOORS: 6 weeks before last frost, 12–14 weeks before first frost for fall harvest

WHEN TO PLANT OUTDOORS: Spring and late summer

READY TO EAT: 50–100 days

MULTI CROPPING: No, single crop

GROWS WELL WITH: Basil, bush bean, cucumber, dill, garlic, hyssop, lettuce, marigold, mint, nasturtium, onion, potato, radish, rosemary, sage, thyme, tomato

DO NOT PLANT WITH: Grape, strawberry, mustard, rue

FOOD TO GROW VARIETIES: 'Liberty', 'Goliath', 'Marathon', 'Bacchus'

WHY TO GROW: I grew up helping my family grow broccoli, not in our garden but as a cash crop in the 30 acres surrounding our home. Broccoli thrives in spring and fall; the challenge is growing broccoli in the summer. Hot, sunny days can quickly push broccoli into bloom—if you see yellow flowers, you're too late! If you harvest broccoli at the right time, you will be rewarded with smaller florets growing again, giving you multiple harvests.

PLANTING: You can direct-sow broccoli seeds and get a decent harvest, but I suggest you only do this for a summer planting to harvest in the fall, as seeds will germinate quickly in the heat. In spring, seed-start indoors if you're so inclined or buy seedlings so you can get a quicker harvest. Plant seedlings in improved soil that you've watered and fertilized. Dig your holes about 7 cm (3 inches) deep; plant so the soil comes up to the base of the first leaves, but no deeper. Add mulch to keep the soil temperature consistent and to maintain moisture levels. Feed with a nitrogen-rich fertilizer about three weeks after planting or once your broccoli plants start to form new leaves. For the best taste, plant your broccoli near celery, onions, and potatoes.

GROWING: Broccoli likes a consistent moisture level so water regularly, especially in hot or dry conditions. Avoid getting the broccoli crowns wet, to prevent mould and mildew. This heavy feeder likes fertilizer right through the growing season: Side-dress with a granular fertilizer or soak with a water-soluble fertilizer until the crowns are ready to harvest. Since broccoli plants have very shallow roots, avoid digging or turning the soil around them. Instead of plucking weeds, prevent them with a thick layer of mulch or use an herbicide.

CHALLENGES: Fussy broccoli likes to be cool and moist and will bolt if it gets stressed because of extreme temperatures or if it dries out. Many bugs like to nibble on broccoli crowns and leaves, including cabbage worms, aphids, flea beetles, cutworms, and thrips. Diseases that can impact broccoli include club root, alternaria leaf spot, black rot, powdery mildew, and white mildew. Most of these pathogens are a result of damp, warm conditions and can be prevented by watering the soil, not the plant, and keeping the soil well nourished. Of all broccoli's issues, you need to worry about club root the most. It will remain in the soil for several years, so you won't be able to grow a brassica vegetable in that spot for a very long time.

HARVESTING: It's tricky to know when your broccoli is just right for picking. You want to get it right—wait too long and your plant may bolt. If you see this start to happen, or if the crowns turn yellow, harvest right away. Otherwise, look for a head that's firm and tight, dark green, and about 10 to 18 cm (4 to 7 inches) wide—don't expect your backyard crowns to grow as big as those at the grocery store. The florets on the outside edge of the head should be the size of a head of a match when the vegetable is ready to pluck.

Harvest by using a sharp knife to cut the head of the broccoli off the plant about 12 cm (5 inches) or more below the head. Use a swift cut, as sawing at the stem can cause damage to your plant. You want it to stay healthy and keep growing, since you can continue to harvest the side shoots, which will grow like smaller heads to the side of where the main head was. Wait until these side florets reach the size of a fist before harvesting.

STORAGE: Broccoli will keep about a week in the refrigerator. As soon as you pick it, rinse it; then soak it in a large bowl of warm water and a few teaspoons of white vinegar for 15 minutes. Rinse and dry, and then store in the fridge, stem down, in a bowl of 4 to 6 cm (1.5 to 2.5 inches) of water that you change daily. It'll keep for more than a week if you cover the head loosely with a plastic bag with a few holes for air circulation. Or you can loosely wrap broccoli heads in damp paper towel and they'll keep for about four days.

To freeze broccoli, blanch it for three minutes in boiling water and then transfer to an ice bath to stop the cooking process. Drain, dry, and store in a plastic freezer bag with all the air removed. It'll keep for up to a year.

Brussels Sprout

WHAT IT IS: Vegetable, annual

HOW HARD TO GROW: Moderate

LIGHT NEEDS: Full sun

SOIL NEEDS: Well drained, moisture retentive, pH 6.8 to 7.0

WATERING NEEDS: High

DIMENSIONS: Height: 90 cm (36 inches); width: 30–40 cm (12–16 inches)

HOW FAR APART TO PLANT: 45–60 cm (18–24 inches)

CONTAINER SIZE: Container planting not recommended

HOW MANY TO PLANT: 1–2 plants per person

WHEN TO SOW INDOORS: 6–8 weeks before last frost

WHEN TO PLANT OUTDOORS: 4 months before first frost

READY TO EAT: 100–120 days from seed, 70–90 days from seedlings

MULTI CROPPING: No, single crop

GROWS WELL WITH: Nasturtium, basil, marigold, potato, thyme, mustard

DO NOT PLANT WITH: Pole bean, strawberry

FOOD TO GROW VARIETIES: 'Catskill', 'Long Island Dwarf Improved'

WHY TO GROW: This member of the brassica family is tolerant of harsh soils, including ones high in salt and limestone. Brussels sprouts are unique growers—their cabbage-like heads appear along the stem of the plant. It is believed that this unusual growing habit was developed through some creative cross-breeding many years ago. Not everyone should try this big, leafy vegetable in the garden. It takes up a lot of space and can shade many plants below it. If you have a small lot and want an easier experience, you might want to buy instead of grow.

PLANTING: Brussels sprouts take a long time to reach harvest; seed starting or buying seedlings will give you a leg up on the growing season. You can direct-sow as well, but your seeds will need as long as four months to reach maturity—forget that! Water your seedling well after planting, soaking the ground to 4 to 8 cm (1.5 to 3 inches) each week, in addition to rain. Feed with an all-purpose fertilizer three weeks after planting.

GROWING: Sprouts begin to form at the base of the stalk around two months after planting. Once there are sprouts formed up half of the stalk, giving you a total of 20 to 30 cm (8 to 12 inches) of growth, snip off the top of the plant to prevent further growing from the top. Now your plant can conserve energy. Since Brussels sprouts have a very shallow root system, avoid disturbing the soil by weeding or hoeing around them. Instead, rely on a thick layer of mulch to discourage weeds and help protect the roots.

CHALLENGES: Brussels sprouts attract numerous small pests: cabbage aphids, flea beetles, large cabbage whites (which start as cabbage worms), diamondback moths, cabbage loopers, thrips, root-knot nematodes, and webworms. They can also develop black rot, powdery mildew, white rust, ring spot, alternaria leaf spot (also called "black spot" or "grey spot"), and rot (also called "white mould"). Watch out for clubroot, fusarium wilt (also called "yellows"), and clerotinia stem rot (also called "white mould"). The only solution for many of these diseases is to discard infected plants to minimize spread to others. (And see chapter 7 for more on protecting your crops from pests and disease.) Yearly crop rotation and keeping gardens clean and free of debris will minimize disease too.

HARVESTING: Harvest the sprouts, starting from the bottom of the stalk when they reach about 3 cm (1 inch) in diameter and are firm and green. Work your way up the stem as the other sprouts reach maturity. Harvest by twisting the head to carefully break it off the stem. Any yellowed leaves around the sprout can be pruned off at the same time. For a sweeter taste, let your sprouts go through a few light frosts—but avoid a serious freeze.

STORAGE: Do not wash sprouts before storing them, only right before use. They'll stay fresh in a plastic bag for up to five days in the refrigerator.

Cabbage

WHAT IT IS: Vegetable, annual

HOW HARD TO GROW: Easy to moderate

LIGHT NEEDS: Full sun

SOIL NEEDS: Well drained, sandy loam, high organic content, pH 6.8 to 7.0

WATERING NEEDS: Consistent moisture but not too wet

DIMENSIONS: Height: 45–60 cm (18–24 inches); width: 30–45 cm (12–18 inches)

HOW FAR APART TO PLANT: 45–90 cm (20–36 inches)

CONTAINER SIZE: Minimum depth: 45 cm (18 inches); diameter 35–40 cm+ (14–16 inches+)

HOW MANY TO PLANT: 4–8 plants per person

WHEN TO SOW INDOORS: 6–8 weeks before last frost

WHEN TO PLANT OUTDOORS: Early spring after threat of hard frost

READY TO EAT: 50–140 days

MULTI CROPPING: No, single crop

GROWS WELL WITH: Bean, cucumber, celery, kale, spinach, celery, onion, potato, thyme, dill, beet root, oregano, camomile, clover

DO NOT PLANT WITH: Strawberry, tomato, pepper, eggplant, rue, grape, cauliflower, broccoli

FOOD TO GROW VARIETIES: Green: 'Golden Cross', 'Savoy', 'Early Jersey'. Red: 'Red Acre'. Napa: 'Chinese Express'

WHY TO GROW: This brassica vegetable is a heavy feeder, but its frost tolerance, ability to stay fresh in storage for a long time, and high nutritional value make it a smart vegetable to grow. Around the world, this is a staple vegetable, and there's no lack of great cabbage recipes, for all types, out there.

PLANTING: If you want to grow from seed, you'll need to start your seeds inside to get a jump-start on cabbage's very long growing season. Or purchase seedlings and plant at least 45 cm (18 inches) apart so your cabbage plants won't compete with each other for nutrients.

GROWING: Fertilize your cabbage by side-dressing with manure or applying a granular slow-release garden fertilizer three to four weeks after planting seedlings—that one application should keep them going for most of the season. Water 4 to 5 cm (2 inches) per week, including rain, or once the top layer of soil feels dry. Do not overwater as cabbages get close to maturity—the heads can split. (You can still eat them once they have split, but they won't keep as long.) In containers, also use a slow-release fertilizer. Monitor the moisture in your containers to ensure they do not dry out.

CHALLENGES: Cabbages are prone to nutrient deficiencies, making them more susceptible to disease and pests. Planting them at the recommended distance apart and using well-fertilized soil that's been amended with composted manure can prevent problems. Bugs such as cutworms, leaf miners, cabbage white butterfly, root maggots, aphids, cabbage worms, and flea beetles may visit your cabbages. Plant some clover nearby to reduce cabbage worms and aphids. Diseases you may notice include downy mildew, powdery mildew, fusarium wilt, root rot, wire rot, necrotic spot, and dampening off (at the seedling stage).

HARVESTING: The heads are ready for harvest as soon as they feel rigid when squeezed. Harvest by cutting the head from the plant using a sharp knife. If you leave the leaves and roots intact after harvest, the plant will grow new heads. To encourage this second round, remove the smallest new heads to grow in, leaving three to four. Harvest this round when the heads are 5 cm (2 inches) in diameter.

STORAGE: Cabbage can be wrapped in plastic and stored in the fridge for up to two weeks. If heads have split, eat these first, as they won't keep for long. If you want to keep them for up to six months, store heads in –1 to 0°C (30 to 32°F) with 90 to 100 per cent humidity, such as in an unheated garage. If your conditions are less than this ideal, the cabbages will still keep for about four months.

Get in the **zone**! See page 396 for a reminder on growing zones. Know your zone for planting any perennial tree or shrub in the garden that you expect to last through the winter. If you want to grow a tropical tree or one that needs a warmer zone, grow it in a container and protect it over the winter by bringing it indoors.

Carrot

WHAT IT IS: Root vegetable, annual

HOW HARD TO GROW: Moderate

LIGHT NEEDS: Full sun

SOIL NEEDS: Loose, well drained, sandy loam, pH 6.0–6.8

WATERING NEEDS: Consistent, 2.5 cm (1 inch) per week

DIMENSIONS: Height: 15–30 cm (6–12 inches); width: 20–30 cm (8–12 inches)

HOW FAR APART TO PLANT: 10–15 cm (4–6 inches); rows: 30 cm (12 inches)

CONTAINER SIZE: Minimum depth: 30 cm (12 inches)

HOW MANY TO PLANT: 15–30 plants per person

WHEN TO SOW INDOORS: Not recommended

WHEN TO PLANT OUTDOORS: 3–4 weeks before last frost

READY TO EAT: 70–80 days

MULTI CROPPING: No, single crop

GROWS WELL WITH: Radish, flax, leaf lettuce, marigold, onion, parsley, tomato (which can stunt growth), leek, bean, beet

DO NOT PLANT WITH: Dill, kohlrabi, parsnip, pea

FOOD TO GROW VARIETIES: 'Tendersweet', 'Yaya Hybrid', 'Gigante Flakkee', 'Purple Dragon' (purple), 'Rainbow Mixed' (mixed in colour)

WHY TO GROW: My hometown of Bradford, Ontario, has a carrot festival every August and our town mascot is a carrot. Bradford and the surrounding area is one of the largest producers of carrots in the country, growing about 220 kg (480 pounds) or more a year. To keep the local economy healthy, I should tell you not to grow your own. But the truth is homegrown always tastes better—hands down—so go for it.

PLANTING: Sow directly into the ground three to four weeks before the last frost and they'll germinate in time to catch the nice spring weather. Carrot seeds are very small. Mix them with a bit of sand to make sowing them a bit easier, purchase seeds with a biodegradable coating that makes them easier to see and plant, or use seed tape. Sow three to four seeds per 3 cm² (1 square inch) area—you'll thin them later. For aesthetic use in the garden, plant carrots as a border around other flowers or plants. Wherever you plant them, the soil needs to be loosened to a depth of 45 to 60 cm (18 to 24 inches) so the carrots can easily grow long and straight. If you're growing from seedlings—go ahead if you find that easier—plant outdoors after the last frost. Avoid adding fresh manure to the soil right before planting or right after, to prevent "legs"—or side shoots—growing from the main carrot root. Instead of manure, go for compost to improve the soil before you plant.

GROWING: Fertilize five to six weeks after sowing with a low-nitrogen fertilizer. Too much nitrogen will cause the plants to increase their top growth instead of building up the carrot itself. When seedlings reach 4 to 5 cm (about 2 inches) tall, thin out smaller ones so the carrots are spaced 10 to 15 cm (4 to 6 inches) apart. To prevent disturbing or damaging the nearby seedlings, simply cut off the greens at soil level and the tiny carrot below will just die off. Mulch your carrot rows well to prevent soil moisture loss and overheating once the tops are thinned, but don't pile mulch against the stems of the carrots.

CHALLENGES: Don't crowd your carrots! Carrots crammed together (or grown in compacted soil) will end up stunted and can develop side-growth legs

or arms. Your biggest other worries are carrot rust flies, root maggots, flea beetles, nematodes (not the same ones used to prevent grubs in the lawn), the disease aster yellows, rabbits, and groundhogs. Plant leeks to prevent rust fly and put up fences if the bigger critters are common in your area.

HARVEST: Carrots can be picked at almost any stage of their growth. Judge the size of your carrots by the diameter of the top of the root you can see peeking out of the ground, not the size of the top greens. Ideally, look for tops of 3 to 5 cm (about 1 to 1.5 inches) in diameter. If your carrots go through a few frosts, it will sweeten their flavour.

STORAGE: Carrots will store for a long time in the fridge—even months if prepared properly. Twist off the greens, make sure your carrots are dry, and store in an airtight container. To freeze, cut the carrots into slices, cubes, or sticks and blanch in boiling water for two minutes, then transfer to an ice bath. Pat them dry and place in an airtight container such as a plastic freezer bag and they'll last six months. You can also store them in sand (see page 167 in chapter 8 for instructions).

Watering is always a challenge, particularly when you're trying to figure out how much to offer via the hose to balance out the rain. Look to your local weather monitoring station (many of them have websites) for recent rainfall totals. Or just use a rain gauge. Either buy one or make one. Instructions are online for homemade gauges you can make using things like a 2 L (2 quart) pop bottle.

Cauliflower

WHAT IT IS: Vegetable, annual

HOW HARD TO GROW: Difficult

LIGHT NEEDS: Full sun

SOIL NEEDS: Rich, well drained, pH 6.5–7.0

WATERING NEEDS: Medium, 2.5–4 cm (1–1.5 inches) per week

DIMENSIONS: Height: 30–45 cm (12–18 inches); width: 30–45 cm (12–18 inches)

HOW FAR APART TO PLANT: 45–60 cm (18–24 inches); rows: 30 cm (12 inches)

CONTAINER SIZE: Container planting not recommended

HOW MANY TO PLANT: 2–3 plants per person

WHEN TO SOW INDOORS: 4–5 weeks before last frost

WHEN TO PLANT OUTDOORS: 2–3 weeks before last frost

READY TO EAT: 45–80 days from seedlings

MULTI CROPPING: No, single crop

GROWS WELL WITH: Celery, celeriac, bean, oregano, spinach, Swiss chard

DO NOT PLANT WITH: Strawberry, rue, pea, potato, nasturtium, tomato, cucumber, radish

FOOD TO GROW VARIETIES: Early: 'Snow Crown', 'Symphony', 'Early Snowball'. Unique: 'Cheddar', 'Romanesco', 'Violet Queen'

WHY TO GROW: This member of the brassica family is not the easiest plant to grow. It demands consistent moisture, temperatures between 15 and 20°C (59 to 68°F), and rich, organic soil. Falter on any of these fronts and you can get something called "buttoning," which is where the head (also called the "curd") stops growing and ends up a useless, inedible button. Traditional varieties take almost three months to harvest, but some early varieties can be harvested in around six weeks, and many of these are more heat tolerant. The colourful varieties make for a stylish-looking garden, and provide options for culinary adventures. But I must warn you—purple cauliflower turns green when you cook it!

PLANTING: Choose a spot in your garden that gets lots of sun and that's easy to access, so you can keep your eye on this finicky grower. Add compost or manure to your planting area. Direct-sow two to four weeks before the last frost, and transplant seedlings one to two weeks before last frost. Cauliflower can tolerate light frosts only—protect it from hard frost or freezing.

GROWING: To keep cauliflower roots moist and protected from extreme temperatures, layer mulch thickly around your plants. Use straw because wood mulches attract earwigs. Water regularly, but do not overdo it. Use my trusted finger touch method: Feel the top 2 cm (about 1 inch) of soil before watering. If it feels dry, water. If not, don't. Prevent mildew in your cauliflower plants by watering the roots only and avoiding the leaves and head. Do not water at night unless necessary.

When the heads are about 2 to 3 cm (about 1 inch) in diameter, carefully pull the leaves up and over the head and then secure them with elastic, tape, or twine—this will protect the head from getting bronzed by the sun. This step is known as blanching, and is only necessary with white cauliflower varieties. Coloured varieties don't need to be blanched, and newer varieties have been bred to grow their leaves over the developing head to provide their own blanching.

CHALLENGES: Cauliflower is very temperature sensitive. In the summer heat, you should provide light shade with a floating row cover that, as a bonus, helps with pests. And cauliflower attracts a few: cabbage worms, aphids, cabbage loopers, cabbage root maggots, leaf miners, caterpillars, and cutworms. Your plants are also at risk for diseases such as club root, which is a soil pathogen that grows a tumour on the stem of the plant near the soil. The tumour cuts off water to the leaves, causing wilt. You can prevent it by avoiding overwatering and

making sure the pH does not go below 6.5—test the soil and add limestone if needed to make it more alkaline. This plant is at risk for black rot, black leg, powdery mildew, and white mildew too. Most of these pathogens are a result of damp, warm conditions and can be prevented by watering properly and taking care of the soil.

HARVESTING: When the curds are about 15 cm (6 inches) in diameter, cut off the head and 5 to 7 cm (2 to 3 inches) of stem. Keep your eye on your cauliflowers and make sure they don't get too large, as the head will start to separate, and you don't want that.

STORAGE: Cauliflower will last for one to two weeks in the fridge if stored in a plastic bag. Heads can be pickled or frozen after blanching.

To keep your cauliflower a beautiful white colour, you'll need to blanch them. Don't worry, this isn't a cooking technique—just a simple gardening one. Simply gather the leaves over the growing head and secure them with an elastic (right).

Celeriac

WHAT IT IS: Vegetable, annual

HOW HARD TO GROW: Easy to moderate

LIGHT NEEDS: Full sun to part shade

SOIL NEEDS: Rich, moist, pH 6.0–7.0

WATERING NEEDS: Consistent

DIMENSIONS: Height: 30 cm (12 inches); width: 30 cm (12 inches)

HOW FAR APART TO PLANT: 20–30 cm (8–12 inches); rows: 50–75 cm (20–30 inches)

CONTAINER SIZE: Container planting not recommended

HOW MANY TO PLANT: 2–3 plants per person

WHEN TO SOW INDOORS: 10 weeks before last frost

WHEN TO PLANT OUTDOORS: 2 weeks before last frost

READY TO EAT: 120 days from seed

MULTI CROPPING: No, single crop

GROWS WELL WITH: Pea, lettuce, spinach, cauliflower, leek

DO NOT PLANT WITH: Cucumber, pumpkin, squash

FOOD TO GROW VARIETIES: 'Diamant', 'Brilliant', 'President'

WHY TO GROW: This is the ugly cousin of celery, but it is much easier to grow. The edible part is the large, brown, hairy root, which tastes like a cross between celery and parsley. You can't munch on it raw the way you would a crispy celery stalk, but it does make an interesting addition to a dish of roasted root vegetables or shredded for a twist in coleslaw. To prepare celeriac, make sure to aggressively peel it right down to the white flesh.

PLANTING: Finding celeriac transplants may be difficult, because it is not a popular backyard crop. So you will likely have to start from seed. Plan well ahead, as it will take four months in total to get to harvest and seeds will take two to three weeks to germinate. To help speed this up, soak the seeds in water overnight and then pat dry before planting. Plant the seeds in fresh potting soil and cover with plastic (to help the soil retain water), poking a few holes in the plastic to allow some airflow. Start hardening off the seedlings when they reach 8 to 10 cm (3 to 4 inches) and nighttime temperatures are above 5°C (41°F). Plant outdoors in full sun or light shade in a plot improved with compost or manure.

GROWING: Mound soil up over the root bulb as it grows. Remove any stalks that grow laterally from the root bulb, keeping only stalks that are growing upright in a tight bunch. Celeriac likes consistent moisture and gentle feeding; water regularly and fertilize with compost, compost tea, or fish emulsion fertilizer. While the celeriac root itself is a tough cookie, you need to be careful with the tender roots that grow around it, so avoid weeding around this root—use a thick layer of mulch instead.

CHALLENGES: This relatively easy-to-grow root has one major issue: its transplants will go readily into false winter dormancy. Be sure seedlings get day and night temperatures above 5°C (41°F) for their first two weeks. Cover them on cooler nights or during frost risk to keep them growing. It's rare for bugs or diseases to affect celeriac.

HARVESTING: Celeriac is ready to come out of the ground when the diameter of the root is 10 to 13 cm (4 to 5 inches), usually in the late fall. The taste of the vegetable is actually improved by a light frost but will be ruined if exposed to anything more than that.

STORAGE: Left whole and wrapped lightly in plastic or newspaper, this root will stay fresh in a crisper drawer in your fridge for several months. Do not cut off the roots or hairs until you are ready to use celeriac.

Celery

WHAT IT IS: Vegetable, annual

HOW HARD TO GROW: Difficult

LIGHT NEEDS: Full sun to part shade

SOIL NEEDS: Rich, moist, organic, pH 6.0–7.0

WATERING NEEDS: Consistent

DIMENSIONS: Height: 45–60 cm (18–24 inches); width: 20 cm (8 inches)

HOW FAR APART TO PLANT: 30 cm (12 inches); rows: 75 cm (30 inches)

CONTAINER SIZE: Container planting not recommended

HOW MANY TO PLANT: 2–4 plants per person

WHEN TO SOW INDOORS: 8–10 weeks before last frost

WHEN TO PLANT OUTDOORS: 2 weeks before last frost

READY TO EAT: 120–150 days

MULTI CROPPING: No, single crop

GROWS WELL WITH: Bean, cabbage family, leek, onion, spinach, snapdragon, cosmos

DO NOT PLANT WITH: Corn, potato, carrot, aster

FOOD TO GROW VARIETIES: 'Pascal', 'Conquistador', 'Alfina'

WHY TO GROW: It makes for a crunchy snack and is famous for being a negative calorie food, but celery is one of the toughest crops to grow at home. Celery takes a very long time to get to harvest, needs a lot of care, and will easily turn bitter. Even on commercial farms, it is grown with a strict regimen of fertilization and irrigation flooding to keep this heavy feeder moist and happy. Look for varieties that are less temperature sensitive and are ready to harvest sooner.

PLANTING: I recommend purchasing and planting celery seedlings—celery is tough enough without starting from seed. Plant homegrown seedlings in full sun or a spot that gets light shade, preferably in the afternoon, in soil improved with compost or manure several weeks before planting.

You can also regrow celery. This has been big on social media. You place the bottom end of a stalk in a bowl of water in a sunny spot, and refresh the water every few days. The heart will begin to thicken and small leaves will emerge. After about eight days, you'll get some roots. At this point, plant the celery base and roots in a pot with nutrient-rich potting soil, with the rooted section under the soil. Water and feed regularly, and place in a sunny spot that doesn't get too hot. Regrown celery will take a while to reach maturity, but growing it this way might be fun to try.

GROWING: Keep the soil consistently moist and fed with compost or natural fertilizers such as compost tea or fish emulsion fertilizer every two to three weeks. Celery has a delicate root system, so weed gently and rely on mulch to prevent weeds. Closer to harvest, about two to three weeks before celery matures, you will need to blanch your

stalks—protect them from the sun—to prevent them from turning green and bitter. Mound dry soil or mulch over the stalks, or wrap them in newspaper or cardboard. Around this time, one light frost will sweeten the flavour. But consecutive or hard frosts will damage the stalks, induce bolting, and make your long-awaited crop inedible.

CHALLENGES: Celery is extremely fussy about temperatures right through its lifespan. At the transplant stage, it needs temperatures above 5°C (41°F) for two weeks, or it'll bolt. During the main growing season, it likes 12 to 21°C (53 to 70°F) and will bolt if the weather gets too hot or too cold. Too much water will lead to root rot and other fungal diseases. Celery is also at risk for early and late blight, fusarium, wilt, root rot, fungal rot, and leaf spot. Mosaic virus is also a problem. It is transmitted by aphids and leads to yellowing of the leaves. To deal with it, remove infected areas, treat with insecticidal soap, and keep your garden free of weeds.

HARVESTING: When the stalks are 20 to 25 cm (8 to 10 inches) tall, they're ready to cut. Start harvesting from the outside stalks and move inward, or cut the entire plant off with a sharp knife just below the soil level.

STORAGE: Wrapped in plastic, celery will last about two weeks in the fridge.

GROWN AND PACKED BY
CULTIVÉES et EMPAQUETÉES PAR
VINELAND
GROWERS

Cherry

WHAT IT IS: Fruit tree, perennial (zones 4–7)

HOW HARD TO GROW: Moderate

LIGHT NEEDS: Full sun

SOIL NEEDS: Well drained, slightly acidic, pH 6.0–7.0

WATERING NEEDS: Consistent; minimal when fruit is ripening

DIMENSIONS: Height: 2–10 m (6–30 feet); width: 2.5–10 m (8–30 feet)

HOW FAR APART TO PLANT: 3.5–7.5 m (11–25 feet)

CONTAINER SIZE: Minimum depth: 60 cm (24 inches); dwarf varieties only; diameter: 60 cm+ (24 inches+)

HOW MANY TO PLANT: Yields 1,000 cherries, or 18–54 kg (40–120 pounds); sweet cherries produce more than sour

WHEN TO SOW INDOORS: Not recommended

WHEN TO PLANT OUTDOORS: Seeds or pits in the late fall; saplings in fall or spring

READY TO EAT: Fruit by year 3, June or July

GROWS WELL WITH: Dill, fennel, rosemary, lavender, mint, nasturtium, thyme

DO NOT PLANT WITH: Grass

FOOD TO GROW VARIETIES: Sweet: 'Stella' (self-pollinating), 'Vandalay' (self-pollinating), 'Sweetheart', 'Symphony', 'Vega' (white cherry). Sour: 'Montmorency'

WHY TO GROW: Sweet cherries right off your own tree are a real delight, but they are a bit challenging to grow. Much easier to raise are sour cherries—also known as tart or pie cherries—which are not great eaten raw but are ideal for cooking in jams and pies. Most traditional varieties of cherry trees require at least two other cherry trees nearby for cross-pollination. Some newer varieties are self-pollinating, so you can grow your own without needing an orchard.

PLANTING: Plant your cherry tree saplings in the fall or spring in a location with good airflow and enough room for the mature tree to expand as the years pass. Avoid areas with heavy, wet soil. Dig a large hole where the entire root ball of the new tree can easily fit, with additional room on the sides to allow the roots to expand after planting—aim for two times the diameter of the root ball or pot. The hole should be deep enough that the root ball sits 2 cm (less than 1 inch) below ground level. Place the tree in the hole and backfill with the original soil mixed with some compost. Aim for a 2:10 compost to native soil ratio. Tamp down the soil and water deeply. New trees may have to be staked for one or two years, especially in windy areas. If you want to grow a dwarf variety in a container, don't use a container made of treated wood.

GROWING: Feed your trees with an all-purpose fertilizer starting in the spring and until the cherries start to ripen, then again after the harvest is complete. Prune in later winter or early spring. Cut off any dead or diseased wood. Different varieties of cherries can benefit from being pruned into certain shapes or forms; research your particular variety.

Cherries need consistent watering as the fruit grows. When the fruit is ripening, you can pull back—a little bit of drought stress can improve the taste, as the sugars will become concentrated. Overwatering during the ripening stage will dilute the flavour and increase the likelihood of disease for the tree overall. Container trees can be overwintered in an unheated garage once the leaves drop. Or keep the container outside in an insulated container so the roots remain frozen all winter long. If they thaw out at any point in the winter and then refreeze, you can lose the tree. Be sure container trees are well pruned so they stay small and manageable.

CHALLENGES: You may need to keep birds from snacking on your ripe cherries. Placing bird netting over your trees before the fruits ripen should help. Cherries planted in wet soils or in areas of poor airflow are highly susceptible to fungal and bacterial

disease such as black knot, brown rot, bacterial canker, fusarium wilts, rots, moulds, and plum curculio. Along with birds, the following critters might also come after your trees and fruit: aphids, caterpillars, and fruit flies. Another hassle: the blossoms and unpicked cherries can be a bit a messy once they have fallen off the tree.

HARVESTING: Snip fully ripened cherries at the cherry stalks with scissors or pruners to protect the shoots for future harvest. If you are planning to freeze the cherries, harvest when they are ripe but still firm to the touch.

STORAGE: Cherries should be eaten or cooked immediately after harvest, but will last a few days in the refrigerator. Avoid freezing sweet cherries you plan to eat raw later on—they'll be too mushy and will only be good for smoothies.

Chicory
(also known as Italian Dandelion)

WHAT IT IS: Vegetable, annual

HOW HARD TO GROW: Easy

LIGHT NEEDS: Full to part shade

SOIL NEEDS: Well drained, moist, fertile, pH 5.5+

WATERING NEEDS: Frequent

DIMENSIONS: Height: 30–60 cm (1–2 feet); width: 15–30 cm (6–12 inches)

HOW FAR APART TO PLANT: Seeds: 10–15 cm (4–6 inches); seedlings: 15–30 cm (6–12 inches); rows: 60 cm (24 inches)

CONTAINER SIZE: Minimum depth: 20 cm (8 inches); diameter: 45 cm (18 inches)

HOW MANY TO PLANT: 2–4 plants per person

WHEN TO SOW INDOORS: 3–4 weeks before last frost date

WHEN TO PLANT OUTDOORS: Early spring or late summer

READY TO EAT: 42–56 days from seed

MULTI CROPPING: No, single crop

GROWS WELL WITH: Most greens, lettuce, arugula

DO NOT PLANT WITH: Bean, pea

FOOD TO GROW VARIETIES: 'San Pasquale', 'Spandona', 'Sugar Loaf'

WHY TO GROW: A popular salad green in Italy that you can steam or eat raw, chicory is a close relative to endive and radicchio. While it tastes similar to the dandelion growing in our lawns, chicory does not produce a yellow dandelion flower. Chicory is a fast-growing green that you can cut at any height and it will keep on growing back. This easy grower does well in pots, raised beds, or the garden.

PLANTING: In early spring, sow chicory seeds directly into the garden about two weeks before the last frost date. Chicory can handle a light frost but should be covered if a hard frost looms. Sow seeds 1 cm (.5 inch) deep and 5 cm (2 inches) apart. Once your seedlings produce three leaves and grow to 10 cm (4 inches) tall, thin your plants. You can eat the plants you pull out. Or just plant seedlings if you can find them.

GROWING: Chicory needs lots of moisture: Water deeply. This cool-season-loving plant will bolt during periods of extended heat—once the plants sprout blue flowers, they'll turn bitter. Remove flower stems immediately when the flowers appear. While this green will grow in almost any soil type and requires very little fertilizer to thrive, add compost during planting and side-dress with composted manure in late summer for the best taste and yields.

CHALLENGES: This easy grower has no serious disease or pest problems. Deer, rabbits, and groundhogs will generally leave chicory alone due to its bitter taste. If there are no other food sources around, they will try it for a snack. Be sure you have some marigolds or leafy greens in your garden to keep your chicory safe—or put up a fence.

HARVESTING: You can pluck your chicory at any stage of growth by removing side leaves or cutting the entire plant. Always harvest before flowering.

STORAGE: Chicory is always best fresh. If you have a bumper crop and you want to share, place an unwashed bunch in a plastic grocery bag in the refrigerator and it'll last up to five days.

Many fruits and vegetables need **pollination** from insects such as bees to offer you good yields. Attract bees to your garden by planting early flowering plants and shrubs such as muscari, rockcress, red currant, lilac, even dandelion and clover. If you don't see bees, or find your fruit isn't growing well, hand-pollinate them yourself with a cotton swab. Once the flowers on your plants are in bloom, just touch them with the swab you've collected pollen on and then touch the other flowers of the same species. (You may need different varieties to cross-pollinate the same type of fruit.)

Collard

WHY TO GROW: Collards are one of the easiest members of the cabbage family to raise in your garden. As a bonus, it offers an ongoing harvest through most of the growing season. If you're a fan of the Southern American cuisine. (where it's grown a lot), then you'll find plenty to do with it in the kitchen.

WHAT IT IS: Leafy green vegetable, annual

HOW HARD TO GROW: Easy

LIGHT NEEDS: Full sun, light shade in hot weather

SOIL NEEDS: Well drained, good organic content, pH 6.5–7.5

WATERING NEEDS: Consistent, minimum 2.5 cm (1 inch) per week

DIMENSIONS: Height: 45–90 cm (18–36 inches); width: 30–60 cm (12–24 inches)

HOW FAR APART TO PLANT: 30–40 cm (12–16 inches); rows: 40–75 cm (16–30 inches)

CONTAINER SIZE: Minimum depth: 20 cm (8 inches); diameter: 25 cm (10 inches)

HOW MANY TO PLANT: 2–4 plants per person

WHEN TO SOW INDOORS: 6–8 weeks before last frost

WHEN TO PLANT OUTDOORS: Seeds 4 weeks before last frost, seedlings 2 weeks before last frost, or seeds 3 months before first frost for fall harvest

READY TO EAT: 85–95 days from seed; 75–85 days from seedlings

MULTI CROPPING: Yes, two crops

GROWS WELL WITH: Beet, onion, broad bean, dill, rosemary, basil, cucumber, marigold, lettuce, hyssop, nasturtium, sage, thyme, potato, mint, camomile, garlic

DO NOT PLANT WITH: Rue, grape, tansy, radish, strawberry

FOOD TO GROW VARIETIES: 'Champion', 'Blue Max', 'Vates'

PLANTING: Improve your full-sun planting bed with some compost or manure. If your soil has poor drainage, add extra compost (but not manure) and some coarse sand to make it better. Direct-sow in the spring or fall—or both for multi cropping—but note your leaves will be even sweeter when they're harvested in the cool fall months. Sow just .5 to 1.25 cm (less than .5 inches) deep and 7 cm (3 inches) apart. Once seedlings reach 10 cm (4 inches) in height, thin them to 15 cm (6 inches) apart. Those plucked seedlings are actually edible. Plant either way in pots and collards will do fine.

GROWING: Collards are drought tolerant, although they prefer consistent moisture and will offer great yields with regular watering—when they dry out they're at higher risk for pest and disease damage. Overwatering is also a problem and may lead to browning of the leaves. Water on a regular basis and use mulch to keep the soil moist around them and protect their shallow roots. To keep collards green and tasty, feed about six weeks into the growing season with a nitrogen-rich fertilizer and more often for collards planted in fast-draining soils, in containers, or during periods of high rainfall. They are fond of acidic soil but will tolerate a pH of 6.0— you just need to watch for club root if you go too alkaline.

CHALLENGES: Collards, like many greens, will bolt if they get too hot. If you start to see flower stalks, snip them off immediately and harvest your greens—it's hard to stop bolting once it starts, but might as well try. Best to just pick your greens before the heat of summer and before things get very chilly in the fall. Collards are only threatened by insects when stressed and in the wrong environment. In those cases, you'll see damage from cutworms, cabbage loopers, cabbage worms, flea beetles, cabbage root maggots, aphids, slugs, snails, and nematodes. Water the soil at the base of the plant in the morning, keeping the leaves dry, to discourage small pests. Similarly, collards are pretty tough when it comes to diseases, but occasionally they can be affected by club rot, black rot, and alternaria. Proper watering, amending the soil, and crop rotation will minimize the risk.

HARVESTING: Collard greens can be picked right up until heavy frost and freezing. In zone 8 or higher, collards can often be harvested right through winter. To keep the plant producing, you can start taking leaves from the outside once the entire plant reaches 25 cm (10 inches) and let the inner leaves keep growing. If you take the whole plant at once, it'll be done. Don't let leaves get too large, as they won't be as tasty. Collards actually taste better after a light frost, so you'll enjoy your fall harvest the most.

STORAGE: Eat right away, if you can; or store collards unwashed in the fridge for about five days. Cooked greens will be fine in the freezer for about a year. To freeze, cut off the stems, wash the greens thoroughly, blanch in boiling water for three minutes, dry, and store in an airtight container.

Pick and squish! Many bugs such as beetles, potato bugs, and caterpillars are best dealt with by hand. Get kids to help and don't be squeamish.

Corn

WHAT IT IS: Vegetable, annual

HOW HARD TO GROW: Moderate

LIGHT NEEDS: Full sun

SOIL NEEDS: Fertile, moist, well drained, pH 6.0–6.8

WATERING NEEDS: Consistent, 5–7 cm (2–3 inches) per week

DIMENSIONS: Height: 1–1.5 m (3–5 feet); width: 30–45 cm (12–18 inches)

HOW FAR APART TO PLANT: 20–30 cm (8–12 inches); rows: 30–60 cm (12–24 inches)

CONTAINER SIZE: Not recommended for container growing

HOW MANY TO PLANT: 3–5 plants per person; yield of 2 ears per stalk

WHEN TO SOW INDOORS: Not recommended

WHEN TO PLANT OUTDOORS: When soil is 15–20°C (59–68°F)

READY TO EAT: 65–90 days

MULTI CROPPING: No, single crop

GROWS WELL WITH: Cucumber, melon, pea, pumpkin, potato, radish, bean, squash, sunflower, parsley, soybean, marigold, amaranth

DO NOT PLANT WITH: Celery, tomato; plant 60 m (20 feet) away

FOOD TO GROW VARIETIES: 'Early Golden Bantam', 'Canadian Early Supersweet', 'Butter Gold SE', 'Peaches and Cream SE'

WHY TO GROW: In Canada, eating your fill of sweet corn in late summer is a must. But growing it yourself is really tough work. Corn is a heavy feeder and attracts some pretty difficult pests. Corn requires cross-pollination with other corn plants. This will happen naturally by wind, but it means you have to grow several corn plants together unless you happen to live next to a cornfield! Without enough pollination, the corncobs will "skip" and have incomplete development via missing kernels. Before you pick a variety to grow, you should know there are three general types of edible corn: normal, sugar-enhanced, and super-sweet.

Normal is labelled "SU" on plant tags and seed packets; it's tolerant of growing stresses, but it doesn't taste as sweet as other varieties unless eaten right after harvest. Cross-pollination with super-sweet corn ruins the taste. Sugar-enhanced is labelled "SE," "SE+," "EH," and "Everlasting Heritage." This is the middle-ground variety, and is somewhat vigorous and stress tolerant; it tastes medium sweet. It will not turn as starchy after harvest as normal corn types but will not last as long as the super-sweet. It is not affected by cross-pollination with other varieties. Super-sweet, which is labelled "SH2" and "shrunken," is up to three times sweeter than the normal and sugar-enhanced varieties and has the slowest sugar-to-starch conversion after harvest. This corn type is not very vigorous and tolerant of stress, and is not at all cold tolerant, so is not recommended for most Canadian regions. The taste will be ruined if this corn type is cross-pollinated with other types of corn.

PLANTING: Corn is best grown in soil that's been improved by compost or manure added the previous fall and allowed to overwinter. Cover the plot with black plastic in the early spring to warm it up. Once the risk of frost has passed direct-sow at the back or north side of your garden so cornstalks won't shade other crops. Seeds can be planted in groups of three or four, 3 cm (about 1 inch) deep or 2 cm (just under 1 inch) for super-sweet. Lay out your plot in rows 30 to 60 cm (12 to 24 inches) apart or in square groupings with 30 by 30 cm (12 by 12 inch) spacing. Consider staggering the planting by two weeks to extend the harvest. Seed close together and thin out smaller seedlings once they are 10 cm (4 inches) tall.

GROWING: Corn demands consistent moisture; overwatering will lead to bland corn and increase the risk of rust and seed corn maggots. Mulch around your corn to keep moisture in the soil and help you control weeds. When you do weed, be careful of corn's delicate roots. Feed your stalks with high-nitrogen fertilizers around mid-July. You can grow this crop in pots, but you need a very large container and you'll still need to plant a decent-size crop to get cross-pollination.

CHALLENGES: Pests really like corn. It attracts cucumber beetles, flea beetles, cutworms, corn borers, and corn earworms. Seed corn maggots are a result of too much manure or organic matter in the soil and overwatering. Corn borers enter through a small hole in the cornstalks. To stop corn borers from damaging your crop, pinch the stalk right below the hole to block off their path to the corncobs. The disease corn smut will lead to greyish growths called "galls" on the corn. Remove them as soon as they form to prevent them from breaking apart and causing further damage. Rust is common to corn crops, and is typically a result of poor airflow and too much water. To minimize, use a soaker hose to be sure you're watering the roots and not the leaves or stems. Raccoons, deer, and squirrels love corn, and deterrents to keep these furry friends away are often more costly than the value of the corn harvest.

HARVESTING: Your corn is ready when the silks on the cobs start to turn brown—about three weeks after the silks emerge. To check for ripeness, poke a hole into a kernel. If the liquid that comes out is the same consistency as skim milk, the cobs are ready. If it is watery, they aren't ready yet, and if it's thick like cream, they are past the harvest and are likely a disappointing meal. Remove the corn ear by pulling it down from the stalk and twisting it as you hold on to the stalk.

STORAGE: The sugars in the corn kernels begin to convert to starch once the cob has been picked from the stalk. Eat right away or lose a whole lot of taste! Some gardeners say you should be boiling the water at the same time you are picking your cobs. Un-husked cobs will store in the fridge for about a week and will do best if they're refrigerated right after picking. To freeze, cut kernels from cobs and store in airtight containers.

Corn smut looks as gross as you would think! Remove diseased cobs as quickly as possible.

Cucumber

WHAT IT IS: Fruit, annual

HOW HARD TO GROW: Easy

LIGHT NEEDS: Full sun to light shade

SOIL NEEDS: Loamy, moist, and well drained, pH 7.0

WATERING NEEDS: Water when the top 14 cm (about 5 inches) of soil is dry

DIMENSIONS: Height: up to 2 m (6 feet) if grown as a vine; width: bush 30–45 cm (12–18 inches); vine grown vertically 30 cm (12 inches); vine grown on the ground 1–2 m² (12–20 feet²)

HOW FAR APART TO PLANT: 45–60 cm (18–24 inches)

CONTAINER SIZE: Minimum depth: 45 cm (18 inches); diameter 45 cm (18 inches)

HOW MANY TO PLANT: 2 plants per person

WHEN TO SOW INDOORS: 4 weeks before last frost

WHEN TO PLANT OUTDOORS: 2 weeks after last frost, when soil is at least 18°C (64°F)

READY TO EAT: 28–56 days

MULTI CROPPING: No, single crop

GROWS WELL WITH: Sunflower, corn, bean, pea, beet, radish, carrot, dill, nasturtium, cabbage, cauliflower, celery, broccoli, marigold, lettuce

DO NOT PLANT WITH: Potato, rue, sage, tomato, basil, melon

FOOD TO GROW VARIETIES: Bush: 'Northern Pickling', 'Champion'. Bush container size: 'Spacemaster', 'Bushy', 'Patio King'. Vine: 'Straight Eight', 'Summer Dance Hybrid'

WHY TO GROW: There are both bush and vine types of cucumbers, and they come in green, yellow, orange, and white varieties. Bush cucumbers are great for containers or small areas. They produce less fruit, making them ideal for a smaller family who do not need a bumper crop of cucumbers. Vine cucumbers require much more space, and they will produce more, so you will have extras for pickling. There are also more varieties of vine cucumbers to choose from compared with bush cucumbers. Grow your vine cucumbers vertically and they'll attract fewer diseases and insects, plus take up a lot less space.

PLANTING: Cucumbers can be started from seed indoors or from purchased seedlings, but their roots are easily damaged, so transplanting can be tricky. You will be just as successful sowing directly outside. Cuke seeds like warm soil, so consider covering your plot in the very early spring with black plastic to heat it up. Sow seeds at a depth of 3 to 4 cm (1 to 1.5 inches) spaced 10 cm (4 inches) apart and thin them when they reach 3 cm (about 1 inch).

GROWING: Depending on the type of cucumber plants you are growing, you may have to encourage pollination. Everything from spraying sugar water on the plants or planting pollinator-friendly flowers nearby will encourage insects such as bees to visit the flowers. When in doubt, become the pollinator by spreading pollen yourself using a cotton swab and going flower to flower; or shake the vines to encourage the spread of pollen. In the greenhouse, to spread pollen I would shake the strings the vines would grow on. If you're worried about pollination, plant newer varieties of seedless cucumbers now available; they are known as parthenocarpic— which means they are self-pollinating.

If you're using a trellis or other structure to grow vine cucumbers vertically, start training the vines to grow upward by gently securing them to the trellis with something that won't cut into them, such as loosely tied pantyhose. The vines will eventually secure themselves.

CHALLENGES: Cucumbers are very picky about temperature, especially soil temperature. Seeds won't germinate in chilly soil and the fruits are easily damaged by frost. Cucumbers attract cucumber beetles (striped and spotted), aphids, whiteflies, flea beetles, and spider mites. They're often at risk for mosaic virus, bacterial wilt, anthracnose, powdery mildew, and downy mildew. Some hybrid varieties ('Salad Bush', 'Monarch', and 'Supersett') are mildew resistant. Mildew is a very common problem for cucumber growers and is almost impossible to prevent.

HARVESTING: If you're pickling, you can pluck your cucumbers at just 8 cm (3 inches) in length or wait until they get to 15 cm (6 inches) or larger for everyday use. Burpless varieties will grow to 25 cm (10 inches) or longer. Harvest when the cucumber is uniformly green. Carefully snip or twist off the fruit from the vine, taking care to not pull or disturb the plant's roots.

STORAGE: Wrapped tightly in plastic, cucumber will last for up to 10 days in the fridge. Pickling is a great way to use your cucumbers and keep them for a year or longer.

Eggplant

This vegetable is great for grilling and a key ingredient in the Italian dish ratatouille. There are about 20 different varieties of eggplant around, in an array of shapes and colours.

WHAT IT IS: Fruit, annual

HOW HARD TO GROW: Difficult

LIGHT NEEDS: Full sun

SOIL NEEDS: Moist, pH 5.5–6.0

WATERING NEEDS: Frequent

DIMENSIONS: Height: 30–90 cm (12–36 inches); width: 30–60 cm (12–24 inches)

HOW FAR APART TO PLANT: 60 cm (24 inches)

CONTAINER SIZE: Minimum depth: 30 cm (12 inches); diameter: 30 cm (12 inches)

HOW MANY TO PLANT: 1–2 plants per person; yields 5–6 per plant

WHEN TO SOW INDOORS: 10–12 weeks before last frost

WHEN TO PLANT OUTDOORS: Seedlings 2 weeks after last frost

READY TO EAT: 60–90 days

MULTI CROPPING: No, single crop

GROWS WELL WITH: Bean, pea, pepper, okra, amaranth

DO NOT PLANT WITH: Potato, tomato, corn

FOOD TO GROW VARIETIES: 'Classic', 'Epic', 'Black Beauty'. Containers: 'Little Fingers', 'Patio Baby'

PLANTING: Eggplant seeds take a long time to germinate so purchase seedlings or seed-start indoors, but begin early. Plant outside in sunny, well-prepared beds that are protected from the wind. If you're growing in a container, make sure your eggplants have lots of space; use a large trough or separate pots for each plant. Since they love heat, choose a container material that retains warmth, such as clay (particularly glazed clay, which helps lock in moisture). Clay pots are also heavier and able to support a full-grown eggplant. Use two parts potting soil to one part sand, and mix in a little compost and fertilizer.

GROWING: There's work to be done during the growing season with your eggplants. Water them well, feed them every two weeks, and stake them when they get taller than 60 cm (24 inches). Eggplants can be super-producers, and every flower will turn into a fruit. You don't want this. You want your plants to be energy efficient and produce just five or six large, healthy fruits. Pinch off any new growth after you get five or six flowers that are evenly distributed across the plant.

CHALLENGES: Eggplants can be a bit tough to grow. They're picky about the soil (it can't be compacted), water (they want lots), and temperature (they like warmth and won't endure a frost). They also bruise easily, so be careful when you handle them. Potato beetles and flea beetles will attack eggplant. Verticillium is the main disease enemy and will stunt the growth of the plant and cause the leaves to wilt. To prevent it, rotate your crops—and remember, eggplant is from the same family as tomatoes, peppers, and potatoes.

HARVESTING: When the skin of your eggplants becomes glossy and firm to the touch, they're ready to pick. If you press your finger into the skin and it comes back without cracking, then it is a good time to harvest. Use pruning shears to snip the eggplant off the stem, leaving a bit of stem on the fruit.

STORAGE: Don't refrigerate your eggplants—that can ruin the flavour. It is best to store them at room temperature in a cool spot out of the sun. Never put your eggplants in plastic bags, as they will rot.

Endive and Escarole

WHAT IT IS: Leafy green vegetable, annual

HOW HARD TO GROW: Easy

LIGHT NEEDS: Full sun, part shade during hot periods

SOIL NEEDS: Humus, fertile, well drained, pH 5.0–6.8

WATERING NEEDS: Consistent, 2.5 cm (1 inch) per week

DIMENSIONS: Height: 15–60 cm (6–24 inches); width: 15–60 cm (6–24 inches)

HOW FAR APART TO PLANT: 4–6 cm (about 2 inches); rows: 30–40 cm+ (12–16 inches)

CONTAINER SIZE: Minimum depth: 10 cm (4 inches); diameter: 25–30 cm (10–12 inches+)

HOW MANY TO PLANT: 2–3 plants per person

WHEN TO SOW INDOORS: 6–8 weeks before last frost

WHEN TO PLANT OUTDOORS: Seeds 4 weeks before last frost; seedlings 2 weeks before last frost; seeds 16 weeks before first frost for fall harvest

READY TO EAT: 65–100 days

MULTI CROPPING: No, single crop

GROWS WELL WITH: Radish, turnip, parsnip, tomato

DO NOT PLANT WITH: Pumpkin, squash

FOOD TO GROW VARIETIES: Endive: 'Verde A Cuore Pieno', 'Salad King RS'. Escarole: 'Full Heart Batavian'

WHY TO GROW: The difference between endive and escarole is the leaves. Endive has curly leaves with a milder flavour, while escarole has a wider, smoother leaf and is slightly more bitter. These greens are fairly easy to grow, and because they are frost tolerant, they can be started early in the season. Endive makes for a pretty addition to ornamental plantings—and it's still edible no matter where you plant it.

PLANTING: Purchase seedlings, seed-start inside, or direct-sow—seeds should germinate in about a week. Plant outside in a plot improved with compost or manure. For summer plantings, locate your greens in a partially shaded area to keep them cool and prevent bolting on toasty days. When growing in containers, make sure your container has good drainage.

GROWING: Mulch the soil around your greens to hold in moisture and keep the delicate roots cool. Since endive and escarole can be a little bitter, if you want a milder flavour, you can blanch the leaves starting two weeks before harvest. Simply wrap the leaves with white plastic or cardboard—or grow a self-blanching variety. If it rains while you are blanching, remove your covers and dry off the leaves to prevent rust or rot. Once things are dry, you can put the covers back on. For your late-summer crop, allowing a few frosts will sweeten and enhance the flavour.

CHALLENGES: These greens will bolt if they get exposed to too much heat. Offer them some shade in the heat of the summer with a light blanket or place them close to a taller plant that will protect them a little. They can attract slugs, snails, aphids, cutworms, rabbits, and groundhogs. On the disease front, these are easy-to-grow crops with few risks. Seedlings can develop dampening off. Only in very poor growing conditions can they develop botrytis and mildews.

HARVESTING: To harvest the entire plant, cut off the head at the base with a sharp knife. You can also collect the leaves a few at a time, from the outside in, as the plant grows. Don't wait too long—delaying the harvest leads to tough leaves and a bitter taste.

STORAGE: These greens will store for about a week in the fridge in a breathable plastic bag. Wash just before eating.

Fig

WHAT IT IS: Fruit tree, perennial (zone 8)

HOW HARD TO GROW: Easy

LIGHT NEEDS: Full sun

SOIL NEEDS: Well drained, fertile, pH 6.0–6.5

WATERING NEEDS: Average, 2.5–4 cm (1–1.5 inches) per week

DIMENSIONS: Height: 3–9 m (10–30 feet); width: 3–4.5 m (10–15 feet)

HOW FAR APART TO PLANT: 6 m (20 feet) from other trees

CONTAINER SIZE: Minimum depth: 60 cm (24 inches); diameter: 60 cm (24 inches)

HOW MANY TO PLANT: 1 tree per 4 people; yields 100–200

WHEN TO SOW INDOORS: Can be grown from cuttings indoors

WHEN TO PLANT OUTDOORS: Spring

READY TO EAT: Fruit in fourth year, spring and fall

MULTI CROPPING: No, single crop

GROWS WELL WITH: Rue, marigold, strawberry

DO NOT PLANT WITH: Trees or tall plants that will offer shade

FOOD TO GROW VARIETIES: 'Brown Turkey', 'Celeste', 'Brunswick'

WHY TO GROW: When I was a kid, there were always several fig trees growing in our greenhouses. I remember the twisted, gnarled branches spreading out to cover a corner of the greenhouse with huge, green leaves. What fun it was to be the first to pick the fresh, ripe fruit before anyone else got it! Fig trees are deciduous trees native to tropical and semi-tropical climates, but they can be safely grown in Canada if you protect them over the winter. Figs are actually quite easy to grow, and they give your yard a tropical feel. The varieties I list at left can handle our chilly climate and are self-pollinating. You can expect fruit when your tree is about four years old. Be patient—your tree will be with you for as long as 30 years!

PLANTING: Unless you are living in a relatively balmy part of Canada where winter temperatures don't dip below −10°C (14°F), I recommend planting figs in a container. Start with a pot a little larger than the one the sapling came in. As the tree grows, about every two years, replace the pot with one about 5 cm (2 inches) larger. Fill the bottom of the container with potting soil, remove the plant from its original pot, and score around the roots. Place the root in the pot and fill the pot with soil, allowing a little room on top for water to collect. Put the potted tree in an area of your yard that receives at least six hours of sun a day.

GROWING: This tropical grower loves water, so keep it moist. Top the soil with mulch—even in a container —to retain moisture. Your plant should grow about 30 cm (1 foot) per year. While figs don't need food when planted in the ground, container figs need nutrition through balanced fertilizer. From early spring through to fall, offer it a monthly application of a water-soluble fertilizer or use a slow-release granular fertilizer that will offer consistent food for months. In the fall, move your plant, pot and all, into a garage or shed, cover with mulch or an old blanket, and water occasionally throughout the winter. If you are lucky enough to have a warm area such as a greenhouse or enclosed pool to store your fig tree, remember that it still needs a dormant period, so keep it in an area with cooler temperatures for at least a few weeks so it can have a rest.

The year after planting, trim away all but four or five of the strongest branches—these branches will be the fruiting wood. As your tree grows, trim away any branches that are not on these boughs and any damaged branches and branches that grow across the middle instead of straight out. Prune fig trees when dormant in fall or winter.

CHALLENGES: You may need to adjust your fertilizing routine: Too much nitrogen will produce beautiful foliage but very little fruit or fruit that fails to ripen. If that happens, ease off on your regular feedings. Another challenge is proper watering: Allowing your tree to become dry and then adding lots of water can cause the fruit or the bark to split. Let your tree dry out just a little between waterings, and offer more in the summer when the tree is producing fruit. During winter dormancy, water just a bare minimum. Figs can attract common fungal diseases such as rust and blight. Fig mosaic is a virus caused by a mite. Spotting of the leaves is the first sign, followed by marred fruit that may fall before ripening. There is no treatment, the tree has to be destroyed. A tree that fails to thrive is usually infected with root-knot nematodes. These too are impossible to kill.

HARVESTING: Your figs are ready to harvest when they look full and heavy and are slightly soft to the touch. Nectar sometimes appears on the tip of the fig's underside. Figs need to stay on the tree until they are fully ripe; they do not ripen after they are picked. Handle the ripened figs gently, as they bruise easily, and cut the fruit from the tree. Leave the stem with the fruit to delay spoilage.

STORAGE: Store figs in a single layer in the fridge for up to five days. Figs also freeze well. After washing, place the figs in a single layer on a cookie sheet, freeze until solid, and then store in freezer bags for up to three years. Figs can also be dried in the sun or a dehydrator and then frozen.

Garlic

WHAT IT IS: Root vegetable, perennial (zones 2–8)

HOW HARD TO GROW: Easy

LIGHT NEEDS: Full sun

SOIL NEEDS: Well-drained loam, avoid clay or sand, pH 6.0–7.0

WATERING NEEDS: Infrequent

DIMENSIONS: Height: 60–90 cm (24–36 inches); width: 10–15 cm (4–6 inches)

HOW FAR APART TO PLANT: 15 cm (6 inches); rows: 20 cm (8 inches)

CONTAINER SIZE: Not recommended for container growing

HOW MANY TO PLANT: 5–10 plants per person (I like garlic)

WHEN TO SOW INDOORS: Not recommended

WHEN TO PLANT OUTDOORS: Early spring or fall

READY TO EAT: Plant in fall, harvest late the following summer

MULTI CROPPING: No, single crop

GROWS WELL WITH: Fruit trees, tomato, pepper, eggplant, potato, cabbage, cauliflower, broccoli, kale

DO NOT PLANT WITH: Bean, pea

FOOD TO GROW VARIETIES: 'Asiatic', 'Creole', 'Porcelain', 'Purple Stripe', 'Glazed Purple Stripe', 'Marbled Purple Stripe', 'Rocambole', 'Turban'

WHY TO GROW: Garlic is a dream backyard crop. It's used constantly in the kitchen, it's easy to grow, and it repels aphids. Nothing tastes quite like fresh garlic from the garden, and you also get to harvest the delicious scapes, which are the seed heads. There are two main types of garlic: hardneck and softneck. Hardneck types produce a flower and are the best choices for colder climates. Softneck garlic is best suited to warmer climates and is grown by large commercial producers in places like California. The varieties I list at left are all hardneck; my favourite is 'Purple Stripe'.

PLANTING: Garlic is one of the few crops that do best when planted in the fall after the first frost. This seems odd, but you get used to it. Select an area with full sun and well-drained soil. Avoid planting in clay or sand. Purchase seed garlic from a garden centre— it looks like regular garlic, but it's not!—and separate the cloves without removing the protective papery husk. Dig down about 20 cm (8 inches) and loosen the soil in the planting area. Push your clove, pointy side up, into the earth, about 5 cm (2 inches) down. After planting, mulch the bed with 10 cm (4 inches) of clean straw to insulate the cloves against winter freeze-thaw cycles. To plant in a container in the fall, sink your pots into the ground or group them in a corner of the yard protected from wind and where snow collects—snow provides insulation.

GROWING: Over the winter, your garlic cloves will root down. They'll start growing upward in spring and eventually mature in late summer. In the spring, after the risk of frost has passed, remove the straw mulch. As soon as you see your garlic growing, apply a generous side dressing of blood meal. In the late spring or early summer, snap off the scapes (if you are growing hardneck garlic) and cook them up. This allows the garlic plant to focus on growing the bulb, plus gives you a tasty treat.

CHALLENGES: Garlic is so easy. It hardly needs any water and in fact repels a lot of pests. Furry creatures seldom target it. Keep your garlic plot free of weeds and it should grow beautifully. Garlic is only truly at risk for white rot, which you can see at harvest as a white fungus growing on the bulbs and roots. If you spot it, discard the garlic in the garbage, not the compost pile, and disinfect your tools and wash your hands to reduce the spread. Never grow garlic or anything else from the allium family—shallots, onions—in that location. White rot can last for up to 20 years in your soil.

HARVEST: Late summer when the bottom three leaves on your plant have yellowed and the top six leaves are still green is the perfect time to harvest your garlic. Gently pull out one bulb to ensure it has swollen to a mature size—it will look like a full bulb. If it does, remove remaining garlic by lifting bulbs with a garden fork. Trim the white, dangling roots to 1 cm (.25 inch) and brush off any soil. Braid leaves in groups of three to six bulbs and hang in a shaded location with good airflow. Bulbs should dry for at least two weeks before eating or storing.

STORAGE: Garlic can be stored for up to a year in a cool, dry, dark location. Garlic likes to be stored on a counter or in a cold cellar, never in a refrigerator.

Grape

WHAT IT IS: Fruit vine, perennial (zone 4)

HOW HARD TO GROW: Medium

LIGHT NEEDS: Full sun

SOIL NEEDS: Well drained, pH 6.0–6.5

WATERING NEEDS: Low to average, 3 cm (1 inch) a week

DIMENSIONS: Height: 1.5–2 m (5–6 feet);
width: 1–2 m (3–6 feet)

HOW FAR APART TO PLANT: 2 m (6 feet)

CONTAINER SIZE: Container planting not recommended

HOW MANY TO PLANT: 15–30 bunches per vine

WHEN TO SOW INDOORS: n/a

WHEN TO PLANT OUTDOORS: Early spring

READY TO EAT: Fruit in third year; 150–165 days

MULTI CROPPING: Yes

GROWS WELL WITH: Hyssop, oregano, bean, pea, basil, mustard, chive, blackberry, calendula

DO NOT PLANT WITH: Lettuce, cabbage, collard green, radish, garlic

FOOD TO GROW VARIETIES: 'Concord' (blue), 'Kay Gray' (white), 'Valiant' (blue), 'Swenson Red' (red)

WHY TO GROW: If you simply adore eating fresh grapes or make juice or wine regularly, go ahead and plant this crop. But this perennial vine takes up a lot of space and is a fair amount of work—you will be pruning a lot. Still, once you understand how to prune your grapevine, grapes are quite easy to grow and the work just becomes part of your annual routine. There are numerous varieties of grapes, and they come in green, red, purple, yellow, and white.

PLANTING: Buy year-old plants from a garden centre. Soak the roots for up to two hours before planting and trim away any broken or very long roots. Choose a very sunny, hot location, preferably on a slope, with loose soil and excellent air circulation, and erect a support structure. (You may want to read up on how to grow vertically on page 70.) Dig a 30 by 30 cm (12 by 12 inch) hole near the base of your trellis or other support structure. Gently place the roots in the hole, making sure your plant sits a little bit deeper in the soil than it did in the container or bag it came in. Backfill, gently tamp down the area, and water. Prune your newly planted grapevine canes back so there are only two or three buds showing above the soil level. Add a good layer of mulch around the base.

GROWING: From here, it's all about feeding and pruning. Do not fertilize in your first year of growing, but do add a bit of topsoil around the area of the planting hole.

There are two types of pruning techniques for grapevines: cane and spur. Cane pruning provides the best protection against frost and cold winters, so this is the method we fill focus on.

For the first year, you let your vine grow freely. If you get good growth in that first season (you won't have grapes yet), then in late winter when your grapevine is dormant choose one or two of the strongest canes and prune back the rest. These will be the main supports for your vine. Let them grow just to the top height of your support structure, and cut off any longer parts so as to promote lateral growth. This lateral growth will be your vine's "arms." Choose one or two of the strongest "arms" to focus on and train them to grow sideways by fastening your vine to the support with a soft material such as horticultural tape or old pantyhose—do not use wire, which will cut the stems. Pinch or prune back any blossoms or suckers growing from the base of your vine to allow it to put all of its energy into growing roots and those main vines. However, if your vine did not grow well that first year, just prune the entire thing back to two to three buds above soil level. The vine will start all over again in its second year, and you can delay creating those main support vines until the second winter.

When the grapes start to grow in the second year, focus on the vertical and horizontal support canes selected in the first year. Lightly fertilize

your vine and continue to pinch or prune back any blossoms or suckers growing from the base.

In the third year, after winter has passed, choose four to five shoots growing from the horizontal arms and prune those back to two to three buds above their base. These will be your fruit-producing stems. Prune everything else. Continue to prune back any suckers growing from the base in the third year, focusing the vine growth on the support canes and the lateral "arms," and continue fertilizing lightly.

In the fruit-producing years, maintain good airflow through the vines to prevent disease. If the leaf canopy is too heavy, prune back some leaves. If grapes do not seem to be ripening, pinch back a few leaves around them to allow more sunlight in.

CHALLENGES: To get good yields on your grapevine, you need to do a lot of pruning. Be on the alert for white flies, lead hoppers, ants, grape berry moths, aphids, Japanese beetles, birds, raccoons, opossums, and skunks. Birds love grapes too, but they don't go for Concord—that's one of the reasons this variety is so popular. Grapes can come down with downy mildew, powdery mildew, black rot, botrytis, and gall phylloxera. Crown gall affects roots and lower stems of grapes. This disease is not fatal, but it will impact yields; it produces growths called "black galls." You need to cover the soil around your vine's base with black plastic and let the sun kill the bacterium that causes the disease.

HARVEST: Grapes will change colour long before they are ripe. To know when to harvest them, you need to do a taste test. Once the first frost hits, the leaves will die back and the grapes will no longer ripen and will need to be harvested.

STORAGE: Grapes will stay firm for up to two weeks in the refrigerator. Rinse and dry them, and keep them in a well-ventilated container. Of course they'll last a lot longer when made into jam and juice, or when fermented and turned into wine.

Kale

WHAT IT IS: Leafy green vegetable, annual

HOW HARD TO GROW: Easy

LIGHT NEEDS: Full sun to part shade

SOIL NEEDS: Well drained, moist, fertile, pH 5.5–6.8

WATERING NEEDS: Frequent

DIMENSIONS: Height: 30–60 cm (12–24 inches); width: 20–30 cm (8–12 inches)

HOW FAR APART TO PLANT: 45–60 cm (18–24 inches)

CONTAINER SIZE: Minimum depth: 20 cm (8 inches); diameter: 30–35 cm+ (12–14 inches+)

HOW MANY TO PLANT: 4 plants per person

WHEN TO SOW INDOORS: 6–8 weeks before last frost

WHEN TO PLANT OUTDOORS: Spring or late summer

READY TO EAT: 30–40 days from seedlings

MULTI CROPPING: No, single plant

GROWS WELL WITH: Basil, bean, dill, garlic, hyssop, lettuce, marigold, mint, onion, radish, rosemary, sage, thyme, tomato

DO NOT PLANT WITH: Grape

FOOD TO GROW VARIETIES: 'Dwarf Blue Curled', 'Blue Knight' (a hybrid)

WHY TO GROW: Kale has become incredibly popular for its great health benefits, and luckily, it's pretty great in the garden too. It's one of the most cold tolerant of all its fellow brassicas (cabbage, broccoli, and cauliflower) and is capable of surviving temperatures as low as −10°C (14°F). Kale comes in various shapes and forms; some look showy and make a great addition to an ornamental arrangement. There are six types, divided into groups by their leaf shape: curly (also called Scots), plain, rape kale, leaf, and spear kale (a hybrid of curly and plain), and Cavolo Nero (also called black cabbage, Tuscan, Lacinato, and dinosaur). No matter what your kale looks like, all varieties are edible—even those so popular in decorative fall containers.

PLANTING: You can start kale seed indoors or direct-sow into the garden, but if you're new to growing, I suggest purchasing seedlings and planting in early to mid-spring outdoors. (And you can get additional crops by planting again—for best results and a delicious fall crop wait until the late summer when the weather is cooler.) Plant your kale in full sun in a location where the soil is well drained. Partner your kale with some tomatoes. Your greens will be harvested first and then your tomato plants can take over kale's location—it's a smart use of limited garden space.

GROWING: Go ahead—fertilize your kale if you like. But if you plant it in rich soil, it won't need it. If you opt to feed, be gentle by using a compost tea, fish emulsion, or general garden fertilizer. Keep the kale watered during dry periods, monitor for insects and disease, and remove any leaves that are yellowing or appear sickly.

That's it—I told you kale was easy to grow!

CHALLENGES: Kale likes it cool, and heat can be a problem. In the heat of the summer, consider putting up a shade cover. Like all brassica vegetables, kale often falls victims to moths, cabbage worms, cabbage loopers, cutworms, and slugs. Deer, rabbits, groundhogs, mice, and moles will stop by for a bite, so prevent big critters if they often visit your garden (see page 37).

HARVESTING: Like most greens, kale offers a continuous harvest if you pluck the side leaves only and let the plant keep growing. Start picking your kale when the plant is about 20 cm (8 inches) tall. If you want to harvest the whole plant, cut the stem 5 cm (2 inches) above the soil. For your late-summer planting, it's fine to let your kale go through a light frost—that will sweeten the flavour.

STORAGE: Fresh is best, so eat what you pick and wash just before using. If you need to store a bumper crop, place it unwashed in a loose, breathable bag; it will last for up to a week in the refrigerator.

Cool, shadier weather is better for kale—if it gets too hot, it will bolt (left). Under the right conditions, though, it will keep growing as you pick (above).

Kohlrabi

WHAT IT IS: Vegetable, biennial grown as an annual

HOW HARD TO GROW: Easy

LIGHT NEEDS: Full sun

SOIL NEEDS: Moist, pH 6.0–7.0

WATERING NEEDS: Frequent

DIMENSIONS: Height: 20–30 cm (8–12 inches); width: 20–30 cm (8–12 inches)

HOW FAR APART TO PLANT: 20–30 cm (8–12 inches)

CONTAINER SIZE: Container planting not recommended

HOW MANY TO PLANT: 4–5 plants per person

WHEN TO SOW INDOORS: 4–6 weeks before last frost; 10 weeks before first frost for fall harvest

WHEN TO PLANT OUTDOORS: 2 weeks before last frost; 6 weeks before first frost for fall harvest

READY TO EAT: 45–65 days from seedlings

MULTI CROPPING: No, single crop

GROWS WELL WITH: Beet, celery, herbs, onion, potato

DO NOT PLANT WITH: Pole bean, strawberry, tomato

FOOD TO GROW VARIETIES: 'Early Purple Vienna', 'Early White Vienna', 'Eden', 'Grand Duke'

WHY TO GROW: *Kohlrabi* originally hails from Germany and literally translates to "cabbage turnip." It's also sometimes called a "space cabbage" because of its unique shape—it looks almost like a hot air balloon. You eat the bulb-like stem after you peel the vegetable, and it tastes somewhere between a cabbage and broccoli. Kohlrabi is a popular alternative crop to turnip because it is a little tougher in the heat and high winds. This easy grower does not need deep soil and can weather cold temperatures. In fact, it is during the cooler weather that your kohlrabi will thrive and offer you the best yields and taste.

PLANTING: You can direct-sow into the garden just two weeks before the last frost or plant seedlings at the same time. (You can also seed-start indoors if you like.) Pick a sunny location improved with about 5 cm (2 inches) of compost and some fertilizer worked into the soil well with a pitchfork. If you do get a frost, cover your seedlings. Side-dress your new plants with fertilizer three weeks after planting. For fall kohlrabi, plant seedlings in a sheltered area six weeks before you expect the first fall frost to hit. The shelter will help the plants endure early frosts better.

GROWING: This plant has shallow roots, so you need to weed gently by hand. Offer your kohlrabi about 2.5 cm (1 inch) of water a week and use grass clippings or straw as mulch to prevent weeds and hold in moisture. If your leaves start to touch each other, prune them so they're spaced about 10 cm (4 inches) apart. If your goal is to grow your kohlrabies larger, you'll need to prune back even more so they have about 20 cm (8 inches) between plants.

CHALLENGES: This easy grower does not like the cold and will bolt below 7°C (45°F). Hot weather will lead to tough stems. Kohlrabi attracts the same pests and diseases as its other brassica friends: aphids, flea beetles, cabbage worms, cabbage loopers, cutworms, leaf miners, caterpillars, root maggots, cabbage white butterfly larvae, white rush, down mildew, and powdery mildew. Prevent with good crop rotation; as well as to keep pesky flea beetles under control, use floating row covers for seedlings until they get to 10 cm (4 inches).

HARVESTING: Start harvesting your kohlrabies when the round, bulbous stems are about 2.5 cm (1 inch) in diameter. You can pick them later too, up until they reach 8 cm (3 inches) in diameter. Pull up on the plant. Leave the roots behind and cut 2.5 cm (1 inch) below the stem.

STORAGE: Kohlrabi can last three weeks or longer in the refrigerator when stored in the crisper drawer. If you want to go for long-term storage, remove the leaves but leave the skin on and put the kohlrabi in a cool, dark place. Peel, dice, and blanch this vegetable before freezing.

Garden vigilance is key—look for early signs of rot, which can happen if water pools after an early spring rain.

Leek

WHAT IT IS: Vegetable, biennial grown as an annual

HOW HARD TO GROW: Easy to moderate

LIGHT NEEDS: Full sun to part shade

SOIL NEEDS: Rich, well drained, fertile, pH 6.0–6.8

WATERING NEEDS: Consistent, 3 cm (1 inch) per week

DIMENSIONS: Height: 24–65 cm (10–26 inches); width: 2–8 cm (1–3 inches)

HOW FAR APART TO PLANT: 10 cm (4 inches)

CONTAINER SIZE: Minimum depth: 30 cm (12 inches); you need a large container so you can mound the soil during blanching

HOW MANY TO PLANT: 10 plants per person

WHEN TO SOW INDOORS: 8–10 weeks before last frost

WHEN TO PLANT OUTDOORS: Seeds 4 weeks before last frost; seedlings 2 weeks before last frost

READY TO EAT: 50–125 days

MULTI CROPPING: No, single crop

GROWS WELL WITH: Apple, carrot, celery, onion

DO NOT PLANT WITH: Pea, bean

FOOD TO GROW VARIETIES: Short season: 'King Richard'. Long season: 'Lancelot'

WHY TO GROW: This is the mildest member of the onion family and it comes in two general varieties. Short-season leeks are planted in the early spring for a summer harvest. Long-season varieties have a longer time to maturity, so they are planted in the spring for fall harvest and will grow right up until the ground freezes.

PLANTING: Plant your leeks in well-drained soil that's been improved with compost or manure—ideally, get the bed ready the previous fall. Leeks do not like competition, so be sure you start out with a weed-free area. For direct sowing, plant four weeks before the last frost, placing your seeds 3 cm (1 inch) deep and 3 cm (1 inch) apart. After six weeks, thin to about one plant every 2 cm (.75 inch), then later to 10 cm (4 inches). If you're planting seedlings, dig a hole or trench 15–20 cm (6–8 inches) deep and plant your leek seedlings so just a few centimetres of the tips are above soil level.

GROWING: Leeks have a small root system and need consistent moisture; aim for 3–4 cm (1–1.5 inches) per week, including rain, for average soils; sandy soils may need more. Leeks have to be blanched to get a white, tender base and a sweet flavour. Two weeks before harvest, mound soil up over the stems.

CHALLENGES: Leeks are relatively easy to grow and rarely attract trouble. They can be at risk for thrips, onion maggot, purple blotch, leaf blight, and botrytis.

HARVESTING: Pull your leeks before they are mature to get a mild-tasting onion similar to scallions or spring onions. They're fully mature and perfect for cooking at 3–4 cm (1–1.5 inch) in diameter. Leftover leeks? You can actually replant them the following spring, since leeks are a biennial. Just dig up a leek, preserving the soil ball around the roots. Store the plant and roots at 0°C (32°F) in a humid location. In the spring, replant your leeks. I often find these become my biggest, healthiest crops.

I have friends who have planted leek roots from the grocery store, and they also work, even after the top foliage was used for cooking. So I guess you can have your leek and plant it too!

STORAGE: To keep them in the fridge for up to two weeks, clean and dry them, and then store in a plastic bag in a crisper drawer. For longer storage, cut off the roots and the green leaves to 3–4 cm (1–1.5 inches) above the base. Store upside down in a wooden box or crate filled with sawdust, where they will last for up to eight weeks. To freeze, remove the roots and leaves and freeze in freezer bags.

I mention two kinds of **blanching** in this book. One is just briefly boiling a ripe vegetable before you freeze it. The other, which is more complex, is about protecting vegetables such as celery, leeks, endive, and escarole from the sun and helping them develop their colour and taste right before harvest. Usually, about two weeks before harvest, cover such vegetables with newspaper, cardboard, soil, or mulch until they are ripe.

Lettuce

WHAT IT IS: Leafy green vegetable, annual

HOW HARD TO GROW: Easy to moderate

LIGHT NEEDS: Full sun to part shade

SOIL NEEDS: Fertile, moist, well drained, pH 6.0–7.0

WATERING NEEDS: Average, 3 cm (1 inch) per week, more in windier locations

DIMENSIONS: Height: 15–45 cm (6–18 inches); width: 30–45 cm (12–18 inches)

HOW FAR APART TO PLANT: 15–25 cm (6–10 inches)

CONTAINER SIZE: Minimum depth: 10 cm (4 inches); diameter: 20–30 cm (8–12 inches)

HOW MANY TO PLANT: 6–10 plants per person

WHEN TO SOW INDOORS: 4–6 weeks before last frost date

WHEN TO PLANT OUTDOORS: Around last frost date

READY TO EAT: 45–90 days

MULTI CROPPING: No, single crop

GROWS WELL WITH: Beet, bean, onion, radish, broccoli, carrot, chive, garlic, strawberry, cilantro, cucumber

DO NOT PLANT WITH: Celery, cabbage, parsley

FOOD TO GROW VARIETIES: Green leaf: 'Grand Rapids'. Red leaf: 'Red Sails'. Boston: 'Adriana'. Romaine: 'Coastal Star'. Head: 'Iceberg' (left).

WHY TO GROW: Lettuce is not difficult to grow, and nothing impresses guests more than a salad made entirely from a backyard crop—possibly harvested in front of their eyes. There are four types of lettuce: romaine (or cos); loose-leaf or leaf; butterhead (also known as Boston or loose head); and crisphead (such as 'Iceberg'). The term *mesclun mix* describes a combination of lettuces and greens such as radicchio, dandelion leaves, or other lettuce-like vegetables. You should know that romaine and leaf lettuce are more heat tolerant, whereas crisphead and butterhead are more cold tolerant. All types can withstand a light frost, and none is a particular fan of really hot weather—all will bolt when the mercury rises. I like planting my lettuces close to bigger growers like tomatoes that will help shade them in the dog days of summer.

PLANTING: Plant lettuce in the ground or a container—ideally, in a location that will get a little shade in the height of the summer. If your soil has good nitrogen content, great. If not, apply a high-nitrogen fertilizer to encourage green growth. Consider staggering your plantings every two weeks or so to get a nice, long lettuce harvest.

If you seed-start inside or purchase seedlings, put them in the ground around the time of the last frost. Direct-sow about a month before the last frost. The seeds need light to germinate, so they should only be planted slightly below the soil surface. When each seedling has sprouted three to four leaves, the seedlings can be thinned. In general, aim for a spacing of 30–40 cm (12–16 inches) for romaine; 15–20 cm (6–8 inches) for butter and head; and 10–15 cm (4–6 inches) for leaf. Leaf lettuce will adapt to the space you offer, so sometimes you can push it a bit tighter.

GROWING: Your lettuce needs consistent moisture—and more water in windy locations—but take care not to waterlog your delicate plants. Watch lettuce religiously as the season warms up. When lettuce bolts, it does so very quickly. If your plants start sending up a stem that will soon flower, remove the entire plant immediately and place in the refrigerator to try to prevent the leaves from turning bitter.

CHALLENGES: Aside from watching for bolting in the summer heat, keep your eye out for slugs, snails, earwigs, rabbits, flea beetles, aphids, cutworms, cabbage loopers, and leaf miners. Diseases that target lettuce include root rot, leaf spot, dampening off (at the seedling stage), fusarium, and mosaic virus.

HARVESTING: Leafier lettuce can be harvested all at once, or you can pick the outer leaves, letting the inner ones grow, for an ongoing harvest. Head lettuce should be harvested whole once it has firmed up. You can feel for this by applying a little bit of pressure to the head—squeezing too hard will damage the inner leaves. Cut the heads off just above the base with a sharp knife.

STORAGE: Lettuce is one of the few backyard crops that cannot be frozen, canned, or preserved in any way. It'll last up to one week—longer for some varieties—stored loosely in a plastic bag in the fridge. Wash lettuce just before use.

Head lettuce (bottom left) is a perfect salad addition, but make sure you pick and enjoy before it starts to bolt like this romaine (bottom right).

Melon

WHAT IT IS: Fruit vine, annual

HOW HARD TO GROW: Moderate

LIGHT NEEDS: Full sun

SOIL NEEDS: Sandy loam, pH 6.0–6.8 but can tolerate as low as 5.0

WATERING NEEDS: Moderate, 4–8 cm (2–3 inches) per week

DIMENSIONS: Height: 30 cm (12 inches); width: 1.5–3 m (5–10 feet)

HOW FAR APART TO PLANT: 2–2.5 m (6–8 feet)

CONTAINER SIZE: Container planting not recommended

HOW MANY TO PLANT: 1 plant per 2 people

WHEN TO SOW INDOORS: 1 month before planting

WHEN TO PLANT OUTDOORS: 2 weeks after last frost

READY TO EAT: 70–90 days (longer in cooler weather)

MULTI CROPPING: No, single crop

GROWS WELL WITH: Corn, pea, pumpkin, radish, nasturtium, oregano, camomile, savory

DO NOT PLANT WITH: Other melon, squash, cucumber, black walnut

FOOD TO GROW VARIETIES: Watermelon: 'Sugar Baby', 'Early Canadian Improved'. Cantaloupe: 'Delicious', 'Hale's Best Jumbo', 'Minnesota'

WHY TO GROW: What's summer without big mouthfuls of summer melons—watermelons, cantaloupes, honeydew, and others—preferably eaten outside. Getting these sweet treats out of your own garden is even better. These cousins to squash, pumpkins, and cucumbers need a long, hot season to produce fruit, but you can grow them in Canada if you take some care. For watermelons, you should know there are about 1,200 varieties. They come in seeded, seedless, mini, yellow, and orange varieties. Whatever you do, look for a short-season variety to get good results in our chilly climate. Cantaloupes are great to grow. And give honeydew or muskmelons a try—in fact, the latter are the easiest melons to grow of all. Look for a short-season variety and you should be good.

PLANTING: Prepare a bed with some compost or manure in a sunny and hot section of your garden. Forget containers unless you have very large ones that will hold these sprawling plants. Some gardeners have planted melons right into their compost piles, which are usually in sunny locations and come loaded with nutrients. To warm up your soil faster in the spring, cover it with black plastic for a few weeks. Wait until the threat of frost has long passed and the soil is a toasty 21°C (70°F). If you're growing vertically—an option for cantaloupes and other smaller melons but not watermelon—prepare a support that is 1.5 to 2 m (5–7 feet) high and 2.5–3 m (8–10 feet) wide. Weed the area well and add mulch—weeding when the plants have filled in will be difficult. If you are growing your melons in a wet area, consider planting them in hills or mounds so their roots and stems don't stay too wet. If you are in a drier area, you can do the opposite and plant them in a slight depression so they can catch more water.

GROWING: Like many fruits, pollination is major factor in getting great yields. Melons have both female and male flowers; the males will be the first to bloom. If the flowers are not pollinated, they will not produce fruit. Bees in your garden should do the pollination for you, but if you're low on helpful insects, you can do the pollinating using a cotton swab. You pretty much act like a bee, going flower to flower, transferring pollen on your swab. Later in the growing season, once a few fruit have begun to form, prune off any new flowers so the plant can direct its energy to growing the existing melons. Do not prune back any new leaf growth. Note that most leaves will wilt in the afternoon heat, but that does not mean they need water. If they are wilted in the morning or later on in the evening, they need watering. When you do add water, do so in the morning and water the roots only. Consider side-dressing with rich compost every few weeks to feed the melons. As the melons grow heavy, particularly when you're growing vertically, you'll need to support them. Secure the fruit with a sling made of anything that will not cut into the fruit or vine, such as rubberized tape or old pantyhose, and fasten it to your supporting structure. Once your melons start to ripen, ease off on watering.

CHALLENGES: Melons can start to rot where they touch the earth, so prevent this by slipping a piece of cardboard, straw, or a few pieces of newspaper under them. Be aware that aphids, cucumber beetles, squash vine borer moths, and mice could target your melons. Watch for fusarium wilt, alternaria leaf spot, powdery mildew, downy mildew, anthracnose, and stem blight. Watering the leaves of melon plants is the biggest no-no, as that will lead to powdery mildew.

HARVESTING: Both watermelon and cantaloupe will not continue to ripen, or get any sweeter, after being picked. For watermelons, harvest when the part of the melon that rests on the soil has turned from white to yellow. If you knock on the melon gently and hear a hollow sound, you're good to go. If the tendrils on the plant are green, it isn't ripe. If they are half dead, your melons are ripe, and if they are completely dead, they have overripened. For cantaloupes, the netting or patterning on the rind will become more pronounced at it ripens and the fruit will easily separate from the vine.

STORAGE: Uncut, your watermelons should stay fresh in the fridge for two weeks, while cantaloupes will be okay for one week. Once cut up, both will last about four days wrapped in plastic and refrigerated. To freeze, cut them into cubes and store in a plastic bag, then use later for shakes and smoothies.

Warm soil temperatures are a must for some seeds to germinate or seedlings to thrive. Easy trick: Lay down some **black plastic** on your garden bed for a few weeks in the early spring, and the soil below will become extra warmed by the sun.

Onion

WHAT IT IS: Root vegetable, biennial grown as an annual

HOW HARD TO GROW: Moderate

LIGHT NEEDS: Full sun

SOIL NEEDS: Any; does best in well-drained loam; clay can impact taste; pH 6.5–6.8

WATERING NEEDS: Average to high

DIMENSIONS: Height: 15–75 cm (6–30 inches); width: 5–15 cm (2–6 inches)

HOW FAR APART TO PLANT: 5–15 cm (2–6 inches); rows: 30 cm (12 inches)

CONTAINER SIZE: Minimum depth for scallion: 15 cm (6 inches); Spanish: 45 cm (18 inches)

HOW MANY TO PLANT: 10 plants per person

WHEN TO SOW INDOORS: 6–8 weeks before planting outdoors

WHEN TO PLANT OUTDOORS: 3–4 weeks before last frost

READY TO EAT: 35–180 days

MULTI CROPPING: No, single crop

GROWS WELL WITH: Strawberry, lettuce, brassicas, beet, carrot, leek, kohlrabi, tomato; camomile and/or summer savory to improve flavour

DO NOT PLANT WITH: Pea, pole and bush bean, asparagus, sage

FOOD TO GROW VARIETIES: Early: 'Norstart', 'Alpine'; late: 'Milestone', 'Fortress'. Red: 'Red Zeppelin'; Spanish: 'Sierra Blanca', 'Candy, Montero'. Shallots: 'Golden Gourmet', 'Atlantic', 'Dutch Yellow'. Scallions: 'Tokyo Long White', 'Red Welsh'

WHY TO GROW: Onions are one of the most versatile cooking ingredients, so naturally food gardeners want to grow this indispensable crop. Onions are grouped into three general types: short day, intermediate, and long day. These names refer to the length of daylight they do best in. In Canada, we have long summer days around the summer solstice, so long-day varieties thrive here. Intermediate onions will also grow here, but not as well.

As for all the onion varieties out there, sit back—there are many. Yellow, red, white, shallots, and scallions. Yellow onions are the most commonly used; they have the strongest flavour and the longest storage time. Red onions, also known as brown or purple, have a milder, sweeter flavour and can be eaten raw. White onions are used for cooking. Shallots are a smaller version of typical onions and are mostly associated with French cuisine. They have a very strong taste if eaten raw but offer up a mild garlicky flavour when cooked. Scallions (also known as green or spring onions) are derived from regular onions, mostly white. They are harvested earlier, before the bulb forms or when it's very small, and you eat both the small white bulb and the long, mildly flavourful greens.

PLANTING: You can buy onions in seed form; in seed sets, which are small, dry onion bulbs; or as seedlings. Start by amending soil with 5 cm (2 inches) of compost and mix evenly into the soil to make sure there are no clumps. For the best-tasting onions, plant in sandy loam soil or raised beds. If you're growing from seed, plant your seeds 1.5 to 2.5 cm (less than 1 inch) deep, 10 cm (4 inches) apart. Plant your sowing set at 5 cm (2 inches) deep with the tips of the bulbs just breaking through the soil level. For transplants, plant about 2 weeks

before the last frost. Thin your seeds or seed sets as they emerge. For full onions, you'll need 15 cm (6 inches) between plants. If you're harvesting the tops for scallions, aim for 5 cm (2 inches) apart; shallots need 10 cm (4 inches).

GROWING: Your onions will appreciate feedings high in phosphorous—this nutrient feeds and strengthens roots. If you get a period of warm weather, followed by cool weather and then warm weather again, your onions might bolt. Remove any flower stalks as soon as they start to develop, to preserve the crop—the flavour and the vigour may already be affected, but you have to try. Keep your onions nice and moist throughout the growing season, but avoid overdoing it and turning the soil soggy. As your onions get closer to harvest, when their leaves begin to turn yellow, reduce water and stop feeding them.

CHALLENGES: Along with bolting, you can get splitting bulbs and shaking, which is when the inner leaves turn yellow and the bulb collapses underground into a ball of liquid goo. Prevent this with good air circulation and drainage—the worst thing for onions is to sit in water. The two major diseases affecting onions are blight and purple blotch. Blight you'll identify by the leaves turning pale green and then yellow. Purple blotch causes purple lesions on leaves. Heavy dew and humid, wet weather cause this disease, and all you can do is prevent it by planting in well-drained soil and running your rows in the same direction as the prevailing wind to keep up good air circulation.

Larger critters won't eat onions, which makes them a great crop to grow in rural locations. Watch out for smaller pests such as thrips, onion maggots/onion flies, and onion leaf miners (also known as leaf moths).

HARVESTING: Onions are ready to harvest when the leaves bend or fold over. Wait one week and then pull the entire plant out of the soil. To cure onions, store in a warm, dry place until the skin starts to dry out. Once the leaves have dried, cut the stems 3 cm (about 1 inch) above the bulb. For shallots, you'll be looking at about 90 days to harvest; pull them when the greens start to wither, fall over, and die around mid to late summer. Dig up the bulbs, shake off the dirt, braid the tops, and let the shallots dry. Scallions can be harvested about four weeks after planting sets or seedlings, or eight weeks after planting by seed. Harvest when the green leaves are around 18 cm (7 inches) tall, before the bulbs get too large, by removing the entire plant.

STORAGE: Red or purple sweet onions have a short storage time of about three weeks. Other varieties can be stored longer, up to four months if you can keep them cool and dry. Store shallots in a mesh bag in a cool, dry spot and they'll be fine for about four months. Put your scallions upright in a container with 5 cm (2 inches) of water, cover the tops with a plastic bag, and refrigerate. Replace the water every few days, and they'll last for 7 to 10 days.

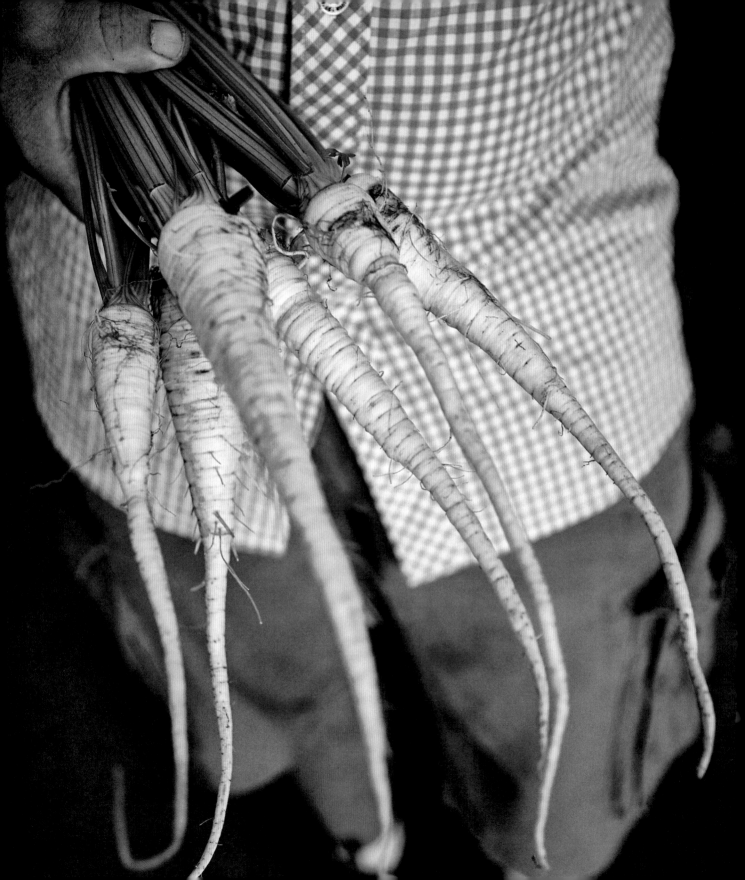

Parsnip

WHAT IT IS: Root vegetable, biennial grown as an annual

HOW HARD TO GROW: Easy

LIGHT NEEDS: Full to part sun

SOIL NEEDS: Sandy, loamy, pH 6.0–6.8

WATERING NEEDS: Average, 2.5 cm (1 inch) per week

DIMENSIONS: Height: 90 cm (3 feet); width: 10–15 cm (4–6 inches)

HOW FAR APART TO PLANT: 10 cm (4 inches); rows: 30 cm (12 inches)

CONTAINER SIZE: Minimum depth: 30–45 cm (12–18 inches)

HOW MANY TO PLANT: 5–10 per person; yields 1 per plant

WHEN TO SOW INDOORS: Not recommended

WHEN TO PLANT OUTDOORS: 2–3 weeks before the last frost date, as soon as the soil can be worked

READY TO EAT: 120 days

MULTI CROPPING: No, single plant

GROWS WELL WITH: Bush bean, garlic, marigold, onion, rose, tomato

DO NOT PLANT WITH: Cabbage, kale, Brussels sprout, tomato

FOOD TO GROW VARIETIES: Short-rooted: 'Avonresister'. Medium-rooted: 'Cobham Improved Marrow'. Long-rooted: 'Gladiator', 'Harris Early Model'

WHY TO GROW: Once the weather turns cooler, we look to roasting winter vegetables and making warm soups and stews. The sweet, nutty flavour of parsnips makes them a worthy addition to your fall repertoire. Parsnips are biennial root vegetables, grown as an annual in our Canadian climate. Don't let that long time to maturity throw you off. You leave this root vegetable in the ground after a frost and the cold sweetens the taste. In fact, parsnips can be left in the soil all winter and harvested the following spring as soon as the ground thaws. I give you a list of varieties at left, but my real favourites are 'Harris Early Model' and 'Gladiator' because they harvest so early, as quick as 100 days. If your soil is poor, go for 'Avonresister', as it can grow in any conditions.

PLANTING: Parsnips take a long time to grow, so get working the soil as soon as it's workable and not frozen anymore. Add 5–10 cm (2–4 inches) of compost on the soil and dig it in to a depth of 30–40 cm (12–15 inches). For successful germination use only fresh seed—parsnip seed does not store well. Sow the seeds 1.25 cm (.5 inch) apart and 1.25 cm (.5 inch) deep in rows 30 cm (12 inches) apart. Water well. About two weeks after the plants emerge, thin them so they are about 10 cm (4 inches) apart.

GROWING: Give your parsnips consistent water through the growing season or you risk them turning tough. Midway through the season, around June, add a layer of manure or compost to your plot—that's all the food they need to get by.

CHALLENGES: Don't let your parsnips get too big, don't space them too far apart in the garden, and don't skip the step above where I suggest you work the soil before you plant. Loose, improved soil at the

time of planting will encourage them to grow deeply so they'll be thin, not large and tough. Monitor for aphids—they'll hang out on the underside of leaves. Wash them away with a strong blast from the hose or use insecticidal soap. Chewed leaves are a sign of slugs. Saucers of beer in the soil will attract and then drown them. Yellowed leaves or a mottled pattern on the leaves are signs of disease. Remove affected plants.

HARVESTING: Your parsnips are ready to harvest when the foliage reaches about 30 cm (12 inches) in height. Ideally, leave them in the ground for about two weeks after the first frost but before the ground freezes. Pull parsnips up by digging initially with a spade or fork, being careful not to damage the root. It helps to trim the foliage off first. The vegetable should be around 5 cm (2 inches) wide and 30 cm (12 inches) long.

STORAGE: A good way to store parsnips is simply to leave them in the ground! Harvest some of your crop for winter use and leave the rest for the spring, covered with an extra layer of soil and mulch. These parsnips must be removed as soon as the ground thaws or they will begin to grow again.

The parsnips harvested in the fall or early winter will store well in the fridge in a plastic bag for months. They can also be kept buried in sand in a cool location (see page 167). To freeze them, wash, peel, and cut into small chunks. Blanch them for three minutes, cool in an ice bath, drain, and place in freezer bags. Frozen, they will keep for six months.

Homegrown sometimes doesn't look at all like a parsnip from the grocery store but it tastes even better! This parsnip was transplanted as a seedling—hence the funny shape.

Pea

WHAT IT IS: Legume, annual

HOW HARD TO GROW: Easy

LIGHT NEEDS: Full sun

SOIL NEEDS: Moist, fertile, well drained, pH 5.8–7.0

WATERING NEEDS: Moderate, water weekly

DIMENSIONS: Height: 90–180 cm (36–72 inches); width: 30–100 cm (12–40 inches)

HOW FAR APART TO PLANT: Sow very close together; rows: 40 cm (16 inches)

CONTAINER SIZE: Minimum depth: 20 cm (10 inches); diameter: 25 cm+ (10 inches+)

HOW MANY TO PLANT: 3–5 per person

WHEN TO SOW INDOORS: Not recommended

WHEN TO PLANT OUTDOORS: Seeds 1–2 weeks before last frost

READY TO EAT: 84–100 days

MULTI CROPPING: 1–3 crops per season

GROWS WELL WITH: Bean, corn, carrot, cucumber radish, turnip

DO NOT PLANT WITH: Anything from the onion family: garlic, onion, shallot

FOOD TO GROW VARIETIES: Shelling: 'Mr. Big', 'Laxton Progress'. Snap: 'Sugar Snap', 'Super Spring'. Snow: 'Snowflake', 'Edible Podded Snow'

WHY TO GROW: Garden-fresh peas are delicious and one of those easy crops that kids enjoy helping grow. There are three basic types of peas: shelling peas (garden or green), which you take out of the shell to eat; snap peas, which are totally edible, pod and all; and the smaller snow peas, which are also completely edible. Shelling peas come in earlier varieties that are ready in 12 weeks. Instead of staggering the sowing time with peas, I recommend using varieties that mature at different times. Get your peas started nice and early in the spring; they love the cool weather. If you want a fall crop, sow some early variety shelling peas in midsummer. Peas are best grown vertically—and they hardly take up any space—so plant them in containers or in the ground with a support nearby.

PLANTING: Prepare a sunny area with lots of compost; peas like rich soil. Sow your seeds in early spring as soon as the soil is warm enough to work. Sow thickly in rows and cover with 2.5 cm (1 inch) of soil. Seeding thickly will prevent the growth of weeds and there will be no need to thin seedlings out later. Water frequently after seeding. Keep your eye on your seeds once they've germinated. If there's a risk of frost in those early weeks, cover them up.

GROWING: Peas don't need to be fed. In fact, if you fertilize them, you can end up with a lush plant with few pods. (If you're growing in potting soil in a container, give your peas regular feedings with an all-purpose fertilizer.) For most of the growing season, particularly when flowers and pods are forming, water heavily just once a week, then more often in the heat of the summer. When vines begin to grow, mulch to protect peas' shallow roots, and offer support for the vines. Use a fence or trellis or get posts at your garden centre that you can string twine between. As your plants grow up, guide them through the twine.

CHALLENGES: Birds love pea seeds. Discourage birds from hanging out in your vegetable garden by placing a plastic owl or a big balloon with an eye on it near your newly planted peas. Also, peas are a cool weather plant, so you need to give them extra care over the hot summer months with watering and perhaps even shading. If your soil does not drain well, you can get root rot. Downy mildew and powdery mildew can affect pea plants. Reduce the risk of these fungal diseases by purchasing seed varieties that are resistant. Cucumber beetles and army worms are both chewers that will leave holes in the leaves and vines, and don't be surprised if aphids stop by too.

HARVEST: Peas mature from the bottom of the plant up. When picking peas, hold the vine with one hand and gently pull the pod with the other so you don't damage the plant. Pick often, as that will encourage more production.

Shelling peas are ready when the pods become rounded and bright green. They will taste sweet; pick and eat them right away to enjoy that sweet-ness—it goes away in a few hours as the sugars turn to starch. Once the pod is a dull green, the peas are overripe. Snow peas are ready when the pods are bright green, flat, and easily bent. Snap peas are ready when they snap as you bend them and the peas in the pod are just beginning to show.

After harvest, leave the roots of your pea plants in the soil. They can stay all winter and you can till them in next spring; pea roots contain nitrogen and will nourish the soil.

STORAGE: Peas are best steamed right after pick-ing. If you have a bumper crop, blanch them, cool them in an ice bath, dry, and place in freezer bags, then freeze.

Spraying your plants regularly with **insecticidal soap** can help prevent and treat many bug infestations. This safe product prevents and eliminates small, soft-bodied insects such as aphids, whiteflies, spider mites, and mealy bugs. You can buy it or even make your own. (See page 135 in chapter 7 for more.)

Peach and Nectarine

WHAT IT IS: Fruit tree, perennial (zones 5–8)

HOW HARD TO GROW: Easy to moderate

LIGHT NEEDS: Full sun

SOIL NEEDS: Well drained, pH 6.5

WATERING NEEDS: Deep and frequent in spring

DIMENSIONS: Peach height: standard 8 m (25 feet); dwarf 2.5–3 m (8–10 feet). Nectarine height: standard 9 m (30 feet); dwarf 2.5–3.5 m (8–12 feet).

HOW FAR APART TO PLANT: Peach: standard 3.5–6 m (12–20 feet); dwarf 2–3 m (7–10 feet). Nectarine: standard 4–5 m (13–16 feet); dwarf: 3–3.5 m (10–12 feet)

CONTAINER SIZE: Minimum depth: 60 cm (24 inches); diameter: 60 cm

HOW MANY TO PLANT: Yields 50–150 per tree

WHEN TO SOW INDOORS: n/a

WHEN TO PLANT OUTDOORS: Spring

READY TO EAT: Fruit in third or fourth season, late summer

MULTI CROPPING: No, single crop

GROWS WELL WITH: Basil, onion, garlic, tansy

DO NOT PLANT WITH: Black walnut, hawthorn, pine

FOOD TO GROW VARIETIES: Peach: 'Reliance', 'Contender', 'Red Haven', 'Intrepid'. Peach dwarf: 'Empress Peach'. Nectarine: 'Harflame', 'Harblaze', 'Fantasia'. Nectarine dwarf: 'Golden Prolific'

WHY TO GROW: Everyone loves the sweetness of a summer peach or nectarine (this less fuzzy fruit is, in fact, a naturally occurring mutation of the peach). But can we really grow our own? Southern Ontario and parts of British Columbia are great for raising these fruits, but in any zone below 5 it's pretty risky. Peaches and nectarines require a long, warm growing season. Choose the right variety—the ones I list at left are cold hardy and self-pollinating. Or consider a dwarf variety and grow it in a container. Even dwarf trees need to be pruned back to keep the size down, but they can produce an abundance of fruit and will endure the winter in your garage or shed.

PLANTING: Choose a sunny spot in your garden with good drainage, preferably one with eastern exposure that warms up earlier in the spring and is less likely to be zapped by a late frost. Plant your peach or nectarine tree in early spring as soon as the ground can be worked. Prepare the soil by amending it with compost, manure, or peat moss to a depth of about 1 m (3 feet). Dig a hole a few inches larger than the root ball. Before placing the root in the hole, score around the root with a knife. Six weeks after you plant, feed your tree with a balanced fertilizer (10-10-10). If you're putting a dwarf tree in a container, be sure there is adequate drainage. Drill holes in the base or line the bottom of the container with gravel or empty water bottles (do both if you want really great drainage). Don't overfill the pot with soil—leave some space at the top for water. If you plan on moving the container around your yard to catch the sun and for winter storage, consider one with wheels on the bottom—this tree will become quite heavy as it grows.

GROWING: Water the plant deeply and frequently while it's blooming and producing fruit, and water consistently through the rest of the season. Use sawdust or wood chips to mulch around the base of the tree to keep weeds out and moisture in. In your peach tree's second year, fertilize in spring and midsummer, and after that just every spring. If you fertilize in late summer, the new root growth could be damaged by winter. After planting, you should prune down to a height of 75 cm (30 inches), and then prune a one-year-old plant down to 90 cm (36 inches). Reduce a two-year-old tree to four well-spaced branches, and shorten each by a third. You want the branches of your mature tree well spaced for air circulation and sturdy enough to support fruit. As the tree matures, prune in early spring, removing branches that grow inward and any small shoots (suckers) along the trunk and at the base of the plant. Once you get fruit in the spring, thin it so each small peach is 15–20 cm (6–8 inches) apart. Keep the area around the tree free of debris and weeds, and remove any rotted fruits—they are a breeding ground for bugs and disease.

CHALLENGES: In Canada, our climate puts us at a disadvantage. Peaches and nectarines like a long, warm growing season, and harsh temperature can damage the tree severely. You will need to protect your tree from cold winters by mulching. The blossoms can get damaged by unexpected frosts in spring. Be sure your variety will bloom when you're free and clear of frost. It helps to plant in a toasty part of your yard. In late winter or early spring, spray your tree with a dormant oil to kill overwintering insects such as scale. Mites and aphids can be washed away with a hard blast from the hose. Spraying with lime sulphur can protect from bacterial diseases like canker, brown rot, and leaf spot. Prevent winter damage from rodents gnawing on the tender bark of young trees by wrapping the base of the tree with plastic guards.

HARVESTING: After three or four years, your tree will bear fruit. It's time to harvest when they turn from green to golden and are slightly soft to the touch. Let them ripen on the tree to become very sweet. To pick, just gently twist the ripe fruit from the tree.

STORAGE: You can store peaches and nectarines on the counter until they are fully ripe. They ripen extra fast placed in a brown paper bag or beside some bananas. Then move them to the fridge, placed in paper or plastic bags with holes cut in them. If you have too much fruit to deal with (lucky you), wash, peel, and slice it, then arrange the slices in a single layer on a tray lines with parchment paper and place in the freezer. Once frozen, transfer the fruit to freezer bags. It will last for at least one year and will be good for smoothies and baking.

Pear

WHAT IT IS: Fruit tree, perennial (zones 3–10)

HOW HARD TO GROW: Easy

LIGHT NEEDS: Full sun

SOIL NEEDS: Well drained, pH 6.0–6.5

WATERING NEEDS: Deep and frequent in spring

DIMENSIONS: Pear height: standard 8 m (25 feet); semi-dwarf 3.5–4.5 m (12–15 feet); dwarf 1.5–2 m (5–6 feet)

HOW FAR APART TO PLANT: Standard 7.5 (25 feet); semi-dwarf 3.5–4.5 m (12–15 feet); dwarf 3 m (10 feet)

CONTAINER SIZE: Not recommended for container growing

HOW MANY TO PLANT: Yields 100–300 per plant

WHEN TO SOW INDOORS: n/a

WHEN TO PLANT OUTDOORS: Spring

READY TO EAT: Summer to late summer

GROWS WELL WITH: Nasturtium, dill, clover

DO NOT PLANT WITH: Legumes

FOOD TO GROW VARIETIES: Zone 5: 'Anjou', 'Bartlett', 'Bosc'. Zone 4: 'Clapp's Favorite', 'Conference'. Zone 3: 'Flemish Beauty', 'Summercrisp'. Choose dwarf or semi-dwarf varieties: 'Bartlett', 'Bosc', 'Comice', 'Kieffer'

WHY TO GROW: For anyone wanting to start growing fruit, the pear is a good choice. Pear trees offer beautiful blossoms in spring, a wonderful canopy of foliage in summer, and a harvest of fruit to follow. They tolerate our winters and will grow for up to 50 years. Like other fruit trees, you can grow a dwarf or a semi-dwarf in a container as well. No need to bring a pear tree in a pot inside over the winter; just move it to a protected area out of harsh winds. Note that many popular varieties come in smaller versions, so you can pick the pears you like in the tree size you need.

PLANTING: Pear trees are not self-pollinating, so you have to purchase two different varieties. Unless your neighbour has a pear tree, you need to have enough space for two in an area receiving full sun for at least six hours per day.

Prepare the soil by digging in some compost, peat, or manure. Dig a hole a few inches larger than the root ball. To untangle any circling roots, carefully score the roots to loosen them. Place the root in the hole, refill the hole with soil, and tamp down with your feet. Ideally, the covered-up planting hole will be a bit below soil level, as this leaves a little space for water to collect. Place a stake close to the tree and tie it to the trunk. It is also a good idea to add a tree guard to protect the tender bark from rodents. Water the tree well. Mulch around the base to retain moisture and keep weed growth under control.

GROWING: Your tree should not require fertilizer for the first few years if it was planted in good soil. Once it begins producing, start giving it a balanced fertilizer (10-10-10) in early spring each year. If the leaves turn yellow, feed it more. Prune your tree after planting. Cut a one-year-old tree back to 90 cm (36 inches) in total height, and reduce a two-year-old tree to four well-spaced branches and shorten each by a third. You want good air circulation and a tree strong enough to support fruit. As the tree matures, prune in early spring every year, removing branches that grow inward and any small shoots (called "suckers") that grow along the trunk and at the base of the tree. Thin the fruit when it begins to appear; keep pears about 20 cm (8 inches) apart so they don't touch when mature.

CHALLENGES: Pear psylla is the biggest threat to pear trees. It is an overwintering insect that destroys the foliage and fruit; sticky residue and black marks on foliage and fruit are signs of infestation. Dormant oil sprayed before the buds open can help prevent it. Mites can also be controlled by dormant oil spray. Fire blight is a bacterial disease that turns the foliage red first, then brown on the branch. It can be controlled by pruning any infected branches and destroying them before the disease spreads to other plants.

HARVESTING: Unlike other fruits, pears ripen from the inside out, so when they finally appear ripe, they are already too far gone. To tell if your pear is ready to come off the tree, hold a piece of fruit in your hand and lift it until it is in a horizontal position. If it easily comes off the tree, it's time. Your harvested pears will be too hard to eat, so let them ripen on your counter.

STORAGE: Store your pre-ripened pears in the fridge for as long as a few weeks. Before eating, pull them out of the fridge and store at room temperature until ripe. You can also cold store them in a dark area with a temperature of 4°C (38°F) for a couple of months. Canning is another option for storing an abundant crop.

As with apple trees, you can buy pear trees that have been grafted to grow several delicious varieties at once.

Pepper

WHAT IT IS: Fruit, perennial grown as an annual

HOW HARD TO GROW: Moderate

LIGHT NEEDS: Full sun

SOIL NEEDS: Rich, well drained, pH 5.5–6.8

WATERING NEEDS: Deeply and infrequently

DIMENSIONS: Height: 45–60 cm (1.5–2 feet); width: 60 cm (2 feet)

HOW FAR APART TO PLANT: 45–60 cm (1.5–2 feet); rows: 60–90 cm (2–3 feet)

CONTAINER SIZE: Minimum depth: 30–45 cm (12–18 inches); diameter: 30–40 cm (12–16 inches)

HOW MANY TO PLANT: 2–3 plants per person

WHEN TO SOW INDOORS: Not recommended

WHEN TO PLANT OUTDOORS: 2 weeks after last frost when soil is 18°C (65°F)

READY TO EAT: 50–100 days

MULTI CROPPING: No, single crop

GROWS WELL WITH: Tomato, eggplant, basil, carrot, garlic, onion, parsley, radish

DO NOT PLANT WITH: Fennel, kohlrabi

FOOD TO GROW VARIETIES: Sweet bell: 'California Wonder' (green), 'Bell Boy' (green), 'Golden Bell' (yellow), 'Chesapeake' (red), 'Red Star' (red). Sweet: 'Ethem Sweet Banana', 'Nardello', 'Naples Shepherd Pepper', 'Early Pimento', 'Biscayne Cubanelle'. Hot: 'Cayenne Long Slim', 'Ring of Fire Cayenne', 'Jalapeno Major League', Super Hungarian Hot', 'Sweet Heat', 'Ghost Chili'

WHY TO GROW: Peppers have been spicing up gardens around the world for centuries. A tender perennial grown as an annual in Canada, the pepper is part of the nightshade family, which includes tomatoes, potatoes, and eggplants. Although thought of as a vegetable, it is actually a fruit, because the plant grows from seed and produces flowers. There are hundreds of varieties of peppers, which come in all colours, shapes, and sizes: red, green, yellow, orange—even brown, white, and purple. Some peppers are loaded with capsaicin, a chemical that causes a burning sensation when it comes into contact with our skin—these varieties are better known as hot peppers, or chili peppers. Canadian gardeners love to grow peppers, but they can be challenging here. They take a very long time to mature, and some growers end up facing fall frost before they've got their harvest in.

PLANTING: Peppers like it hot and need protection from frost and wind, so choose your garden plot and situate your container accordingly. Prepare your soil with some compost in the early spring and then wait for the soil to warm up. Plant from purchased seedlings—peppers are very difficult to seed-start and take too long to mature to direct-sow. I always look for the biggest plants available to ensure I get peppers in our short growing season.

GROWING: Water your peppers deeply and infrequently, never allowing the plants to dry out. Water the roots only; keep the foliage dry. Surround your plants with mulch to maintain warm soil temperatures, help retain moisture, and prevent soil from splashing on the foliage during intense rains; this will reduce the risk of disease. Four weeks after you plant, side-dress in-ground peppers with a layer of composted manure, or fertilize container peppers with a general purpose (20-20-20) or fish emulsion fertilizer.

CHALLENGES: Peppers love sun and heat, and these tender plants need protection from cold wind, frosty nights, and thunderstorms. Luckily, they're not a huge draw for bugs, but peppers can sometimes attract aphids and whiteflies. Cutworms threaten younger plants, while hornworms damage the foliage of more mature pepper plants—both can be picked off by hand. Excessive moisture can lead to fungal diseases on peppers. If you have yellowing leaves that drop and poor growth, you've got fungus. Most newer varieties of peppers are now disease resistant, so you should not have many problems.

HARVESTING: Pick your peppers in the summer before the risk of frost looms. Let the fruit reach full size and colour. Remove peppers by twisting and plucking or cutting them from the stem.

STORAGE: Fresh peppers can last for weeks in the refrigerator and will even keep for up to a week at room temperature when left out of direct light and kept dry. Peppers lose flavour when frozen, but roasting them prior to freezing will help.

Peppers can be sun-dried, air-dried, baked, or dehydrated and stored in airtight containers for months. To sun-dry hot peppers, wash first and dry with a paper towel. Then use a sewing needle and thread to string 20 to 30 of them together by pushing the needle through their stems and afterward tying the ends of the thread together. Hang indoors in direct sunlight until dry. Remove any peppers that turn black.

Plum

WHAT IT IS: Fruit tree, perennial (zone 2)

HOW HARD TO GROW: Easy

LIGHT NEEDS: Full sun

SOIL NEEDS: Fertile, well drained, pH 5.5–6.5

WATERING NEEDS: Deep and frequent in spring

DIMENSIONS: Height: 4–5 m (13–16 feet);
width: 4 m (13 feet)

HOW FAR APART TO PLANT: 3.5–4.5 m (12–15 feet)

CONTAINER SIZE: Minimum depth: 60 cm (24 inches);
same in diameter

HOW MANY TO PLANT: Yields 200–500 per tree

WHEN TO SOW INDOORS: n/a

WHEN TO PLANT: Spring

MULTI CROPPING: No, single crop

READY TO EAT: Fruit in the fourth season, summer

GROWS WELL WITH: Nasturtium, rosemary, caraway,
thyme, catnip (plant catnip in pots)

DO NOT PLANT WITH: Cucumber

FOOD TO GROW VARIETIES: European: 'Valor', 'Italian',
'Mount Royal', 'Reine Claude'. Japanese: 'Early Golden',
'Tora, Shiro', 'Tecumseh'. Canadian cherry plums:
'Convoy', 'Manor'

WHY TO GROW: No plum in your grocery store—plums there are all picked before they are fully ripened—can compare with the flavour of a tree-ripened plum. A plum tree is a good choice as a first fruit tree, as they are pretty adaptable to most conditions. They don't get too big and they offer you scented white blossoms in the spring. You can even grow one in a container if you are prepared to move it to a garage or shed in the winter months.

There are several types of plums: Japanese are large, rounded, and very juicy; Europeans are oval, almost heart shaped, and very sweet; and native varieties tend to be smaller but heartier. All types come in many colours and varieties. Native varieties of plums are the best for the Canadian winter; they will actually regrow from the ground after a harsh winter. Unfortunately, they do not self-pollinate, so you will have to purchase two types of Canadian plums—do the same with Japanese.

PLANTING: Find a spot in your garden with full sun and good drainage—avoid a spot exposed to wind and where moisture may linger. Prepare the soil by digging in compost, manure, or peat moss. Dig a hole slightly bigger than the root ball, replace the soil around the root, and press down with your foot, leaving an indentation to catch water. After planting, water well. Stake the tree, mulch it, and wrap a tree guard around the base. For container planting, go for a sizable container, preferably one with wheels for moving the plant for winter storage.

GROWING: Prune after planting. Take a one-year-old tree to 90 cm (36 inches) in total height, and reduce a two-year-old tree to four well-spaced branches and shorten each by a third. As the tree matures, prune in early spring, removing branches that grow inward and any small shoots along the trunk and at the base of the plant. You will not have to fertilize a new planting, but when your tree begins to bear fruit in year four, apply a balanced fertilizer (10-10-10) or manure in early spring. Thin the plums when they begin to form so they won't touch when they ripen.

Young fruit trees need a little help staying upright. **Stake** them against the prevailing winds, or take two stakes and attach the tree to the stake using a material that won't cut into the tender bark. Stake for two to three years.

CHALLENGES: As with all fruit trees in our climate, the blooms of plum trees can be killed by an early frost, thereby affecting the production of fruit. There is not much you can do about an unexpected late-spring frost—just be sure you choose a variety that's ideal for your zone. Diseases that may impact plum trees include silver leaf, honey fungus, bacterial canker, plum aphids, and moths.

HARVESTING: Leave the plums on the trees until they are completely ripe; they will be brightly coloured and slightly soft to touch. Plums should come off the tree quite easily with a gentle twist.

STORAGE: Plums will keep in the refrigerator for up to two weeks.

Potato

WHAT IT IS: Root vegetable, annual

HOW HARD TO GROW: Moderate

LIGHT NEEDS: Full sun

SOIL NEEDS: Loose, fertile, well drained, pH 5.3–6.0

WATERING NEEDS: Average to moist

DIMENSIONS: Height: 30–45 cm (12–18 inches); width: 30–60 cm (12–24 inches)

HOW FAR APART TO PLANT: 30–45 cm (12–18 inches)

CONTAINER SIZE: Minimum depth: 40–60 cm (18–24 inches); diameter: 25 cm+ (10 inches+)

HOW MANY TO PLANT: One plant yields 1–2 kg (3–5 pounds)

WHEN TO SOW INDOORS: n/a

WHEN TO PLANT OUTDOORS: 2–4 weeks before last frost

READY TO EAT: Early crop: 65 days; mid-season crop: 75–80 days; late crop: 90+ days

MULTI CROPPING: No, single crop

GROWS WELL WITH: Bean, broccoli, Brussels sprout, cabbage, cauliflower, Chinese cabbage, corn, eggplant, horseradish, kale, kohlrabi, pea

DO NOT PLANT WITH: Pumpkin, squash, onion, cucumber, sunflower, tomato, raspberry

FOOD TO GROW VARIETIES: 'Yukon Gold', 'All Blue', 'French Fingerling', 'Red Pontiac', 'Russet'

WHY TO GROW: If you grow potatoes, you will use them in the kitchen, no worries there. From mashed potatoes to french fries, everyone loves a spud! While potato plants can give you great yields, they are not the lowest-maintenance plant to grow. They really struggle with both bugs and disease. Remember the Great Famine in Ireland? Many people starved because of potato blight. If you can deal with the unique growing habits of potatoes and keep your eye on the challenges, you can be okay. Potatoes like a lot of loose, acidic soil to grow in, but they don't seem to mind when I play around with them and grow them in a potato bag or recycling bin of potting mix.

PLANTING: Get your soil ready. You can mix raw manure in the fall so it can age over the winter, or just prepare your beds a few weeks before the last frost with some compost or composted manure. The best and easiest way to grow this tuber is from seed potatoes purchased at a garden centre. Do not use grocery store potatoes, as they are often sprayed with chemicals to prevent sprouting and increase shelf life. Plant small seed potatoes (less than 6 cm/2.5 inches long) directly and cut larger ones into cubes, making sure each cube has two eyes. After cutting, dry your potato cubes over-night. Next, spread seed potatoes out in the sun for a few days. Then plant them. In heavier clay soils, plant the seed potatoes 10 cm (4 inches) deep. In lighter loamy or sandy soils, go a bit deeper to 15–20 cm (6–8 inches). Cover with about 8 cm (3 inches) of soil.

GROWING: Keep your newly planted potatoes good and moist until the sprouts push above the ground, giving them about 6 cm (2 inches) of water per week, including rain. Use a soaker hose so you don't get leaves and stems wet. Once the plants mature at the end of the season and the skins start to brown, slow down on the water. As the tubers develop at the base of the plant, mound about 5 cm (2 inches) of soil over them, repeating each week. You don't want the tubers exposed to the sun, so this task will be ongoing until harvest. Feed your growing potatoes with a fertilizer higher in phosphorus and potassium to encourage tuber growth, not the growth of the upper greens. Container plants should thrive, but they definitely need that regular feeding.

CHALLENGES: Potatoes like acidic soil, and when things become too alkaline, they are at risk for disease. Also, if the tubers are exposed to the sun, their skin turns green and they become inedible. Keep mounding that soil over them each and every week. Bugs that target potatoes include potato beetles, aphids, flea beetles, white grubs, and corn borers. Diseases include scab, early and late blight, white and grey mould, black leg, bacterial wilt, rust, fusarium, powdery mildew, stem and root rot, mosaic virus, and leaf roll virus. Most can be prevented by overall good garden care: weeding, watering the roots, and being tidy.

HARVESTING: New potatoes can be harvested around the same time the plants begin to flower, usually in August. Start harvesting the smaller potatoes as needed, making sure to leave others in the ground for later harvest. Dig up the remaining tubers after the tops have begun to wilt, and before the first hard frost—they can endure light frosts.

STORAGE: Brush off any dirt—do not wash your potatoes—before storage. Store them unwashed in a cool, dark place, for two weeks to allow the skins to cure. Then, for longer-term storage, dust off any dirt and put your spuds into bins, baskets, or boxes with good ventilation (perforated sides are great). Cover your potatoes with newspaper and put them in a cool, dry space such as a root cellar or garage where the temperature is around 5° C (41°F). Check them often and discard any that have begun to rot; the remaining tubers should keep for two months.

Seed potatoes (top, opposite) can be grown in ground or in special growing bags (left). When the greens start to bend and wilt (bottom, opposite) your potatoes are ready to pick.

Pumpkin

WHAT IT IS: Vegetable, annual

HOW HARD TO GROW: Easy

LIGHT NEEDS: Full sun to part shade

SOIL NEEDS: Rich in organic matter, pH 6.0–6.8

WATERING NEEDS: Can withstand short periods of dry; check soil moisture and water as required

DIMENSIONS: Height: 30–45 cm (12–18 inches); width: 9 m+ (30 feet+)

HOW FAR APART TO PLANT: Traditional: 60 cm (2 feet); miniature: 1.5 m (5 feet)

CONTAINER SIZE: Container planting not recommended

HOW MANY TO PLANT: Yields 3–5 per plant

WHEN TO SOW INDOORS: 4 weeks before last frost

WHEN TO PLANT OUTDOORS: After last frost when soil is 21°C (70°F)

READY TO EAT: 95–120 days

MULTI CROPPING: No, single crop

GROWS WELL WITH: Corn, squash

DO NOT PLANT WITH: Potato

FOOD TO GROW VARIETIES: Large: 'Dill's Atlantic Giant'. Medium: 'Jack O' Lantern', 'Magic Lantern'. White: 'New Moon'. Pie: 'Small Sugar'

WHY TO GROW: If you have a lot of space, growing your own pumpkin can be a lot of fun. There are more than 50 varieties and they come in light and dark orange, white, yellow, even bluish green. Pumpkins are actually a winter squash because they can be stored over the winter, whereas summer squash are eaten when they are young and freshly harvested. (See more about the difference under Squash on page 367.) Bush, semi-bush, and miniature pumpkin types do not grow large vines like the heirloom varieties. Their smaller size makes them sweeter and ideal for baking and cooking. For a bit of fun, you can carefully carve a name or message into the pumpkin when it is small and the skin is soft. As the pumpkin grows, the carving will grow with it. When it is ready for harvest you will have your own personally branded pumpkin. To grow a giant pumpkin, which is something of an art form, you have to use a giant variety. 'Dill's Atlantic Giant' gets to thousands of pounds, while 'Big Max' only grows to a hundred. These big beasts need lots of feeding and water, and they're pretty hard to get off the vine and move too.

PLANTING: Choose a hill for your pumpkins if you have a wet yard. If you are in a dryer area, do the opposite and plant them in a slight depression so they can catch more water. Pumpkin seeds can be started indoors, but sowing directly outside is usually the best approach. Prepare the planting bed with a thick layer of compost mixed well into the soil and spread out over the growing area; pumpkins are hungry and need lots of nutrition to grow. Mulch the bed with straw to conserve moisture. These vegetables grow so large I don't think a container is a good idea.

GROWING: To produce fruit, your pumpkins need pollination. They have both female and male flowers; the males will bloom first and the females will later, and only for a day. If you can't attract bees, you can hand-pollinate with a cotton swab. Once your pumpkins are growing—their vines will grow vigorously and wander all over your yard—and a few fruits have started to form, prune off any new flowers or vines so the plant's energy can be directed to growing the existing pumpkins. Be careful about watering—too much can lead to disease and rot. Most leaves will wilt in the afternoon in the heat, but only if they're still looking sad in the morning do they need water. When you do add water, be careful to not get any on the leaves. Side-dress every month with rich compost. As the pumpkins start to ripen, ease off on watering. Carefully slip a piece of cardboard or a few pieces of newspaper under the pumpkins to prevent them from rotting on the moist ground. Prune off any leaves that shade the fruit, so they can get some sunshine while they ripen.

CHALLENGES: You need a *lot* of space with pumpkins. They can attract whiteflies, aphids, earwigs, cucumber beetles, mice, squash bugs, squash vine borers, and stem borers. Pumpkins are prone to powdery mildew, and sometimes downy mildew, bacterial wilt, and the fungal disease anthracnose. It starts as yellow or brown spots on leaves, and can expand and impact the fruit. It can be treated with a fungicide.

HARVESTING: It's time to harvest your pumpkins when they have turned their end colour (orange is most common) and the skin/shell has hardened. The vine will typically start to die back slightly when the pumpkins are ready. To harvest, use a sharp knife to cut as much of the stem off the vine as possible.

STORAGE: Leave pumpkins in the sun for up to two weeks to harden before storing, but take inside on cool fall nights so they're not subjected to frost. After, store in a cool, dry place and make sure they are not leaning against anything or touching one another. They'll keep for months. Keep the stem intact to prevent it rotting down into the fruit.

Radish

WHAT IT IS: Vegetable, annual

HOW HARD TO GROW: Easy

LIGHT NEEDS: Full sun to part shade

SOIL NEEDS: Average fertility, well drained, pH 5.8–7.0

WATERING NEEDS: Consistent moisture, no drying or soaking

DIMENSIONS: Height: 15–20 cm (6–8 inches); width: 10–15 cm (4–6 inches)

HOW FAR APART TO PLANT: 8–10 cm (3–4 inches)

CONTAINER SIZE: Minimum depth: 15 cm (6 inches)

HOW MANY TO PLANT: 10 plants per person

WHEN TO SOW INDOORS: Not recommended

WHEN TO PLANT OUTDOORS: 4–6 weeks before last frost

READY TO EAT: 3–4 weeks for spring varieties; 6–8 weeks for summer varieties; 8–10 weeks for winter varieties

GROWS WELL WITH: Carrot, melon, basil, parsley, cucumber, beet, bush bean, pole bean, potato, chervil, lettuce, pea, spinach, squash, onion, cilantro

DO NOT PLANT WITH: Hyssop, cauliflower, cabbage, turnip, Brussels sprout

FOOD TO GROW VARIETIES: Spring: 'Champion', 'Fireball', 'Pearl' (white). Winter: 'Daikon' (long white root), 'Spanish' (black)

WHY TO GROW: Radishes are one of the easiest plants to grow in your vegetable garden. They can be planted early in the season, as soon as the ground thaws, and they mature quickly, so you won't have to wait until the end of summer to enjoy your harvest. This makes them a great crop to grow with kids impatient to see results! The radish gets even better: It keeps insects busy and away from other crops (radishes are not bothered by light munching). They are used to lure flea beetles from broccoli and leaf miners from spinach. They also break up the soil for weaker root vegetables such as carrots, and they take up very little room, so they can be planted close to crops that mature slowly. On top of all those great attributes, their seeds can stay viable for up to five years, so old, forgotten seeds will still perform for you. Radishes really are the workhorses of the vegetable garden.

All you really need to do is decide which ones to grow. Basically, there are spring and winter types. Spring radishes are round or cylindrical and grow to maturity in cool spring weather in just a month. Late-maturing spring radishes (which are also considered a summer type) take a little longer to grow— as long as two months—and won't bolt in the heat like the regular spring type. Winter radishes take up to two months to be ready to eat, but they can withstand the heat (they'll actually bolt if left for a long time in the cold). These cylindrical vegetables grow up to 45 cm (18 inches) long and can weigh 2.5 kg (6 pounds).

PLANTING: Prepare your plot: Radishes like well-drained soil without too much in the way of nutrients. They're not fond of dry, sandy soils or mucky, rich soils. Root maggots are a problem, so amend your soil with a little bit of wood ash, which turns them off. As soon as the ground has thawed, sow your seeds about 3 cm (1 inch) deep and 4 to 6 cm (about 2 inches) apart. To make your life a whole lot easier, use seed tape and avoid fumbling with these tiny seeds! They are quick to germinate and will start growing in under six days. Once they emerge, thin them to 8 to 10 cm (3 to 4 inches). Those thinned plants will be great in salads. Plant a few rounds of radishes two weeks apart so you have an ongoing harvest.

It feels painful to pull healthy sprouts, but you must thin radish seedlines for success!

GROWING: Radishes are really easy to grow, but they are particular about moisture. Don't waterlog them or let them totally dry out. That goes double for your container radishes, as soilless mix does not hold moisture well.

CHALLENGES: Radishes mature so fast you can miss the harvest. Keep an eye on them so they don't get overripe—they get tough and taste overly spicy when they've gone too far. Overcrowding or lack of water can lead to misshapen radishes, and too much heat (for spring types) can lead to bolting. Bugs that like radishes include flea beetles, cabbage maggots, and rot maggots. Don't worry if your radishes get eaten by aphids; this vegetable can endure it and keep the pest from other plants. Radishes are relatively disease-free, but black root, leaf spot, and downy mildew can sometimes strike when growing conditions are not ideal.

HARVESTING: Know the maturity date of your radishes and get them out of the ground on time. They're ready to pluck when there are roots growing from the radish and when the tops are 3 cm (1 inch) in diameter for spring and summer varieties. Winter radishes can be grown much larger without sacrificing taste.

STORAGE: Spring varieties will last about two weeks in the fridge. Cut off the leaves immediately after harvest and store in plastic bags in the crisper. When you want to eat them, just scrub them clean—no need to peel. Winter radishes can be stored over the winter in moist sand in a root cellar at temperatures close to freezing. When you're ready to prepare your winter radishes, you must peel them.

Raspberry

WHAT IT IS: Fruit, perennial (zones 2–7)

HOW HARD TO GROW: Easy

LIGHT NEEDS: Full sun to light shade

SOIL NEEDS: Fertile, pH 5.6 to 6.2

WATERING NEEDS: Low to average, 3 cm (1 inch) per week

DIMENSIONS: Height: 100–120 cm (40–48 inches); width: 100–120 cm (40–48 inches)

HOW FAR APART TO PLANT: 1 m (3 feet)

CONTAINER SIZE: Minimum depth: 30 cm (12 inches); diameter: 35–40 cm (14–16 inches)

HOW MANY TO PLANT: 10–20 per person; yields 1 L (1 quart) per plant

WHEN TO SOW INDOORS: n/a

WHEN TO PLANT OUTSIDE: 1 month before last frost; 1 month before first frost for fall planting (fall is best for red raspberries)

READY TO EAT: Fruit in second year; fall and spring for everbearing varieties

MULTI CROPPING: No, single crop

GROWS WELL WITH: Garlic, turnip, tansy

DO NOT PLANT WITH: Tomato, potato, eggplant, strawberry

FOOD TO GROW VARIETIES: Red: 'Boyne', 'Festival', 'Killarney', 'Nova'. Everbearing: 'Heritage'. Black: 'Bristol', 'Jewel'

WHY TO GROW: Did you ever pick wild raspberries along the edges of fields and forests as a kid? This rich, sweet berry is a true sign of summer and nothing beats fresh. Most varieties of raspberries will grow just about anywhere. In fact, these vigorous spreaders may take some effort to tame and keep contained. That's not so fun—even thorn-less raspberries are prickly. FYI, raspberries have perennial root systems, but their shoots or canes are biennial.

First, let's sort out the types. They're organized primarily by colour: red, purple, and black. But note that yellow raspberries are really just a version of red. Purple are a hybrid of red and black. In Canada, you won't do well with black; they don't overwinter here, are not overly productive, and are at risk for local insects and disease. Each of these colours has been made into various cultivars such as thorn-less, those with bigger berries, or those that come in different shades and hues. Red varieties spread the most vigorously via suckers from the main plant and from the roots. They will send suckers out underground and will quickly spread into areas you didn't plan to have them. Purple and black raspberries only send suckers from the main plant.

They're also grouped by when they bloom: everbearing (which produce in the spring and fall) and summer bearing. Summer-bearing raspberries (available for red, black, and purple) will only produce one crop per year—in late spring and into summer—and only on the second-year canes. Some lingo for you: First-year shoots are called "primocane" (first cane) and second-year shoots are called "floricane" (flowering cane). Primocanes have green stems and the floricanes have brown, woodier stems. For everbearing raspberries, primocanes will grow and produce fruit on the fall of the first year, go dormant over the winter, and then produce

a second crop on the same canes in the following spring. Once they have produced their second spring harvest, they will no longer produce fruit and should be pruned off.

PLANTING: Prepare your soil beds by adding compost or well-aged manure a few weeks before planting or in the previous season. Make sure to remove all weeds. You purchase raspberry plants as bare-root canes or with the roots bagged or potted with soil. When planting, bury the canes 4 cm (1.5 inches) deeper than the crown (where the stems meet the roots). Some people advise cutting the canes back after planting to 20 cm (8 inches) above the soil, but most canes come already pruned when you buy them from the garden centre. If you are transplanting a bush, then you need to prune it back this far—but never transplant wild raspberries from natural areas, as they can bring disease and pests into your garden. Mulch the planting area well. Raspberries thrive in containers, but if your winter is extremely cold, your raspberry bush may not survive. Consider burying your container in the ground to help insulate the roots. The best variety for containers is 'Boyne'.

GROWING: Remove any blossoms in the first year of growth; these won't produce fruit, and cutting the blossoms will help the plant focus on getting established. Also cut back any suckers—which are sprouts that pop up around the base of the main plant—as they grow. If you want to grow the raspberries on a trellis or support, get this ready early on before the plant gets too big. Trying to build or install a support around a thick, thorny raspberry bush is not much fun.

In the late winter or early spring, cut back all fruit-bearing canes for summer-bearing raspberries—they're done and won't produce fruit anymore—as well as the canes that have produced their second spring crop for everbearing raspberries, as they are done too. In the spring, regardless of their type, prune back any canes that are weak or were roughed up by winter weather.

CHALLENGES: Like other berries, red raspberries can really spread via their root suckers. Red raspberries need to be pruned carefully or planted in an area that restricts their growth. Varieties with thorny stems make pulling the suckers even more of a challenge. Black raspberries are more susceptible to bugs and disease than are the red, yellow, and purple varieties. Guests that might stop by include cane borers, Japanese beetles, spider mites, fruit worms, birds, rabbits, and deer. You may find other, harmless, insects on the fruit, so inspect or rinse before eating from any of the canes. Diseases common to raspberries include verticillium wilt, leaf and fruit rot, and powdery mildew, many of which can be prevented by watering properly and keeping the patch weeded.

HARVESTING: Raspberries are ready to come off the plant and eat when they can be pulled from their stems with little or no effort. If you have to yank them off, they aren't ripe yet.

STORAGE: Raspberries will stay fresh in the fridge for about five days. Freeze them so they'll last a lot longer; they can be used for smoothies and baking. Spread them in a single layer on a cookie sheet, freeze, then transfer to an airtight container and they'll keep for months.

Rhubarb

WHAT IT IS: Vegetable, perennial (zones 3–8)

HOW HARD TO GROW: Easy

LIGHT NEEDS: Full sun

SOIL NEEDS: Well drained, fertile, pH 5.5–6.5

WATERING NEEDS: Medium

DIMENSIONS: Height: 1 m (3 feet); width: 1.25 m (4 feet)

HOW FAR APART TO PLANT: 60–120 cm (2–4 feet); rows: 1 m (3 feet)

CONTAINER SIZE: Minimum depth: 30 cm (12 inches); diameter: 45 cm (18 inches)

HOW MANY TO PLANT: 1–2 per family of 4

WHEN TO SOW INDOORS: Not recommended

WHEN TO PLANT OUTDOORS: Early spring

READY TO EAT: Harvest starts in second year, spring through summer

MULTI CROPPING: No, single crop

GROWS WELL WITH: Onion, garlic, cabbage, broccoli

DO NOT PLANT WITH: Legumes, any plant it can shade

FOOD TO GROW VARIETIES: 'Canada Red', 'Crimson Red', 'MacDonald', 'Victoria'

WHY TO GROW: Ah, early-summer memories of dipping a stalk of rhubarb into a cupful of sugar before munching it. Our backyard always had a rhubarb plant growing in the back corner. No one gave that plant a lick of attention, yet it always yielded enough for several pies and then produced a funky flower. Rhubarb is a drought-resistant perennial vegetable (even though it is thought of as a fruit) grown from a rhizome that produces green or red celery-like stalks with a large, ribbed leaf. Rhubarb should not be harvested in the first year, but once the plant is established, it has a long harvest period, with new stalks growing where old stalks were picked. One plant can produce for eight to twenty years! Just be warned that the leaves of the rhubarb plant are not edible—they contain oxalic acid and are poisonous.

PLANTING: In early spring, as soon as the soil is workable, choose a sunny location with well-drained soil. Pick a place you're sure about—this is a long-lasting perennial! Work some organic compost into the soil to a deepness of about 24 cm (10 inches). Rhubarb plants are sold as crowns—which is just another name for roots—and they need to get in the ground early, while they are still dormant and the roots have not begun to grow outward. Place your crown in a hole twice its depth and width. Surround the root with a mixture of soil, compost, or peat moss; cover with 5 cm (2 inches) of soil; and tamp down around the plant but leave the soil looser on top of the crown. Water and mulch.

GROWING: In the early years, remove seed stalks when they appear in summer to help the plant conserve energy. I leave seed stalks on mature plants. I find it doesn't seem to cause any harm and I think the spiky rhubarb flowers look cool. After several years, once your rhubarb plant is getting big and threatening to take over a corner of the yard, divide it in the early spring or fall when the weather is cool and the plant is dormant. Dig up the root and cut it with a knife. Each section should have three to five eyes (small growths where leaves emerge). You can replant these sections, give them away, or just throw them out.

CHALLENGES: This is one tough plant that's resistant to insects, disease, and drought. As long as there is full sun and the area is kept free of debris and weeds, you'll have few problems. The only true maintenance rhubarb requires is cutting away and discarding any stalks damaged by frost early in the season. These soft, mushy stalks can cause the poisonous oxalic acid in the leaves to migrate to the stem, making them poisonous as well.

HARVESTING: Remember, don't try to harvest your plant in its first year. Starting in year two, you will know rhubarb is ready for eating when the stalks are about 30 cm (12 inches) long. Pull the stalk very gently off the plant so the whole of the stalk pops out. Discard the leaves onto the compost pile. Don't use any stalks that are soft or mushy. At harvest, never strip the plant completely but leave a few stalks to keep it growing. New stalks will replace the ones you just harvested, and you can expect more rhubarb in eight to ten weeks. At the end of the harvest season, when frost approaches, cut the plant back and remove all plant debris. Cover the crown with mulch containing manure or compost—the rhubarb will be protected from winter weather and the soil will get a light feeding too.

STORAGE: Rhubarb stems will last in the fridge for about five days in a plastic bag. Stewed in sugar water, rhubarb will last up to a week. To freeze it, wash and dry, then cut into 2.5 cm (1 inch) pieces and throw into freezer bags. Alternatively, you can blanch the rhubarb for one minute in boiling water, then immediately immerse in cold water to retain its colour and nutrients. Dust it with sugar, put it in freezer bags, and place in the freezer.

A rhubarb crown.

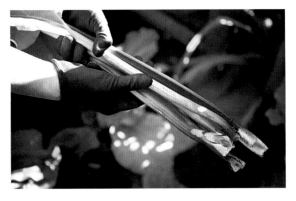

Spinach

WHAT IT IS: Leafy green vegetable, annual

HOW HARD TO GROW: Easy

LIGHT NEEDS: Full sun or light shade

SOIL NEEDS: Fertile, moist, well drained, pH 7.0 or above

WATERING NEEDS: Average

DIMENSIONS: Height: 20–25 cm (8–10 inches); width: 15–20 cm (6–8 inches)

HOW FAR APART TO PLANT: 20 cm (8 inches)

CONTAINER SIZE: Minimum depth: 15 cm (6 inches)

HOW MANY TO PLANT: 15 plants per person

WHEN TO SOW INDOORS: Not recommended

WHEN TO PLANT OUTDOORS: 4–6 weeks before last frost; mid to late summer for fall harvest

READY TO EAT: 35–50 days

MULTI CROPPING: No, single crop

GROWS WELL WITH: Asparagus, Brussels sprout, cabbage, celery, dill, eggplant, lettuce, onions, pea, pepper, radish, strawberry, tomato

DO NOT PLANT WITH: n/a

FOOD TO GROW VARIETIES: 'Renegade', 'Perpetual', 'King of Denmark', 'Long Standing Bloomsdale'

WHY TO GROW: Spinach is one of the healthiest and most versatile greens; you can eat it raw or cooked in a range of dishes. It starts from seeds that are either round and smooth or prickly. The look of the seed often doesn't correspond to the type of spinach you get. Smooth spinach can sometimes grow from prickly seeds, and vice versa—you can only know by reading the seed packet. This cool-loving crop goes into the ground early—farmers often say you plant your spinach when the lilacs get their first leaves—and harvests by summer. Spinach has a shallow root system and does well in very small gardens or containers, and it's quick enough to harvest to get two crops in one season. I love growing spinach in raised beds, as it grows faster in the toasty soil and you can sow and harvest without straining your back.

PLANTING: Spinach grows beautifully from seed right in the ground. You can start seeds indoors or buy seedlings, but spinach roots are very delicate and they do not transplant well. Spinach seeds are finicky, so always buy fresh and don't bother with seed packets left over from last year. Before sowing, soak your seeds overnight in water to speed up germination. In advance, amend your bed with a good layer of compost. If you're planting in containers, use potting soil but feed your plants through the growing season. Sow seeds 1 cm (.5 inch) deep and 2 cm (1 inch) apart. You can also broadcast them over your planting area (see page 98 in chapter 5 for details). Water and mulch. Once your seedlings reach 7 cm (3.5 inches) tall, thin them so neighbouring plants do not touch. If your bed becomes cluttered because you have too many spinach plants later on, thin again, aiming for about 20 cm (8 inches) distance. For a second crop, sow six to eight weeks before the first frost in fall.

GROWING: Spinach plants don't need much care. Consider giving them some light shade in the heat of the summer so they don't bolt. If they seem to be growing a little too slowly or if the leaves are turning light green or yellow—this means they're lacking in nitrogen or iron—give them some all-purpose or nitrogen-rich granular or water-soluble fertilizer to help. Always keep your spinach plants well watered and evenly moist. In just a few weeks, presto—you are ready to harvest.

CHALLENGES: Sometimes spinach seedlings don't emerge because the seeds were sown too shallow. Make sure that your seeds are covered with a good layer of soil at planting. High temperatures or dry conditions can sometimes lead to a drying of the seeds and they may not germinate. Make sure you start your direct seeding in cool weather and keep your seedlings moist. Bugs that like spinach include leaf miners, flea beetles, cutworms, cabbage loopers, snails, and slugs. Diseases common to this green are mildews and anthracnose. Avoid rust disease by watering your beds during the day so they have time to dry by evening, and avoid upsetting rust spores by not working in the garden when it's wet. If the veins in your spinach leaves turn yellow, it means leaf hoppers have infected them with mycoplasma disease. Remove infected plants, try to keep weeds under control, and water the roots only, not the leaves.

HARVESTING: You are ready to harvest your spinach when there are about six big leaves on your plant. Pick as needed and make sure that you take equally from all plants. (No spinach wants to be left out!)

STORAGE: Although you may be tempted to wash your spinach before you store it in the refrigerator, it is best if you don't—moisture during storage can cause rot. Place your spinach in a resealable bag and squeeze out as much air as you can, and your spinach should keep for five days. Don't put your leaves near ethylene-producing fruit (such as bananas and apples), as it will rot quicker. To freeze spinach, blanch it first in boiling water and then cool it in an ice bath. Dry your leaves (maybe use a salad spinner) and place them in freezer bags.

Right: Different varieties of spinach have vastly different looking sprouts. Don't be alarmed if you think you planted spinach and it looks like grass is coming up!

Squash

WHAT IT IS: Fruit, annual

HOW HARD TO GROW: Easy

LIGHT NEEDS: Full sun to light shade

SOIL NEEDS: Fertile, moist, well drained, pH 6.5–7.5 for summer squash, 5.5–7.5 for winter

WATERING NEEDS: Regular

DIMENSIONS: Depends on the variety

HOW FAR APART TO PLANT: 60 cm–3 m (2–10 feet)

CONTAINER SIZE: Minimum depth: 30 cm (12 inches); diameter: 45 cm (18 inches)

HOW MANY TO PLANT: 1 plant per person

WHEN TO SOW INDOORS: 3–4 weeks before last frost

WHEN TO PLANT OUTDOORS: 1 week after last frost and when soil is warm

READY TO EAT: 60 days for summer squash; 75–125 days for winter

MULTI CROPPING: No, single crop

GROWS WELL WITH: Summer savory, basil, catnip, other aromatic herbs

DO NOT PLANT WITH: Potato, fennel

FOOD TO GROW VARIETIES: Summer: 'Peter Pan Hybrid', 'Sunburst', 'Sundance', 'Dixie', 'Early Golden Summer Crookneck'. Winter: 'Acorn Table Queen', 'Buttercup', 'Butternut', 'Spaghetti'

WHY TO GROW: In the garden, squash are always a favourite. Pumpkins and zucchini are types of squash—but there are so many more, including ones you can't even eat but often see decorating the Thanksgiving table (we call those ones "gourds"). They are divided into two main types. Winter squash, which include pumpkins (see more on page 347), are so designated because they can be stored right through the winter. They tend to take a lot of time to mature and are harvested in the fall. These grow off large, sprawling plants and are best grown vertically (see more on vertical gardening on page 70). Summer squash—zucchini falls in this category, it has its own listing on page 383—are easy to grow and should be eaten soon after harvest, as they don't keep for long. They grow in large bushes and don't spread quite as far across your yard. They're the best type for container growing.

PLANTING: Although it's often said you should grow your squash on hills or mounds for better drainage, I don't think this is necessary in well-amended soil. Or grow in a raised bed; such plots heat up quickly in spring and have good drainage. Squash seedlings do not transplant well, so I suggest you direct-sow, which you can do after the risk of frost has passed up until the middle of summer for a fall harvest. Since squash needs a lot of food, before you plant mix a good amount of compost into the soil. Water and mulch. Once your seedlings sprout and develop three to five leaves, thin them out to the distance recommended on the seed packet—it will vary widely depending on the variety you are planting. Don't scrimp on space. Squash needs lots of room to grow, and winter varieties will appreciate something to climb.

GROWING: I told you squash are a fruit: they need pollination. If you don't see any fruit after 45 days, you may have a problem. Hand-pollinate using a cotton swab to collect pollen from the male flowers—male flowers tend to bloom before the female ones and will have longer stems—then take the swab and transfer the pollen to the female flowers. Female blooms will be located toward the centre of the plant, and below their blossom will have the beginnings of a fruit that looks like a little bulge. The female plants are the ones that will develop into the full fruit. Once winter squash varieties start to grow, add a nitrogen-enriched fertilizer.

CHALLENGES: Along with having pollination issues, squash can attract mildew and wilt. Small critters that might stop by include stem borers, whiteflies, squash bugs, squash borers, and vine borers. The worst are cucumber beetles. Destroy them if you see them, as they will increase the risk of wilt. Ants also like damaged squash and mice will get inside the fruit to harvest seeds in the fall. So never leave half-rotted squash lying around—keep that garden tidy. Gophers like this fruit too; line your bed with wire mesh to keep them out.

HARVESTING: With both summer and winter varieties, harvest by cutting the stem with sharp garden shears about 5 cm (2 inches) above the fruit. Don't carry squash by the stems—they may seem tough, but they can be damaged this way and a damaged fruit will rot quickly.

Let a summer squash grow on the vine until it gets to be between 15 and 20 cm (6 to 8 inches) and when the skin can still be easily broken by a thumbnail. The more you pick, the more you will get from the plant. In fact, you will probably have to check on your summer squash plot daily. If you like the blossoms—they are edible—harvest those too, but only the male, as the female will turn into more fruit.

As for a winter squash, let it ripen fully on the vine. Harvest when the rind is hard (a thick skin means it'll store better) and the squash has turned a deep colour—often the vine will begin to die back at this time. Make sure you harvest all your winter squash before the first frost. Again, they may look tough, but even a light frost can damage the fruit.

STORAGE: Your summer squash can go soft if you aren't careful. Either eat a summer squash right away, or place it unwashed in a plastic bag, remove all the air, and store it in the crisper, where it should last two weeks. Winter squash is, of course, meant to be stored all winter, but you need to cure it first. Place the fruits in a full-sun window or a warm spot for 10 to 14 days. Flip occasionally so they cure on all sides. Acorn squash won't store well; don't cure it. Just eat it right away or store it in the fridge like a summer squash.

Strawberry

WHAT IT IS: Fruit, perennial (zones 2–10)

HOW HARD TO GROW: Difficult

LIGHT NEEDS: Full sun

SOIL NEEDS: Moist, slightly acidic, pH 6.0–6.8

WATERING NEEDS: Average, but do not soak

DIMENSIONS: Height: 15–30 cm (6–12 inches); width: 45 cm (18 inches)

HOW FAR APART TO PLANT: 30 cm (12 inches); rows: 1 m (39 inches)

CONTAINER SIZE: Minimum depth: 20 cm (8 inches); diameter: 30–35 cm+ (12–14 inches+)

HOW MANY TO PLANT: 2–4 plants per person

WHEN TO SOW INDOORS: 10–12 weeks before last frost; not recommended

WHEN TO PLANT OUTDOORS: Spring or fall

READY TO EAT: 4–6 weeks after the fruit blossoms

MULTI CROPPING: No, single crop

GROWS WELL WITH: Borage, bush bean, caraway, lupine

DO NOT PLANT WITH: Cabbage, broccoli, Brussels sprout, kale, potato, eggplant, pepper, kohlrabi

FOOD TO GROW VARIETIES: June bearing: 'Cambridge Favourite', 'Veestar', 'Kent', 'Sparkle'. Everbearing: 'Finesse', 'Tribute', 'Tristar'. Alpine (wild): 'Mignonette'

WHY TO GROW: If you're thinking of growing a berry shrub, you probably flipped to Strawberry first in this guide. This delicious fruit commands high prices during the local Canadian harvest—why not skip the middleman and grow your own? There are many different types of strawberries, but the most common are June bearing, which give you a lot of fruit in late spring to midsummer, and everbearing, which offer less fruit but will give you a harvest from late spring to early fall. You are quite welcome to grow your strawberries from seed, but it will take you a year before you get any fruit. Best to just buy some strawberry plants from your garden centre and get a head start on the harvest. Go ahead and plant this perennial in containers—you'll have to overwinter strawberries in the shed or garage, as the roots can be damaged by the cold. This is not a forever perennial; you need to replace your plants every three years, as they stop producing well at that point.

PLANTING: Best to grow from garden centre seedlings; really scrutinize the plants you're buying to be sure they're good and healthy. Improve your soil with some compost. Dig a hole, put the plant in, and surround it firmly with soil. Be sure you do not plant the crown of the plant—this is where the fruit grows from!

GROWING: The biggest trick to growing strawberries is to get the watering right. They like regular moisture but will spoil if you drown them. Always water during the day, as nighttime watering encourages disease. June-bearing varieties will need fertilizer six weeks after planting, and everbearing every month. Choose a fertilizer high in ammonia nitrate for the best results. Once your strawberry shrubs get established, remove the first growth of flowers to help the plant conserve energy. Also remove the runners—the shoots, branches, or twigs coming from the root—to help the plant become strong.

CHALLENGES: These somewhat delicate perennials can be damaged by snow or heavy rain. After a few light frosts but before the temperature dips below −5°C (23°F), cover them with clean straw for some winter protection. Strawberry plants can develop grey mould, red stele, wilt, fungi, leaf spot, blight, and root rot. Bugs such as spider mites, grasshoppers, and earwigs can bother strawberries. Water the roots, not the plant, and always during the day to prevent diseases and bugs. Birds adore the sweet fruit, so you may need to cover your plants with mesh or hang something noisy like a wind chime in the garden to encourage them to fly on.

HARVESTING: Only pick ripe berries—really red ones—from your plant. Do not pull the strawberry to remove it, but instead cut it at the stem. You will be able to harvest strawberries frequently once they start to grow. It is best if you harvest your strawberries in the morning and put them directly in the fridge. After the harvest, tidy up well—rotting fruit attracts pests and disease. Clear dead foliage, apply a slow-release fertilizer, and use mulch.

STORAGE: Eat your harvest right away if you can. Store unwashed berries in the fridge and they'll keep for a few days. Frozen, they'll last for about three months and make a sweet ingredient for smoothies and baking.

Swiss Chard

WHAT IT IS: Leafy green vegetable, annual

HOW HARD TO GROW: Easy

LIGHT NEEDS: Full sun to part sun

SOIL NEEDS: Well drained and fertile, pH 6.0–7.0, best in slightly alkaline soils

WATERING NEEDS: Average, 2.5 cm (1 inch) per week

DIMENSIONS: Height: 30–90 cm (12–36 inches); width: 15–60 cm (6–24 inches)

HOW FAR APART TO PLANT: 30 cm (12 inches); rows: 60 cm (24 inches)

CONTAINER SIZE: Minimum depth: 15 cm (6 inches)

HOW MANY TO PLANT: 2–3 plants per person

WHEN TO SOW INDOORS: 4–6 weeks before last frost

WHEN TO PLANT OUTDOORS: After last frost

READY TO EAT: 28 days

MULTI CROPPING: Yes, multiple harvests from one plant

GROWS WELL WITH: Bean, cabbage family, onion, tomato, root crops, lettuce, radish, celery, mint

DO NOT PLANT WITH: Cucurbit, melon, corn, herbs, potato

FOOD TO GROW VARIETIES: 'Peppermint' (pink and white), 'Rhubarb Chard' (red stems), 'Silverado' (white stems), 'Bright Lights' (multicoloured)

WHY TO GROW: Swiss chard is very easy to grow and one of my favourite recommendations for first-time food growers. This leafy green is pretty enough to grow in ornamental containers for your front walk—I like 'Bright Lights' for that job. The different varieties offer an array of stem colours, but all of them have big, green, nutritious leaves. Swiss chard is more heat tolerant than spinach and can be used as a substitute in most recipes, so give it a try, particularly if you're multi-cropping and need a late-season plant that won't take up a lot of space.

PLANTING: You can plant from garden centre seedlings, but I prefer to direct-sow outside after the risk of frost has passed. The seeds are teeny, so buy seed tape—it's so much easier. First, amend your planting area with 4 to 6 cm (2 inches) of compost. Plant seeds 2 cm (.75 inch) deep and 5 cm (2 inches) apart. When sprouts grow to 4 to 6 cm (2 inches), thin them so the plants are 30 cm (12 inches) apart. The thinned plants are edible and can be used in soups or salads. When your plants reach 15 to 20 cm (6 to 8 inches), fertilize with a high-nitrogen fertilizer. Keep the area weed-free and add mulch. If plants start to fade midsummer, harvest them right away. You can plant a second crop for a late harvest—plant it right in the middle of summer and the seeds should germinate quickly. Swiss chard should thrive in containers big or small. The challenge is to keep them moist and happy. The big leaves of chard act like kites in the wind, so the plants sometimes topple over, container and all, in high winds. Be sure you weight down any light container with a bottom third of rocks or old pot shards—that helps improve drainage too.

GROWING: Chard enjoys rich soils and will benefit from a side dressing with nitrogen-rich amendments like blood meal or composted manure. In containers, I recommend using slow-release all-purpose garden food so your greens get food every time they are watered. That should be often—this vegetable needs a steady supply of water no matter where it's planted, roughly 2.5 cm (1 inch) a week. To reduce weeds and maintain moisture, mulch your Swiss chard well.

CHALLENGES: This leafy green attracts the usual culprits: slugs, leaf miners, caterpillars, aphids, rabbits, and deer. Put up a fence if these bigger critters are often in your neighbourhood—Swiss chard leaves are tasty and critters will take them down. Rarely, you can develop powdery mildew, downy mildew, and root rot, but you should be fine if you water the soil, not the plant, and avoid waterlogging it.

HARVESTING: When your leaves get to 12 to 20 cm (5 to 8 inches) tall, they're ready to harvest. Carefully remove the outer leaves first, and the plant will keep on growing and giving. Leaves can be harvested throughout the summer, and the remaining plant can be cut off at the base before a heavy frost or freeze.

STORAGE: Swiss chard will last for about five days in a plastic, breathable bag in the refrigerator crisper. This green does not freeze well. Best to eat it as you pick it.

Tomato

WHAT IT IS: Fruit, annual

HOW HARD TO GROW: Easy to moderate

LIGHT NEEDS: Full sun

SOIL NEEDS: Well drained, fertile, loam, pH 6.0–7.0

WATERING NEEDS: Frequent

DIMENSIONS: Height: bush 90–150 cm (3–5 feet); vine 150–240 cm (5–8 feet); patio 30–60 cm (1–2 feet); cherry 30–150 cm (1–5 feet). Width: 30–120 cm (1–4 feet)

HOW FAR APART TO PLANT: 60–120 cm (2–4 feet)

CONTAINER: Minimum depth: 40 cm (16 inches); diameter: 40 cm (16 inches)

HOW MANY TO PLANT: 1 plant per person

WHEN TO SOW INDOORS: 6–8 weeks before last frost

WHEN TO PLANT OUTDOORS: After last frost

READY TO EAT: 60–80 days

MULTI CROPPING: No, single crop

GROWS WELL WITH: Chive, nasturtium, basil, carrot, pepper, sage, onion, lettuce, garlic, parsley

DO NOT PLANT WITH: Corn, potato, kohlrabi, apricot, dill, fennel, cabbage, cauliflower, walnut

FOOD TO GROW VARIETIES: Bush: 'Early Girl', 'Roma'. Vine: 'Big Beef', 'Brandywine'. Cherry: 'Sugar Snack', 'Black Cherry', 'Juliet Hybrid', 'Patio'

WHY TO GROW: Tomatoes are, hands down, the most popular backyard crop in the world. They're so versatile—eat them fresh or can them into sauces. For this Canadian boy who grew up in an Italian family, I couldn't imagine a meal without tomatoes. They're not the easiest plant around to grow, but people figure them out! To have more success your first year, start by knowing the types. Bush tomatoes (also called "determinate") don't sprawl, so they're perfect for small spaces or pots. But their fruit ripens all at once. Vine style (called "indeterminate") need space, staking, and some extra time. But the effort is often worth it, as this type produces tomatoes continually from late summer until killing frost in the fall. Cherry tomatoes are beloved by kids and are the perfect starter plant for new gardeners—they're really easy and thrive in containers. Heirloom tomatoes taste amazing. But they can be very challenging for first-time food growers. If you can, choose tomato varieties that are resistant to disease. On the tag or seed packet, look for the letters VFN to indicate your tomatoes will be resistant to verticillium wilt (V), fusarium wilt (F), and root-knot nematodes (N). Tomatoes love heat and sun. If you don't have a spot in your yard or on your patio that gets six hours of direct afternoon light, I would suggest growing something else and buying your tomatoes.

PLANTING: Sow seeds indoors if you like—tomatoes take too long to mature in the ground outside—or simply buy seedlings from your garden centre. They likely have an ample selection. Plant after the last frost or get a jump-start on the season by planting early and being prepared to cover your new seedlings if you get the risk of overnight frost. (See page 122 in chapter 6 for how to protect against frost.) Before planting, remove the lower leaves from the seedling. Then carefully remove the plant from its pot and place the root ball in your planting hole so that the tomato plant is lying sideways, with its foliage hanging out over the side of the hole. Bury the bottom part of the stem, which is the part of the plant where you removed the lower leaves. Be sure all the leaves are above ground level. The buried part of the stem will actually send out roots.

GROWING: Tomatoes cannot be left alone during the growing season. First, they are heavy feeders, and won't produce fruit without lots of nutrients. Organic gardeners must improve the soil heavily before planting and use natural feeders such as compost tea during the growing season. Ideally, use a water-soluble fertilizer of about 15-15-30 composition every two weeks, or a calcium-enriched slow-release fertilizer when you plant. If your garden soil is very rich and was prepared well in advance, you might be able get away without feeding. But in containers it's a total must because potting soil lacks nutrients.

As tomatoes grow, they'll require staking for support, particularly vine varieties. And you must also "sucker" them. Suckers are clusters of leaves in the spot where branches and stems meet. They almost look like little tomatoes growing from the stem. Pinch them off with your fingers—they steal energy from the plant (hence their name).

Once your plant flowers, remove some of them from your plant. You will not have as many fruits, true, but the ones you get will be bigger and healthier. Sometimes just the weight of the fruit can break a branch—thin some out! Note that this fruit needs pollination. If you have no bees, particularly if you are growing on a high-rise balcony, you may need to do the work of bees yourself by using a cotton swab to transfer pollen from bloom to bloom.

When your tomato plants reach a height of 65 to 90 cm (2 to 3 feet), strip the leaves from the bottom 25 cm (10 inches) of the plant. This will reduce disease, as these leaves will be the first to develop fungus, plus they rarely bear fruit and are just using up energy.

Plant tomato seedlings on their side—they'll straighten up (left) and soon need the support of cages (centre). When the plants start to branch out, make sure to pinch off any suckers (right).

CHALLENGES: Water, water, water. Tomato plants need moisture to form fruit; dry weather stresses them out and leads them to drop their fruit and develop blossom-end rot. You should mulch your plants with clean straw to both hold in moisture and reduce weeds, but also to reduce splash back of soil onto the foliage of tomatoes. This can transfer soil-borne pathogens onto tomatoes and increase the risk of disease. Tomatoes are at risk for quite a few conditions, including fusarium wilt. This is a fungal disease that causes yellowing on the bottom of leaves and eventually wilts the entire plant and destroys fruit production. Plants showing any sign of wilt should be removed immediately and thrown out in the garbage, not in the composter. Tomatoes are also at risk for blossom-end rot. Prevent it by adding eggshells to your soil to enrich it with calcium.

Bugs that might infect tomatoes include white-flies, tomato hornworms, beetles, and slugs. Not done yet! Voles and mice love tomatoes. The key to control here is to keep the fruit high above the ground by staking the plant. Try mousetraps too. Raccoons might eat your tomatoes. Good luck controlling them. I say let them have a few.

HARVEST: The best tomatoes are those allowed to ripen on the vine. A ripe tomato is firm and fully coloured. To harvest, grasp the tomato firmly and gently twist it off. If frost is looming, hurry up and harvest as many tomatoes as you can. Take any green ones and place them in a bag with one ripe tomato. It'll release ethylene gas, helping to ripen its neighbours.

STORAGE: Here is a pet peeve of mine: storing tomatoes in the refrigerator. Never do it! You've worked so hard for that homegrown flavour, and placing tomatoes in the refrigerator is a flavour killer. Tomatoes must be stored on the counter out of direct light. Check them often for signs of rot and discard those starting to go. They should keep for about a week. Tomatoes can be frozen directly in plastic freezer bags. It should go without saying that they can well alone or in sauces.

Zucchini

WHAT IT IS: Fruit, annual

HOW HARD TO GROW: Easy

LIGHT NEEDS: Full sun or light shade

SOIL NEEDS: Any soil, but prefers well drained and fertile, pH 6.0–7.5

WATERING NEEDS: Average

DIMENSIONS: Height: 45–60 cm (18–24 inches); width: 60–90 cm (24–36 inches)

HOW FAR APART TO PLANT: 70–90 cm (28–36 inches); rows: 1.5 m (5 feet)

CONTAINER SIZE: Minimum depth: 40 cm (16 inches); diameter: 30–35 cm (12–14 inches)

HOW MANY TO PLANT: 1 plant per 4 people (you get lots!)

WHEN TO SOW INDOORS: 3–4 weeks before last frost

WHEN TO PLANT: 1–2 weeks after last frost

READY TO EAT: 35–55 days

MULTI CROPPING: No, single crop

GROWS WELL WITH: Nasturtium, corn, bean, pea, borage, mint, pumpkin, melon, lovage, marjoram

DO NOT PLANT WITH: Potato

FOOD TO GROW VARIETIES: 'Aristocrat', 'Ambassador', 'Cocozelle', 'Black Zucchini', 'Gold Rush' (yellow)

WHY TO GROW: Zucchini are really just a summer squash (so look to the Squash section on page 367 for more tips) and one of the easiest of their kind to grow—plus, they're a versatile ingredient in the kitchen. They come in dark green, light green, yellow, and striped green. While zucchini do take up a bit of space, they offer up a pretty flower before they sprout fruit, don't need much care, and are, overall, well behaved. Your zucchini can cross-pollinate with other squash—pumpkin, acorn, and crookneck—if they are planted near each other. Cross-pollination is not a big deal unless you plan on saving the seeds from your zucs to grow next year.

PLANTING: You can plant with seedlings—purchased, or seed-started yourself—outside once the ground has toasted up to 21°C (70°F) or direct-sow into a bed improved with compost mixed evenly into the soil. Plant in hills or in rows. Space your rows 1.5 m (5 feet) apart; for hill planting you can place them a bit closer together. If you are direct-sowing, plant three to four seeds per planting area, and when the plants reach 60 to 80 cm (2 to 3 feet) tall, snip off the weakest, leaving one to two plants per area. Don't thin by pulling, as you risk disturbing roots.

GROWING: Zucchini have both male and female flowers. The males will be the first to bloom. They have a longer stem and act as bait for bees, enticing the insect to return later on and pollinate the plant. Female flowers have a bulge at the base of the flower. There is typically a ratio of 3:1 male-to-female flowers, and only the females bear fruit, so don't be discouraged when the majority of flowers on your plant do not turn into zucchini. If the flowers are not pollinated, they will not produce fruit. If you don't have any bees, you may need to hand-pollinate using a cotton swab—but bees do a better job. Weed often around your plants. As your zucchini start to ripen, ease off on watering.

CHALLENGES: Zucchini are not fussy about much, but they do dislike too much water. A rainy year or overwatering with the hose will make the fruits grow too large, and they'll be watery in texture and flavour. The leaves may wilt in the afternoon sun; that's the normal way they cope with the heat. Only water if they stay wilted in the morning. Critters that might visit include aphids, cucumber beetles, spider mites, whiteflies, ants, and mice. Zucchini are at risk for powdery and downy mildews (but note that this plant's leaves naturally have white markings on them that are often mistaken for mildew), bacterial wilt, viral disease, and scab. Keeping the area tidy and free of weeds and rotting fruit, plus watering the soil and not the plant, can prevent a lot of problems in your patch. Mounding soil around the base of the plant but not against the stem will discourage squash borers from laying eggs.

HARVEST: Remove zucchini from the plant by cutting them off with a sharp knife and leaving about 4 to 6 cm (about 2 inches) of stem on the zucchini. They are best harvested when they are around 15 to 20 cm (6 to 8 inches) long. Every variety is different, so check the seed packet or plant tag to find out the mature size. Harvest gently—this fruit bruises easily, which can reduce how long it will store and stay fresh.

STORAGE: A raw, unwashed zucchini will keep for about a week in the fridge in a breathable plastic bag in the crisper drawer. After zucchini are cooked, they only last about two days. You can also cube and freeze them in airtight containers, and they'll keep a few months.

Food to Grow Herb Guide

Herbs are heavenly! Why? They are easy to grow in both gardens and pots, provide a huge amount of harvest for a small footprint, and can be harvested multiple times a year. They are both flavourful and medicinal, and they can make even the most boring meal a culinary delight. But herbs bought in the grocery store cost a lot, and you don't always use the whole bunch in time. Fresh is best—nothing compares with fresh herbs.

Each and every growing season I plant several pots of herbs on our deck right near the barbecue and the kitchen door—my mom grows hers just outside her back door too. I find that when I grow them in a convenient place, I use them more. Only grow what you use in your cooking. At my house, we plant big pots of basil, flat-leaf (Italian) parsley, rosemary, mint, and oregano. This year, for fun, we tried stevia. The bigger the pot the more the harvest and the more forgiving the herbs are if I'm not around to water. Nothing frustrates me more than seeing designer pictures of tiny pots of herbs outdoors on a table—sure, they look pretty, but they will die when they dry out constantly.

Here are some things you need to know about growing herbs:

Light: They love full sun. Parsley and lemon balm will tolerate some shade or indirect light. Plants like cilantro can bolt in the summer heat.

Temperature: Most herbs are pretty delicate, so plant them outside after the threat of frost has passed. Most do best from seedlings. Try basil and dill from seed, but don't bother with most others.

Moisture: Water your herbs regularly but avoid offering them too much. Root rot can be a problem.

Feeding: In the garden, most herbs don't need fertilizing if they're grown in soil rich in organic matter. Container herbs, like all container plants, need regular feedings. A balanced fertilizer on a regular basis (every two weeks), or a slow-release one, should be all you need. If the leaves on your plants start looking washed out or lack in vigour, feed them!

Basil

Air: Don't overcrowd your herbs. This is tempting in a container arrangement meant to be attractive, but cramped plantings foster disease and bugs.

Pests: Watch for slugs and beetles on basil, powdery mildew on bee balm, and rot on rosemary, but that's pretty much it. The strong smell of herbs keeps many pests away—in fact, mint will repel mice. But always be on the lookout for bunnies. I've had my own parsley patch devoured by those furry friends.

Containers: Grow your pots in containers no smaller than 25 cm (10 inches) and go bigger if you can. Give your herbs space—ideally their own pots. Containers need more watering and more feedings, but they're perfect for herbs: You can move them, they rarely develop weeds, and they're just so easy to harvest.

Harvesting: Most herbs keep growing after you pick them. Always leave a third of the plant behind and it should keep giving. Cut your plants just above a set of leaves. Remove the stem and leave behind a sharp, clean cut where a new set of leaves and stem can form.

Storing: After harvesting, you can store your herbs in a cup of cool water on the counter (with stems in the water only, no leaves) or wrap them in paper towel and put them in the fridge. To dry herbs, place on a drying rack or hang in bunches in a dark, dry place with good air circulation, then store them out of direct light.

Frankie's Favourite Herbs

Basil: This is one of the most popular herbs used in the kitchen but can also be frustrating to grow. It's easily damaged by wind or heavy rainfall. It doesn't like getting too dried out, nor does it want too much water—the roots will rot. There are over 100 different varieties, from traditional 'Genovese' (large green leaf); to fancy-foliage 'Purple Ruffles'; to interesting flavours such as 'Lemon', 'Licorice', or even 'Cinnamon'. Locate basil in full sun out of strong winds and always plant well after the threat of frost. Slugs and beetles will snack on basil. Harvest it regularly and you'll just get more.

> **Weeds** aren't just unattractive—they offer a place for bugs and disease to hang out in your garden. So get weeding.

Chives

Chives: This mild herb is so easy to grow. It's a perennial and will bounce back year after year, even in containers. Most varieties produce edible pinkish-purple flowers in late spring that can be added to salads. You can plant either regular chives or garlic chives; both are delicious. This tough little plant rarely needs fertilizer when planted in the garden.

Cilantro/coriander: This flavourful treat starts off great but withers quickly. It's not an herb I recommend for new or easily frustrated gardeners. A short spell of hot, dry conditions and your cilantro will set seed and that's it! In the spring, plant it in full sun, but in the summer consider moving your cilantro pots into indirect light or shade to keep them going. Or plant a spring crop and another in late summer for a fall harvest to take advantage of the cool weather it likes.

Dill: This easy grower is the only herb I recommend growing from seed and seed only. Direct-sow it into the garden two weeks before the last frost date. About 10 days after sowing, you'll start to see small plants. After 20 days, thin them to 15 to 20 cm (6 to 8 inches) apart. For a continuous supply, sow more seeds a few weeks apart. Dill grows well with cabbage or onions, but keep it away from carrots.

Mint: Do not—I repeat, do not—put mint in your garden! (Lemon balm either.) This invasive perennial will take over and soon your entire garden will be mint. Instead, in pots, try out 'Chocolate', 'Peppermint', 'Spearmint', 'Pineapple Mint', 'Apple Mint', 'Grapefruit Mint', and others. Mint will overwinter in a pot and come back the next year.

Coriander

Dill

Mint

Oregano: This perennial herb doubles as a hardy ground cover. Oregano is pretty tough and can go lengthy periods without watering. A good choice for the forgetful starting gardener! Recommended varieties are 'Common Oregano' or 'Greek'.

Parsley: This versatile ingredient is easy to grow and will tolerate some shade. Try either flat-leaf (also called Italian) or curly (also called English)— the former has a more peppery taste. In pots, bigger is always better. Go for 25 cm (10 inches) minimum, and I find it grows best on its own. You can grow parsley from seed, but I recommend purchasing seedlings.

Curly parsley

Oregano

Flat, or Italian parsley

Rosemary: This is an evergreen perennial that grows well in Canadian summers but will only overwinter in places south of our border. It does not like its feet wet and can easily develop rot if you overwater it. Go ahead and take it indoors this winter, but note that it loves humidity, so it may not endure a dry house.

Stevia: The new and hip sugar replacement is actually an herb you can grow. Seriously, it tastes like sugar and you can use it as a sweetener. It's very easy to grow in full sun and does very well in pots.

Thyme: If you're not so great at watering, grow thyme! It puts up with very dry conditions and overall is really easy to grow. This perennial ground cover should come back next year and offer both herbs for your kitchen and a pretty look in your garden.

Rosemary

Stevia

Thyme

What's That? Key Gardening Terms

Forgive us gardeners—we use a lot of lingo. Some of it makes total sense. The rest can come across as gibberish to newcomers to gardening. Here are some terms to help you better understand this book, and food gardening in general:

Annual: A plant that completes its entire life cycle, from seed germination to seedling, full-grown plant, and production of seed, in one season. This term also describes plants that will not survive through our cold Canadian winters. Examples: leaf lettuce, tomatoes, peppers, radishes.

Biennial: A plant that requires two years from seed germination to production of seed to complete its life cycle. Although we harvest beets, cabbage, carrots, and chard annually, they are technically biennials—we just treat them as annuals in food gardens in Canada. If you let them go to seed, they may seed themselves and reappear the following year.

Blanching: Some crops need protection from the sun at the end of their growing period to get the colour and taste we're used to; cover them about two weeks before harvest with cardboard or soil. Examples: asparagus, leeks, endive, escarole.

Bolting: When some plants are stressed by heat or cold, they will sprout a tall flowering stem containing seeds. Food plants like leafy greens do this, and as soon as such plants bolt, the edible part of the plant turns tough and bitter. Unless you plan to collect seeds, you don't want this!

Cultivar: Also known as a variety. This is the name you'll see on the seed packet or plant tag. (Example: 'Early Girl Bush', a type of tomato.) This term can also be used to refer to a plant that has been bred for specific traits such as not being bitter, maturing early, or being resistant to disease.

Deadheading: Removing the spent or finished flowers on annuals and perennials to encourage future buds and extend the blooming season a bit longer. It's also a key part of winter cleanup, as dead plant material is a haven for diseases and bugs.

Dormant spray: Also called "dormant oil." It's a blend of horticultural oil and sulphur that you apply to trees every spring before buds emerge. It helps control diseases and insects that can affect the tree such as scale, mites, and black spot.

Floating row covers: This is a cover for young plants that will prevent pests from laying eggs on them but not block the sun or airflow. Many insects, such as butterflies, are harmless, but their young, once they hatch, will feast on your crops. Use covers purchased at the garden centre, or use a light bedsheet and rig it up to float over your crops without touching them. You often remove covers after a few weeks when hatching season is over and your seedlings need more light to grow.

Fungicide: A chemical-based liquid or powder used to control fungus and disease such as leaf spot and mildew.

Herbicide: A liquid, powder, or granular product made from chemicals used to control weeds. Herbicides can either be selective or non-selective—selective herbicides will not kill certain crops, but non-selective will kill every plant they touch.

Insecticide: A liquid or powdered substance used to kill insects. Look for those with minimal environmental impact—insecticidal soaps, for example.

Miticide: A product, usually in liquid form, used to control or kill mites such as spider mites.

Mulch: A material that you lay over the soil to hold in moisture and prevent weeds from growing. Bark, grass clippings, shredded leaves, straw, and newspaper are typical mulching materials.

N-P-K: The nitrogen (N) to phosphorous (P) to potassium (K) ratio of nutrients in fertilizer. For instance, 20-20-20 indicates 20 per cent nitrogen, 20 per cent phosphorous, and 20 per cent potassium. Think "N-P-K" as meaning "up, down, all-around" to remember which number is which. Nitrogen stimulates green or leafy growth (up), phosphorous promotes flowering and root growth (down), and potassium stimulates the plants' overall health (all-around). These numbers rarely add up to 100 per cent, as other nutrients in fertilizers simply aren't listed.

Perennial: A plant that comes back every year. It will often die back to the root over the winter but will regrow each season. Food plant examples: rhubarb, mint, strawberries. Note that some plants we treat as annuals here are perennials in a warmer climate. For instance, a lime tree would die over the winter in Canada. In Florida, that tree would keep coming back.

Pesticide: A chemical liquid or powder used to control or repel a garden pest, usually bugs.

pH: The pH level indicates the acidity in soil and affects the amount of nutrients that plants can take up. It is measured on a scale of 0 to 14. A pH of 7.0 is neutral. Anything lower is acidic, or sour; anything above is alkaline, or sweet.

Pruning: Selective removal of parts of a plant, usually the branches. Pruning removes dead parts of the plant, helps shape it, and allows the plant to conserve energy so it can stay healthy or bear fruit.

Sow: This simply means planting seeds into soil with the goal of them germinating (turning into plants). You can sow your seeds indoors or outdoors. Direct sowing indicates planting outdoors.

Thinning: After sowing seeds outside, young seedlings often end up growing too close together. When they reach an average of 10 cm (4 inches) tall, pull out the weakest of your seedlings, aiming for the distance recommended on your seed packet. (You often thin very small seedlings after you seed-start them inside.)

Transplants/seedlings: Young plants that have been sown into trays or pots. This is what you call the small plants you buy at the garden centre in the spring—and what you get if you've started seeds indoors. You plant them in the ground outside, usually once the risk of frost has passed.

Weeding: Removing any unwanted plants from the garden. Weeds take resources—soil nutrients, moisture—away from wanted crops; as well, they can harbour bugs and diseases.

Key Climate Terms

Last frost date: This is the date in the spring when frost in your area is highly unlikely, based on average historical data. Frost can hit well before or even after this date, but it's a pretty reliable reference point to begin planting. It's also a helpful date to know when choosing your plants, as it can help you figure out how long the growing season is in your area, and if certain crops will grow in your garden.

First frost date: This is the date that frost first arrives in late summer or late fall, depending on where you live. (For example, the first frost will hit much earlier in northern Alberta than in southern Ontario.) I always mark down the date of first frost in my calendar and make sure it sends an alert to my smart phone so I can rush out to the garden and harvest the last of my produce or cover the things I want to survive out there just a little longer.

Knowing the stretch of time between last frost and first frost in your region is critical. When planning your garden, make sure your growing season matches the needs of the plants you buy.

Hardiness zones: These are the defined geographical areas in which perennial plants can survive. These zones are not useful for annual crops, just those such as trees, shrubs, and plants like asparagus. Hardiness zone maps help gardeners determine if a plant is strong enough to live in their yard based on the weather. Every region of Canada has been assigned a zone number from 0 to 8, zone 8 being the warmest and 0 the coldest. Always know your zone before planting perennials. Note: Canada uses Agri-Food Canada's zone map, but the U.S. follows the USDA's hardiness zone map, and they differ. For example, my hometown is in zone 5 according to the Canadian map and zone 4b on the USDA map. Make sure you know which country's hardiness zone map your seed packet or plant tag is referring to.

Here are the last and first frost dates for some major Canadian cities:

Location	Last Frost	First Frost
St. John's	June 2	Oct 12
Halifax	May 6	Oct 20
Charlottetown	May 17	Oct 9
Fredericton	May 20	Sept 22
Quebec	May 13	Sept 29
Toronto	May 9	Oct 6
Winnipeg	May 25	Sept 22
Regina	May 21	Sept 10
Edmonton	May 7	Sept 23
Vancouver	March 28	Nov 5

A Year in the Garden: A Checklist for the Four Seasons

Gardening happens throughout the year, in weather both freezing and hot. Here's a seasonal guide to tending the best food garden possible.

Spring Checklist

The days are getting toastier, but the nights are still crisp. The snow starts to melt, the sun finally comes out, leaves slowly emerge. The forsythia and grape hyacinth bloom and spirits are high. It's early spring outdoors. It's beautiful and there are tasks to complete in the garden.

Early spring

☐ Choose an appropriate site for your garden.

☐ Remove sod, weeds, and debris from your plot and amend and improve the soil.

☐ Purchase or build containers, raised beds, and other planting structures. Fill them with the appropriate soil.

☐ Select fruits and vegetable plants that are straightforward to grow and that you and your family enjoy eating.

☐ Plan your garden so taller plants won't shade out smaller ones.

☐ When soil temperatures warm to 10°C (50°F), sow seeds of cool-season vegetables such as radishes, spinach, Swiss chard, beets, carrots, and lettuce directly into your garden.

☐ Plant cool-crop seedlings such as kale, cabbage, broccoli, and collards.

☐ Be ready to protect tender growers from frost with a cover of some kind.

☐ Plant perennials such as asparagus, rhubarb, raspberries, and strawberries.

☐ Plant fruit trees.

☐ Prune some of your perennials such as existing raspberries bushes and grapevines.

☐ Think ahead and clear space for your summer crops such as tomatoes.

Mid-spring

☐ Direct-sow crops such as corn, summer squash, cucumbers, peas, and beans.

☐ Plant tomatoes, peppers, and eggplant seedlings. Plant your herbs too.

☐ If you have space, sow a second round of spinach and radishes.

☐ Thin crops such as carrots, beets, and late lettuce.

☐ Be on alert for a late frost. Cover up any crop that won't withstand frost when it threatens overnight.

☐ Protect berry crops from birds.

☐ Monitor for insects and disease.

☐ Protect plants from critters like rabbits, deer, and raccoons.

☐ Harvest green onions, lettuce, and radishes.

☐ Harvest mature asparagus and rhubarb.

☐ Monitor your soil and plants and water if they're dry. Particularly if there's been no rain, water deeply and infrequently. Containers will require more frequent watering.

☐ Keep your garden clean. Weed, remove decaying leaves, and discard any diseased leaves or plants.

☐ Fertilize containers and heavy feeders planted in the garden.

☐ Consider starting a composter. Place it in the sun.

☐ Remove flowers of June-bearing strawberries as soon as they appear. This is necessary just for the first growing season. The plants will now develop a stronger root system.

□ Remove flowers for everbearing and day-neutral strawberries as soon as they appear. Flowers that develop after July 1 can be left on the plants to set fruit for later in the season.

Summer Checklist

The hot, humid days of summer bring bounties of food but also the threat of insects and disease.

Early summer

□ Harvest cool-season vegetables like lettuces, radishes, and spinach.

□ Harvest peas, raspberries, and strawberries.

□ Keep records of harvest dates. This will help plan next year's garden.

□ Monitor for insects and diseases.

□ Harvest herbs and pinch top growth before the plant starts to flower or bolt and ruin the flavour of your aromatic herbs.

□ Carve your name into growing pumpkins; the letters will enlarge as they grow.

□ Tie vines of beans, grapes, and summer squash.

□ Support tomatoes and peppers as they grow.

□ Water most of your crops deeply and infrequently.

□ Weed and add more mulch if needed. Really keep your eye on containers, as they are going to dry out faster than your garden.

□ Remove dead and decaying plants—keep your garden clean.

□ Fertilize, particularly your containers.

Midsummer

□ Monitor for insects and disease.

□ Hand-remove tomato hornworms.

□ Weed. Even if it's hot. Wait until after a rain or do the day after you water, to make it easy on yourself.

□ Remove any dead or diseased plants.

□ Water. Be diligent, especially with tomatoes to prevent blossom-end rot.

□ Harvest herbs often. Remove any developing flowers.

□ Monitor for ripeness daily. There is nothing worse than letting your hard work bolt or spoil on the vine.

□ Harvest zucchini before they get too big. Bigger isn't better for flavour.

□ Harvest berries, leafy greens, cherry tomatoes, beans, peas, and summer squash.

□ Sow succession crops of cool-season plants like spinach, radishes, and lettuces. They'll be ready for fall harvest if you plant now.

Late summer

□ Monitor for insects and disease. Look for symptoms of fungus or blight. Remove any plants showing signs. Discard and clean any tools used during the process.

□ Weed and water.

□ Reduce your use of fertilizer—ripening plants don't need it.

□ Monitor your crops for ripeness. Allow tomatoes, peppers, and eggplants to vine-ripen before you harvest.

□ Wait for the tops of onions and garlic to turn brown and fall over. Harvest as they are ready. Cure them.

□ Keep harvesting your herbs on an ongoing basis.

□ Clean up all debris after you harvest plants. No rotten fruit on the ground! A clean garden is a healthy one.

□ Sow a final crop of leafy greens, radishes, and spinach.

□ Remove lower leaves on Brussels sprouts when bud heads form.

□ Monitor for ripeness and harvest your plants often. Many will produce more.

☐ Water fruit trees deeply and infrequently during dry periods to prevent fruit drop.

Fall Checklist

Leaves change colour, the threat of frost is near, birds migrate south, and we get ready to wrap up the harvest.

Early fall

☐ Monitor your crops and keep harvesting.

☐ Watch the forecast and cover peppers, tomatoes, basil, and eggplants if an early frost threatens.

☐ Harvest winter squash. Allow pumpkins to fully ripen on the vine, but harvest them before a killing frost.

☐ Allow a light frost to settle on crops of kale and collards to sweeten their flavour.

☐ Harvest final crops of leafy greens and carrots, onions, beets, garlic, potatoes, and parsnips.

☐ Harvest and dry or freeze herbs.

☐ Can tomatoes and other fruits and vegetables.

☐ Clean up debris, remove and discard diseased plants, and weed.

☐ With the threat of killing frost, harvest all tomatoes, including green ones, and store in a dark, dry spot (or in a bag with a ripe tomato) for ripening.

☐ Plant garlic three weeks before ground frost expected.

☐ Prune tall canes of small berry bushes to protect them from heavy wet snow in early winter.

☐ Protect fruit trees from rabbit, deer, and rodent damage by wrapping the tree base.

Late fall: after killing frost

☐ Harvest all remaining root vegetables before ground frost locks them in.

☐ Remove all dead plant material; cut back foliage of perennial plants like rhubarb and asparagus.

☐ Amend your soil by applying a generous top dressing of compost or triple mix.

☐ Clean up and empty pots. Store indoors or turn over so they don't crack in the cold.

☐ Clean up all fallen fruit. A clean garden is a healthy one, particularly over the winter.

Winter Checklist

The garden has been put to bed, snow begins to fall, and Old Man Winter threatens a cold blast of air to freeze the ground for another season. Welcome to winter!

Early winter

☐ Clean your gardening tools and store them. Use bleach if your garden had any disease.

☐ Frequently check stored root vegetables and discard those with signs of rot.

☐ Reflect and plan next year's garden.

Winter

☐ Seed catalogues arrive. Have a look, but be certain you're ready to seed-start before purchasing. Purchase seeds for direct sowing and check the yields so you get the right amount (many people buy too many seeds).

☐ Continue to plan next season's garden.

☐ Monitor stored root vegetables for rot.

☐ Make a winter soup out of your harvest.

☐ Use dried herbs.

☐ Enjoy the time off!

Acknowledgements

They say it takes a village to raise a child, and the same can be said when it comes to writing a book! *Food to Grow* is my fourth book, so I've learned that lesson very well by now. At the centre of my village is my family. Endless thanks to my wife, Laurie, and to my boys, Gavin and Matheson, for supporting me once again and pushing me through to finish the final pages. To my parents, Tony and Alyce, who gave me an incredible work ethic and the knowledge to grow everything and anything. To my extended family who work the rich soils of Bradford's Holland Marsh—thank you for inspiring me and also for helping to put food on the tables of so many!

Now to my book family, who I would say are the most incredible gardening book team in the country. Thanks to Shannon Ross, our photographer, who brings vision and beauty to the pages of every book I write. At HarperCollins, to Kate Cassaday, who keeps the project on track, always gently nudging us along to meet deadlines and make the book beyond perfect. To Julia Barret, who focuses our publicity efforts in the media and communities where it's needed most, and to Kelly Hope, who helps pull it all together. Finally to our newest team member, Diane Peters, who after countless coffees and much discussion helped give *Food to Grow* a friendly focus and reminded me of some of the basic information people need to know to grow.

FrankieFlowers.com has become an extension of who I am, a place where readers, gardeners, and just anyone who wants to know can reach out and ask how or what to grow in a garden. This community has informed much of the content in these pages. For this I need to thank both Aileen Barclay and Devon MacPherson, who keep FrankieFlowers.com fresh and keep me following a daily schedule.

To Daniel, Gavin, Ronan, Mackie, and Sandy Costa, who shared their property and landscaping, giving me a place to build some additional raised beds. I've loved working with you to raise some good grub, harvest some honey, and even just hang out with our feathered friends.

To my friends and family at Bradford Greenhouses, Bob Martin of Martin Farms, Monique Kelemen from Toronto Community Garden Network, Riga Farms, Cherry Avenue Farms, Pat Lamanna of Less Mess Soil, Rita DeMontis of *Toronto Sun*, my colleagues at both *Breakfast Television* and *CityLine*, and many more—thank you for your friendship and support and for believing, like I do, that those who grow a garden and connect with the food they eat will not only be healthier but happier, and that is what matters most!

Frankie

When I look back on the journey of creating this book, I am reminded of the amazing team who brought it to life. I am truly blessed and inspired to work with such a talented team as Frankie and Kate and the whole gang at HarperCollins. I was immediately excited by the subject matter, as my family also dabbles in home farming, growing what we can with limited space in our urban garden. It is so rewarding to eat something grown in your own soil that you have nurtured from seed.

Frankie, I would like to thank you most of all for having the vision and creative expertise to make these books truly inspiring and memorable. Your relentless energy and amazing personality make the days a lot of fun and create lasting memories that I cherish. Your sense of humour, your unwavering work ethic, and your sense of family and friendship have bolstered us along the way. Thanks a million, Frankie!

To Kate Cassaday, your intelligence and wisdom have been paramount in bringing this project together. Your insights and clarity of vision helped tremendously, and your ability to see the big picture and keep a firm hand on the tiller has been invaluable, and I know that the success of this book will be in no small part due to you.

To my wife, Robyn, who has supported me with insights and ideas along the way: your good taste and stylish sense have mixed wonderfully in this project. I am blessed to have you—and now Haydyn and Chloe—by my side. And to my family and friends who build me up and yet keep me grounded, thank you for always being a real and true compass.

Finally, to you the reader, please accept my humblest and most heartfelt thanks for reading our book. May it inspire you, feed you, and help you gain a better understanding of farm to table. I know I have certainly learned that there are many unsung heroes in the farming communities who work the land and produce what we eat on a daily basis. Bon appétit!

Shannon

Sources

Most of this book was developed from my own knowledge of food gardening. But I did get a little help.

Idea soil temperature for germination came from Alabama A&M and Auburn universities via www.aces.edu/pubs/docs/A/ANR-1061/ANR-1061.pdf

Instructions for building a wooden compost came from East Sussex County Council via www.eastsussex.gov.uk/NR/rdonlyres/0F4EC-6BC-1F51-453A-949D-5DC1DEEC52BE/0/build_compost_wormery.pdf

Frost dates for Canadian cities came from *The Old Farmer's Almanac* via www.almanac.com/content/frost-chart-canada

Additional Sources

Books

Rodale's Ultimate Encyclopedia of Organic Gardening: The Indispensable Green Resource for Every Gardener, edited by Fern Marshall Bradley, Barbara Ellis, and Ellen Phillips

Lois Hole's Vegetable Favorites: A Rich Vegetable Harvest, by Lois Hole

Websites

www.harvesttotable.com/2011/06/vegetable_crop_yields_plants_p/
www.motherearthnews.com
www.omafra.gov.on.ca/english/index.html